Role of Vocational Education

Role of Vocational Education

Damodar Singh

RANDOM PUBLICATIONS
NEW DELHI (INDIA)

Role of Vocational Education

ISBN 978-93-5111-438-3

Published in 2014 in India by

RANDOM PUBLICATIONS

Reprint, 2016

4376-A/4B, Gali Murari Lal, Ansari Road
New Delhi-110 002
Phone : +91-11-43580356, +91-11-23289044
e-mail: randomexports@gmail.com, sales@randompublications.com,
info@randompublications.com

Type Setting by: Friends Media, Delhi-110089
Digitally Printed at: Replika Press Pvt. Ltd.

Preface

Vocational Education and Training (VET) is an important element of the nation's education initiative. In order for Vocational Education to play its part effectively in the changing national context and for India to enjoy the fruits of the demographic dividend, there is an urgent need to redefine the critical elements of imparting vocational education and training to make them flexible, contemporary, relevant, inclusive and creative. The Government is well aware of the important role of Vocational education and has already taken a number of important initiatives in this area. School-based vocational education in India is currently covered by a centrally sponsored scheme which was mooted in 1988 and was aimed at providing an alternative to the pursuit of higher academic education. Vocational education may be classified as teaching procedural knowledge. This can be contrasted with declarative knowledge, as used in education in a usually broader scientific field, which might concentrate on theory and abstract conceptual knowledge, characteristic of tertiary education. Vocational education can be at the secondary, post-secondary level, further education level and can interact with the apprenticeship system. Increasingly, vocational education can be recognised in terms of recognition of prior learning and partial academic credit towards tertiary education (e.g., at auniversity) as credit; however, it is rarely considered in its own form to fall under the traditional definition of higher education.

Vocational education is related to the age-old apprenticeship system of learning. Apprenticeships are designed for many levels of work from manual trades to high knowledge work. However, as the labour market becomes more specialized and economies demand higher levels of skill, governments and businesses are increasingly investing in the future of vocational education through publicly funded training organizations and subsidized apprenticeship or traineeship initiatives for businesses. At the post-secondary level vocational education is typically provided by an institute of technology, university, or by a local community college. Vocational education has diversified over the 20th century and now exists in industries such as retail, tourism, information technology, funeral services and cosmetics, as well as in the traditional crafts and cottage industries. Every year over two lakh Indian students travel abroad to get foreign degrees. But another number that's growing is that of 'glocal' students — young Indians who aspire to study abroad, but either can't afford it, or haven't secured admission in a foreign college. It's these glocal students that are being targeted by international specialty schools, many of whom have recently started operations in India.

In the preparation of this book, it has been the author's aim to keep in mind not only the requirements of students in this subject but as well the needs of student.

I thank all members of my team who have helped in the preparation of the book. My special thanks go to "Random Publications" who have published the book.

—Damodar Singh

Contents

1

Introduction

Vocational Education

Vocational education (education based on occupation or employment) (also known as vocational education and training or VET) is education that prepares people for specific trades, crafts and careers at various levels from a trade, a craft, technician, or a professional position in engineering, accountancy, nursing, medicine, architecture, pharmacy, law etc. Craft vocations are usually based on manual or practical activities, traditionally non-academic, related to a specific trade, occupation, or *vocation*. It is sometimes referred to as *technical education* as the trainee directly develops expertise in a particular group of techniques. In the UK some higher technician engineering positions that require 4-5 year apprenticeship require academic study to HNC / HND or higher City & Guilds level.

Vocational education may be classified as teaching procedural knowledge. This can be contrasted with declarative knowledge, as used in education in a usually broader scientific field, which might concentrate on theory and abstract conceptual knowledge, characteristic of tertiary education. Vocational education can be at the secondary, post-secondary level, further education level and can interact with the apprenticeship system. Increasingly, vocational education can be recognised in terms of recognition of prior learning and partial academic credit towards tertiary education (e.g., at a university) as credit; however, it is rarely considered in its own form to fall under the traditional definition of higher education.

Vocational education is related to the age-old apprenticeship system of learning. Apprenticeships are designed for many levels of work from manual trades to high knowledge work.However, as the labour market becomes more specialized and economies demand higher levels of skill, governments and businesses are increasingly investing in the future of vocational education through publicly funded training organizations and subsidized apprenticeship or traineeship initiatives for businesses. At the post-secondary level vocational education is typically provided by an institute of technology, university, or by a local community college.

Vocational education has diversified over the 20th century and now exists in industries such as retail, tourism, information technology, funeral services and cosmetics, as well as in the traditional crafts and cottage industries.

VET Internationally

Australia

In Australia vocational education and training is mostly post-secondary and provided through the vocational education and training (VET) system by registered training organisations. There were 24 Technical Colleges in Australia but now only 4 independent Trade Colleges remain with two in Queensland; one in Brisbane and one on the Gold Coast and one in Adelaide and Perth. This system encompasses both public, TAFE, and private providers in a national training framework consisting of the Australian Quality Training Framework, Australian Qualifications Framework and Industry Training Packages which define the assessment standards for the different vocational qualifications.

Australia's apprenticeship system includes both traditional apprenticeships in traditional trades and "traineeships" in other more service-oriented occupations. Both involve a legal contract between the employer and the apprentice and provide a combination of school-based and workplace training. Apprenticeships typically last three to four years, traineeships only one to two years. Apprentices and trainees receive a wage which increases as they progress.

Since the states and territories are responsible for most public delivery and all regulation of providers, a central concept of the system is "national recognition" whereby the assessments and awards of any one registered training organisation must be recognised by all others and the decisions of any state or territory training authority must be recognised by the other states and territories. This allows national portability of qualifications and units of competency.

A crucial feature of the training package (which accounts for about 60% of publicly funded training and almost all apprenticeship training) is that the content of the vocational qualifications is theoretically defined by industry and not by government or training providers. A Training Package is "owned" by one of 11 Industry Skills Councils which are responsible for developing and reviewing the qualifications. The National Centre for Vocational Education Research or NCVER is a not-for-profit company owned by the federal, state and territory ministers responsible for training. It is responsible for collecting, managing, analysing, evaluating and communicating research and statistics about vocational education and training (VET).

The boundaries between Vocational education and tertiary education are becoming more blurred. A number of vocational training providers such as NMIT, BHI and WAI are now offering specialised Bachelor degrees in specific areas not being adequately provided by Universities. Such Applied Courses include in the areas of Equine studies, Winemaking and viticulture, aquaculture, Information Technology, Music, Illustration, Culinary Management and many more.

Commonwealth of Independent States

The largest and the most unified system of vocational education was created in the Soviet Union with the Professional'no-tehnicheskoye uchilische and, Tehnikum. But it became less effective with the transition of the economies of post-Soviet countries to a market economy.

Finland

In Finland, vocational education belongs to secondary education. After the nine-year comprehensive school, almost all students choose to go to either a *lukio* (high school), which is an institution preparing students for tertiary education, or to a vocational school. Both forms of secondary education last three years, and give a formal qualification to enter university or *ammattikorkeakoulu*, i.e. Finnish polytechnics. In certain fields (e.g. the police school, air traffic control personnel training), the entrance requirements of vocational schools include completion of the *lukio*, thus causing the students to complete their secondary education twice.

The education in vocational school is free, and the students from low-income families are eligible for a state student grant. The curriculum is primarily vocational, and the academic part of the curriculum is adapted to the needs of a given course. The vocational schools are mostly maintained by municipalities.

After completing secondary education, one can enter higher vocational schools (*ammattikorkeakoulu*, or *AMK*) or universities. It is also possible for a student to choose both lukio and vocational schooling. The education in such cases last usually from 3 to 4 years.

German-language Areas

Vocational education is an important part of the education systems in Austria, Germany, Liechtenstein and Switzerland (including the French and the Italian speaking parts of the country) and one element of the German model. For example, in Germany a law (the *Berufsausbildungsgesetz*) was passed in 1969 which regulated and unified the vocational training system and codified the shared responsibility of the state, the unions, associations and chambers of trade and industry. The system is very popular in modern Germany: in 2001, two thirds of young people aged under 22 began an apprenticeship, and 78% of them completed it, meaning that approximately 51% of all young people under 22 have completed an apprenticeship. One in three companies offered apprenticeships in 2003; in 2004 the government signed a pledge with industrial unions that all companies except very small ones must take on apprentices.

The vocational education systems in the other German speaking countries are very similar to the German system and a vocational qualification from one country is generally also recognized in the other states within this area.

Hong Kong

In Hong Kong, vocational education is usually for post-secondary 3, 5 and 7 students. The Hong Kong Institute of Vocational Education (IVE) provides training in nine different vocational fields, namely: Applied Science; Business Administration; Child Education and Community Services; Construction; Design; Printing, Textiles and Clothing; Hotel, Service and Tourism Studies; Information Technology; Electrical and Electronic Engineering; and Mechanical, Manufacturing and Industrial Engineering.

Hungary

Normally at the end of elementary school (at age 14) students are directed to one of three types of upper secondary education: one academic track (gymnasium) and two vocational tracks. Vocational secondary schools provide four years of general education and also prepare students for the maturata. These schools combine general education with some specific subjects, referred to as pre-vocational education and career orientation. At that point many students enrol in a post-secondary VET programme often at the same institution, to obtain a vocational qualification, although they may also seek entry to tertiary education.

Vocational training schools (szakiskola) initially provide two years of general education, combined with some pre-vocational education and career orientation, they then choose an occupation, and then receive two or three years of vocational education and training focusing on that occupation – such as bricklayer. Students do not obtain the maturata but a vocational qualification at the end of a successfully completed programme. Demand for vocational training schools, both from the labour market and among students, has declined while it has increased for upper secondary schools delivering the maturata.

India

Vocational training in India is provided on a full-time as well as part-time basis. Full-time programmes are generally offered through I.T.I.s Industrial training institutes. The nodal agency for granting the recognition to the I.T.I.s is NCVT, which is under the Min. of labour, Govt. of India. Part-time programmes are offered through state technical education boards or universities who also offer full-time courses. Vocational training has been successful in India only in industrial training institutes and that too in engineering trades. There are many private institutes in India which offer courses in vocational training and finishing, but most of them have not been recognized by the Government. India is a pioneer in vocational training in Film & Television, and Information Technology. AAFT, Audio Production & Recording ILM Academy. Maharashtra State Government also offers vocational Diplomas in various Trades . Vocational Higher Secondary schools are under MHRD in India. All the state governments runs vocational schools. In the state of Kerala, 389 vocational schools are there with 42 different courses. Commerce & Business, Tourism, Agriculture, Automobile, Air conditioning, Live stock management, Lab Technician are some prominent courses.

Japan

Japanese vocational schools are known as *senmon gakkô*. They are part of Japan's higher education system. They are two-year schools that many students study at after finishing high school (although it is not always required that students graduate from high school). Some have a wide range of majors, others only a few majors. Some examples are computer technology, fashion and English.

South Korea

Vocational high schools offer programmes in five fields: agriculture, technology/engineering, commerce/business, maritime/fishery, and home economics. In principle, all students in the first year of high school (10th grade) follow a common national curriculum, In the second and third years (11th and 12th grades) students are offered courses relevant to their specialisation. In some programmes, students may participate in workplace training through co-operation between schools and local employers. The government is now piloting Vocational Meister Schools in which workplace training is an important part of the programme. Around half of all vocational high schools are private. Private and public schools operate according to similar rules; for example, they charge the same fees for high school education, with an exemption for poorer families.

The number of students in vocational high schools has decreased, from about half of students in 1995 down to about one-quarter today. To make vocational high schools more attractive, in April 2007 the Korean government changed the name of vocational high schools into professional high schools. With the change of the name the government also facilitated the entry of vocational high school graduates to colleges and universities. Most vocational high school students continue into tertiary education; in 2007 43% transferred to junior colleges and 25% to university. At tertiary level, vocational education and training is provided in junior colleges (two- and three-year programmes) and at polytechnic colleges. Education at junior colleges and in two-year programmes in polytechnic colleges leads to an Industrial Associate degree. Polytechnics also provide one-year programmes for craftsmen and master craftsmen and short programmes for employed workers. The requirements for admission to these institutions are in principle the same as those in the rest of tertiary sector (on the basis of the College Scholastic Aptitude Test) but candidates with vocational qualifications are given priority in the admission process. Junior colleges have expanded rapidly in response to demand and in 2006 enrolled around 27% of all tertiary students.

95% of junior college students are in private institutions. Fees charged by private colleges are approximately twice those of public institutions. Polytechnic colleges are state-run institutions under the responsibility of the Ministry of Labour; government funding keeps student fees much lower than those charged by other tertiary institutions. Around 5% of students are enrolled in polytechnic colleges.

Mexico

In Mexico, both federal and state governments are responsible for the administration of vocational education. Federal schools are funded by the federal budget, in addition to their own funding sources. The state governments are responsible for the management of decentralised institutions, such as the State Centres for Scientific and Technological Studies (CECyTE) and Institutes of Training for Work (ICAT). These institutions are funded 50% from the federal budget and 50% from the state budget. The state governments also manage and fund "decentralised institutions of the federation", such as CONALEP schools.

Compulsory education (including primary and lower secondary education) finishes at the age of 15 and about half of those aged 15-to-19 are enrolled full-time or part-time in education. All programmes at upper secondary level require the payment of a tuition fee.

The upper secondary vocational education system in Mexico includes over a dozen subsystems (administrative units within the Upper Secondary Education Undersecretariat of the Ministry of Public Education, responsible for vocational programmes) which differ from each other to varying degrees in content, administration, and target group. The large number of school types and corresponding administrative units within the Ministry of Public Education makes the institutional landscape of vocational education and training complex by international standards.

Vocational education and training provided under the Upper Secondary Education Under secretariat includes three main types of programme:

- "Training for work" (formación para el trabajo) courses at ISCED 2 level are short training programmes, taking typically 3 to 6 months to complete. The curriculum includes 50% theory and 50% practice. After completing the programme, students may enter the labour market. This programme does not provide direct access to tertiary education. Those who complete lower secondary education may choose between two broad options of vocational upper secondary education at ISCED 3 level. Both programmes normally take three years to complete and offer a vocational degree as well as the baccalaureate, which is required for entry into tertiary education.
- The title "technical professional – baccalaureate" (profesional técnico — bachiller) is offered by various subsystems though

one subsystem (CONALEP) includes two thirds of the students. The programme involves 35% general subjects and 65% vocational subjects. Students are required to complete 360 hours of practical training.

- The programme awarding the "technological baccalaureate" (bachillerato tecnológico) and the title "professional technician" (técnico professional) is offered by various subsystems. It includes more general and less vocational education: 60% general subjects and 40% vocational subjects.

The Netherlands

Nearly all of those leaving lower secondary school enter upper secondary education, and around 50% of them follow one of four vocational programmes; technology, economics, agricultural, personal/ social services & health care. These programmes vary from 1 to 4 years (by level; only level 2, 3 and 4 diplomas are considered formal 'start qualifications' for successfully entering the labour market). The programmes can be attended in either of two pathways. One either involving a minimum of 20% of school time (apprenticeship pathway; BBL-BeroepsBegeleidende Leerweg) or the other, involving a maximum of 80% schooltime (BOL -BeroepsOpleidende Leerweg). The remaining time is both cases is apprenticeship/work in a company. So in effect, students have a choice out of 32 trajectories, leading to over 600 professional qualifications. BBL-Apprentices usually receive a wage negotiated in collective agreements.

Employers taking on these apprentices receive a subsidy in the form of a tax reduction on the wages of the apprentice. (WVA-Wet vermindering afdracht). Level 4 graduates of senior secondary VET may go directly to institutes for Higher Profession Education and Training (HBO-Hoger beroepsonderwijs), after which entering university is a possibility. The social partners participate actively in the development of policy. As of January 1, 2012 they formed a foundation for Co operation Vocational Education and Entrepreneurship (St. SBB – stichting Samenwerking Beroepsonderwijs Bedrijfsleven; Its responsibility is to advise the Minister on the development of the national vocational education and training system, based on the full consensus of the constituent members (the representative organisations of schools and of entrepreneurship and their centres of expertise). Special topics are Qualification & Examination, Apprenticeships (BPV-Beroepspraktijkvorming) and (labourmarket) Efficiency of VET. The Centres of Expertices are linked to the four vocational education programmes provided in senior secondary VET on the content of VET programmes and on trends and future skill needs. The Local County Vocational Training represents the VET schools in this foundation and advise on the quality, operations and provision of VET.

New Zealand

New Zealand is served by 39 Industry Training Organisations (ITO). The unique element is that ITOs purchase training as well as set standards and aggregate industry opinion about skills in the labour market. Industry Training, as organised by ITOs, has expanded from apprenticeships to a more true lifelong learning situation with, for example, over 10% of trainees aged 50 or over. Moreover much of the training is generic. This challenges the prevailing idea of vocational education and the standard layperson view that it focuses on apprenticeships.

One source for information in New Zealand is the Industry Training Federation. Another is the Ministry of Education. Polytechnics, Private Training Establishments, Wananga and others also deliver vocational training, amongst other areas.

Norway

Nearly all those leaving lower secondary school enter upper secondary education, and around half follow one of 9 vocational programmes. These programmes typically involve two years in school followed by two years of apprenticeship in a company. The first year provides general education alongside introductory knowledge of the vocational area. During the second year, courses become more trade-specific. Apprentices receive a wage negotiated in collective agreements ranging between 30% and 80% of the wage of a qualified worker; the percentage increasing over the apprenticeship period. Employers taking on apprentices receive a subsidy, equivalent to the cost of one year in school. After the two years vocational school programme some students opt for a third year in the 'general' programme as an alternative to an apprenticeship. Both apprenticeship and a third year of practical training in school lead to the same vocational qualifications. Upper secondary VET graduates may go directly to Vocational Technical Colleges, while those who wish to enter university need to take a supplementary year of education.

The social partners participate actively in the development of policy. The National Council for Vocational Education and Training advises the Minister on the development of the national vocational education and training system. The Advisory Councils for Vocational Education and Training are linked to the nine vocational education programmes provided in upper secondary education and advise on the content of VET programmes and on trends and future skill needs. The National Curriculum groups assist in deciding the contents of the vocational training within the specific occupations. The Local County Vocational Training Committees advise on the quality, provision of VET and career guidance.

Paraguay

In Paraguay, vocational education is known as *Bachillerato Técnico* and is part of the secondary education system. These schools combine general education with some specific subjects, referred to as pre-vocational education and career orientation. After nine years of *Educación Escolar Básica* (Primary School), the student can choose to go to either a *Bachillerato Técnico* (Vocational School) or a *Bachillerato Científico* (High School). Both forms of secondary education last three years, and are usually located in the same campus called *Colegio*. After completing secondary education, one can enter to the universities. It is also possible for a student to choose both Técnico and Científico schooling.

Russia

Sweden: Nearly all of those leaving compulsory schooling immediately enter upper secondary schools, and most complete their upper secondary education in three years. Upper secondary education is divided into 13 vocationally oriented and 4 academic national programmes. Slightly more than half of all students follow vocational programmes. All programmes offer broad general education and basic eligibility to continue studies at the post-secondary level. In addition, there are local programmes specially designed to meet local needs and 'individual' programmes.

A 1992 school reform extended vocational upper secondary programmes by one year, aligning them with three years of general upper secondary education, increasing their general education content, and making core subjects compulsory in all programmes. The core subjects (which occupy around one-third of total teaching time in both vocational and academic programmes) include English, artistic activities, physical education and health, mathematics, natural science, social studies, Swedish or Swedish as a second language, and religious studies. In addition to the core subjects, students pursue optional courses, subjects which are specific to each programme and a special project.

Vocational programmes include 15 weeks of workplace training (Arbetsplatsförlagd utbildning – APU) over the three-year period. Schools are responsible for arranging workplace training and verifying its quality. Most municipalities have advisory bodies: programme councils (programmråd) and vocational councils composed of employers' and employees' representatives from the locality. The councils advise schools on matters such as provision of workplace training courses, equipment purchase and training of supervisors in APU.

Switzerland

Nearly two thirds of those entering upper secondary education enter the vocational education and training system. At this level, vocational education and training is mainly provided through the 'dual system'. Students spend some of their time in a vocational school; some of their time doing an apprenticeship at a host company; and for most programmes, students attend industry courses at an industry training centre to develop complementary practical skills relating to the occupation at hand. Common patterns are for students to spend one-two days per week at the vocational school and three-four days doing the apprenticeship at the host company; alternatively they alternate between some weeks attending classes at the vocational school and some weeks attending industry courses at an industry training centre. A different pattern is to begin the programme with most of the time devoted to in-school education and gradually diminishing the amount of in-school education in favour of more in-company training.

Switzerland draws a distinction between vocational education and training (VET) programmes at upper-secondary level, and professional education and training (PET) programmes, which take place at tertiary B level. In 2007, more than half of the population aged 25–64 had a VET or PET qualification as their highest level of education. In addition, universities of applied sciences (Fachhochschulen) offer vocational education at tertiary A level. Pathways enable people to shift from one part of the education system to another.

Turkey

Students in Turkey may choose vocational high schools after completing the 8-year-long compulsory primary education. Vocational high school graduates may pursue 2 year-long polytechnics or may continue with a related tertiary degree.

Municipalities in Turkey also offer vocational training. The metropolitan municipality of Istanbul, the most populous city in Turkey, offers year long free vocational programs in a wide range of topics through ISMEK, an umbrella organization formed under the municipality.

United Kingdom

The first "Trades School" in the UK was *Stanley Technical Trades School* (now Harris Academy South Norwood) which was designed, built and set up by William Stanley. The initial idea was thought of in 1901, and the school opened in 1907.

The system of vocational education in the UK initially developed independently of the state, with bodies such as the RSA and City & Guilds setting examinations for technical subjects. The Education Act 1944 made provision for a Tripartite System of grammar schools, secondary technical schools and secondary modern schools, but by 1975 only 0.5% of British senior pupils were in technical schools, compared to two-thirds of the equivalent German age group.

Successive recent British Governments have made attempts to promote and expand vocational education. In the 1970s, the Business And Technology Education Council was founded to confer further and higher education awards, particularly to further education colleges in the United Kingdom. In the 1980s and 1990s, the Conservative Government promoted the Youth Training Scheme, National Vocational Qualifications and General National Vocational Qualifications. However, youth training was marginalised as the proportion of young people staying on in full-time education increased.

In 1994, publicly funded Modern Apprenticeships were introduced to provide "quality training on a work-based (educational) route". Numbers of apprentices have grown in recent years and the Department for Children, Schools and Families has stated its intention to make apprenticeships a "mainstream" part of England's education system.

Vocational Education in India

Throughout the post-independence period there have been many attempts to reform the Indian vocational education system and make it more applicable. The list of vocational education policy reforms that have been attempted over the last 60 years is quite extensive. Without raising standards, efforts have been made to go forward with market-oriented reforms to the vocational education system. This study mainly focuses on the present parallel (vocational) education system with the help of the indicative data. This article also proposes certain policy interventions in the parallel educational system.

Vocational education consists basically of practical courses through which one gains skills and experience directly linked to a career in future. It helps students to be skilled and in turn, offers better employment opportunities. These trainings are parallel to the other conventional courses of study (like B. Sc., M. Sc. etc.). Time management and meeting deadlines play an important role in success in a vocational course and during their studies students normally produce a portfolio of evidence (plans, reports, drawings, videos, placements), which is taken as a demonstration of students' capabilities for a job. After finishing the courses, students are often offered placements in jobs. Vocational trainings in a way give students some work related experiences that many employers look for. According to a National Sample Survey Organization (NSSO) report (No. 517, 61/10/03) two types of vocational trainings are available in India: a) Formal and; b) Non-formal. Formal vocational training follows a structured training programme and leads to certificates, diplomas or degrees, recognized by State/Central Government, Public Sector and other reputed concerns. Non-formal vocational training helps in acquiring some marketable expertise, which enables a person to carry out her/his ancestral trade or occupation. In a way through such non-formal vocational training, a person receives vocational training through 'hereditary' sources. Often 'Non-formal' vocational trainings are also received through 'other sources'. In such cases training received by a person to pursue a vocation, is not ancestral and is different from the trade or occupation of his/her ancestors. Data and graphs used here are all indicative, not exhaustive.

Type of Institutions for Vocational Training According to National Sample Survey Organization (NSSO)

Different institutions which impart vocational training can be classified into five categories: (i) Government, (ii) Local body, (iii) Private aided, (iv) Private unaided, and (v) not known. According to a NSSO report vocational training is received by only 10% of persons aged between 15-29 years. Out of this only 2% receive formal training, while non-formal training constitutes the remaining 8%. Out of the formal training received by that particular age group only 3% are employed. Most sought after field of training is computer related training. Only 20% of formal vocational training is received from ITI/ ITCs. In India, technical education and vocational training system follows patterns like graduate - post graduate, engineer - technologists through training colleges, diploma from polytechnics and certificate level training in ITIs through formal apprenticeships.

The Vocational Training in India is Imparted by Mainly two Types of Bodies

- Public Industrial Training Institutes (ITIs)
- Private owned Industrial Training Centres (ITCs)

The Indian Government has invested a lot for the development of skills through ITIs.

The DGE&T generally regulates these ITIs and ITCs at national level and implements policies for vocational training.

Training Statistics of ITI/ITCs - Main Formal Vocational Training Institutes in India

Some of the principal training schemes are:

- The Craftsmen Training Scheme (CTS)
- Apprenticeship Training Scheme (ATS).

According to the Planning commission report for the 11th Five year plan there are about 5,114 Industrial Training Institutes (ITIs) imparting training in 57 engineering and 50 non-engineering trades. Of these, 1,896 are State Government-run ITIs while 3,218 are private. The total seating capacity in these ITIs is 7.42 lakh (4 lakh seats in government ITIs and the remaining 3.42 lakh in private ITCs). This text represent detailed information on the number and capacity of ITIs/ITCs in different states/UTs.

A number of vocational training institutes are being run by private training providers. The formal training system of India starts at Grade 8 and above. According to a report of ILO, the quality of DGE&T's skills development programmes compete with other programmes , such as high vocational schools (10 plus 2 stream), colleges, polytechnics, etc. The share of ITI-based training seems to capture around 10-12 per cent of the total number of school pass outs at Grade10 level.

Some training schemes provide by DGE&T other than Craftsmen Training Scheme (CTS) and Apprenticeship Training Scheme (ATS) are:

- Craft Instructors' Training Scheme(CITS), Advanced Vocational Training Scheme (AVTS)
- Supervisory/Foremen Training Scheme, Staff Training and Research Programme
- Instructional Media Development Programme
- Women's Training Scheme
- Hi-Tech Training Scheme

From the above graphs we may conclude that Tamil Nadu holds the majority stake in private owned ITCs and Maharashtra holds a similar position for Government owned ITIs.

Details about the nature of the training in ITIs etc. are available on the website of

- Ministry of Labour
- National Council for Vocational Training (NCVT)

National Council for Vocational Training', an advisory body, was set up by the Government of India in the year 1956. The National Council is chaired by the Minister of Labour, with members from different Central and State Government Departments, Employers and Workers organizations, Professional and Learned Bodies, All India Council for Technical Education, Scheduled castes and Scheduled tribes, All India Women's Organization, etc. And State Councils for Vocational Training at the State level and Trade Committees have been established to assist the NCVT. Main mandate of the NCVT, according to DGE&T, is to establish and award National Trade Certificates in engineering, non-engineering, building, textile, leather trades and such other trades which are brought within its scope by the Government of India. It also prescribes standards in respect of syllabi, equipment, scales of accommodation, duration of courses and methods of training. It also conducts tests in various trade courses and lays down standards of proficiency required for passing the examination leading to the award of National Trade Certificate etc.

Total Number and Capacity of ITIs and ITCs Per Million Persons in India:

Statistics on persons (per thousand) who attend vocational training, according to duration of training and age groups of trained people:

Despite efforts made to popularize these courses, several problems prevent ITIs/ITCs from reaching common masses and youth.

Paramedical Training Status for Rural India

Paramedical courses are one of the largest sources of vocational educated persons in the field of medical industry. Status of the total paramedical manpower in rural India is given in following graph.

It is clear that out of total 315,746 paramedical workers in rural India, 47% are female health workers. But extension workers are very few; almost 1%. We also need to focus on the availability of Radio Graphers, Pharmacists and Laboratory Technicians for rural India.

To disseminate knowledge of basic health facilities we need to train more paramedical workers for rural India. But unfortunately at present they are few compared to the large size of the rural population.

Status in Schools

Schools also provide vocational training formally at 10 and 12th level. The percentage stake of all major states, providing vocational training in India.

It is observed that states like Punjab, Orissa Tamil Nadu etc. hold approximately 79% stake in number of schools which impart vocational training. And Maharashtra is the foremost, holding more than 16%. Schools have an important role in vocational studies because one can start learning a vocation from his/her schools days. More coverage in school with proper infrastructure can create a large technical group in future, which at present is deficient.

Other Government and private bodies providing vocational training in India:

Khadi and Village Industries Commission (KVIC): The Khadi and Village Industries Commission (KVIC) impart training and awards vocational certificates for the unorganized sectors. KVIC (established in April 1957) is a statutory body established by an Act of Parliament. It took over the work of former All India Khadi and Village Industries Board.

It has the main objective of generating employment; the other objective of producing saleable products; and the wider objective of creating self-reliance amongst the people and building up of strong rural community spirit.

- KVIC is assigned with the proper planning, promotion, organizational implementation of programmes for the development of Khadi and other village industries in rural areas in coordination with other agencies engaged in rural development and are also charged with the responsibility of encouraging and promoting research in the KVI sector.
- KVIC is also entrusted with the task of providing financial assistance to institutions engaged in rural development.

Rural Employment Generation Programme (REGP) is the major programme of KVIC. The main objective of this programme is employment generation in rural areas by setting up new village industries (except those on negative list) by availing loans from banks and margin money (middle end subsidy) being provided by KVIC.

Beneficiaries own contributions should be minimum 10% of project cost for general category and 5% of project cost for special category. Banks will sanction 90% of the project cost in case of general category and 95% for project cost for special category beneficiary. Prime Minister's Employment Generation Programme (PMEGP) as a central scheme to be monitored by the Ministry of Micro, Small and Medium Enterprises (MoMSME). The implementation body will be Khadi and Village Industries Commission (KVIC), a statutory organization under the administrative control of the Ministry of MSME as the single nodal agency at the National level. At the State level, the Scheme will be implemented through State KVIC Directorates, State Khadi and Village Industries Boards (KVIBs) and District Industries Centres (DICs) and banks.

The Government subsidy under the scheme is routed by KVIC through the Banks for similar distribution to the beneficiaries / entrepreneurs in their Bank accounts. The Implementing Agencies, such as KVIC, KVIBs and DICs will associate with different Non Government Organizations (NGOs)/reputed autonomous institutions/ Self Help Groups (SHGs)/ National Small Industries Corporation (NSIC)/Udyami Mitras empanelled under Rajiv Gandhi Udyami Mitra Yojana (RGUMY), Panchayati Raj institutions and other relevant bodies in the implementation of the Scheme. Here training, formally or informally, plays a crucial role for success for the schemes.

List of Training Institutes Providing Support for the Schemes

Micro, Small and Medium Enterprises Development Institutes (MSME-DIs), Tool Rooms and Technical Development Centres (Development Commissioner), National Small Industries Corporation's (NSIC) offices, Incubators and Training cum Incubation Centres (TICs) set up in Public Private Partnership Mode. National level Entrepreneurship Development Institutes like National Institute for Entrepreneurship and Small Business Development (NIESBUD), National Institute for Micro, Small and Medium Enterprises (NIMSME) and Indian Institute of Entrepreneurship (IIE), Guwahati (under MoMSME), and the Entrepreneurship Development Centres (EDCs).

According to the Annual Reports of KVIC in the year 2001-02 and 2004-05, three different categories of training namely, Khadi, Village Industries and EDP training existed.

It is also observed that women's participation has also increased for Khadi training from 52% to 82.1%. But the women's participation fell from 47% to 30.9% and from 41.5% to 20% for Village industries and Other EAP/EDP trainings respectively. Karnataka, Kerala, Madhya Pradesh Maharashtra Orissa, Tamil Nadu, West Bengal, Uttaranchal and UP are the main states where KVIC imparts maximum number of trainings.

Tool Room & Training Centres (DC, MSME): Govt. of India has set up a few Tool Room & Training Centres of large size involving estimated cost of over Rs. 50 crores each, in order to provide facilities for design and manufacture of tools. Govt. of India have decided to assist the State governments by setting up Mini Tool Room and Training Centres.

The main objective of the Mini Tool Room & Training Centres would be-

- Manufacturing jigs, fixtures, cutting tools, gauges, press tools, plastic moulds, forging dies, pressure casting dies and other tools for Small Scale Industries. To provide training facility in tool manufacturing and tool design to generate a work force of skilled workers, supervisors, engineers/designers etc.
- To work as a Nucleus Centre for providing consultancy, information service, documentation etc, for solving problems related to tooling of industries in the region. And to act as a Common Facility Centre for small scale industries and to assist them in product and prototype development.

National Manufacturing Competitive Council (NMCC): This Body was set up by Govt. of India in the year of 2004 as a part of National Common Minimum Programme to help in accelerated growth of GDP, primarily focusing on manufacturing Industry. According to the strategy for National Manufacturing-2006, vocational training plays a key role on this. According to a report by NMCC, if Indian manufacturing has to grow at around 12 percent per annum, it will be necessary for the education and training system to produce at least 1.5 million technically skilled people every year. It is estimated that the country would need an incremental requirement of about 20 million skilled technicians by 2015.

To support the growth of manufacturing, the policy highlights of NMCC on vocational training system are:

- The public sector driven initiative, through The Apprentices Act, 1961 and ITIs (Industrial Training Institutes) has not been able to keep pace with changing requirements. So we need to be taken care of the up-gradation of the Industrial

Training Institutes through public-private partnerships, with training authorities de-linked from certifying ones.

- To initiate some PPP mode operations to establish and operate new demand driven technical training centres through financial and other incentives, with designed industry-managed and government supported, quality control and accreditation systems.
- Two major themes to be taken up on priority basis, namely; 'National Vocational Education Qualification System' and setting up a Vocational Education & Training Institute in each State.
- Private sector manufacturing/engineering organizations will be encouraged to adopt Vocational Education Institutes to meet the challenges. The diploma-holders form the backbone of the manufacturing sector at the 'hands on' level. But for keeping focus on the rapid changes in manufacturing technology it is essential that the polytechnic institutions be strengthened both in terms of the equipment and teaching faculty; with curricula changing to match the emerging needs of the manufacturing sector.

CAPART (Council for Advancement of Rural Technology): CAPART is playing a crucial role in implementing development activities through funding of different voluntary organizations. These voluntary organizations help rural people to enhance livelihood by giving them support through different modes of vocational training and related activities. CAPART has been formed by amalgamating the 'Council for Advancement of Rural Technology' (CART) and 'People's Action for Development India' (PADI). CAPART is an autonomous body registered under the Societies Registration Act 1860, under the aegis of the Ministry of Rural Development, Government of India and it has been a major promoter of rural development in India, assisting over 12,000 voluntary organizations.

SRI, Ranchi (Society for Rural Industrialization): This society has major programme to impart training for the rural people. It mainly focuses on skill development of village youths. Training of trainers and management training are offered to other organizations including the government. The skill training includes courses on communication, personality building and enterprise management. It also offers short training courses on programme management for various National schemes for functionaries of NGOs and of Governments. SRI's tie up with Indian Institute of Science, IIT-Kharagpur and CBRI-Roorkee on cost-effective construction is well known.

Ramakrishna Math and Ramakrishna Mission: Ramakrishna Math was established by Sri Ramakrishna (1836-1886). Ramakrishna Mission is a society (registered) in which monks and devotees of Ramakrishna Math cooperate in conducting various types of social services, mainly in India. It was founded by Sri Ramakrishna's chief apostle, Swami Vivekananda (1863-1902), one of the foremost thinkers and religious leaders of the present age. Ramakrishna Math and Ramakrishna Mission are legally and financially separate from each other but they are closely inter-related in several other ways, and are to be regarded as twin organizations. Vocational training is one of their most valuable inputs in development activity. The rural and tribal activities are mainly classified as:

(i) General;

(ii) Agricultural;

(iii) Educational and Self-reliance training; and

(iv) Medical.

Within the classification of Educational and self-reliance training, free schools are run for children. Adult and non-formal education centres have been set up. Audio-visual shows, farmers' fairs and the like are also organized. And a major activity is to help the formation of self-help groups and training schemes are organized for teaching lathe-turning, carpentry, bee-keeping, pisciculture, dairy-farming and poultry-farming, weaving, incense-stick rolling, etc to enable the rural and tribal community to achieve minimum livelihood.

Some other institutes which impart vocational training like Gandhi Ashram in Wardha and Madurai are also important in this field. We could name a few like Nanaji Deshmukh and many other personalities who had done remarkable work in the vocational education field in rural areas.

Initiatives

The Eleventh Plan has taken an initiative to launch a National Skill Development Mission that may bring some changes in 'Skill Development' programmes and initiatives. The Mission will be operative under Prime Minister's *National Council on Skill Development* for apex level policy directions, and under the *National Skill Development Coordination Board*, and a *National Skill Development Corporation/Trust*. The State governments will engage some of their Departments/Agencies for constituting a State Skill Development Mission. Some chosen private sectors (mainly twenty high growth sectors), will play an important part as the private arm of the Mission with an outlay of Rs 22,800 crores.

Constituents of *Prime Minister's National Council on Skill Development* and *National Skill Development Coordination Board* will be the following:

- *Prime Minister's National Council on Skill Development:* Prime Minister as Chairman; Ministers of Finance, HRD, Industries, Rural Development, Labour & Employment and Housing & Urban Poverty Alleviation; Deputy Chairman, Planning Commission; Chairperson, National Manufacturing Competitive Council; Chairperson of the National Skill Development Corporation; six experts in the area of Skill Development as Members and Private Secretary to Prime Minister as Member-Secretary.
- *National Skill Development Coordination Board:* Deputy Chairman, Planning Commission as Chairman; Chairperson/ Chief Executive Officer of the National Skill Development Corporation, Secretaries of Ministries of Finance, Human Resource Development, Labour and Employment, Rural Development, Housing and Employment, Rural Development, Housing & Urban Poverty Alleviation; Secretaries of Four States by rotation, for a period of two years, three Distinguished Academicians/Subject Area Specialists as Members and Secretary, Planning Commission as the Member-Secretary.

The National Skill Development Corporation will be constituted as Government Equity with a view to obtaining about Rs 15,000 crore from the public and private sectors, and other bilateral and multilateral sources for the promotion of skill development. It will act as a non-profit company under the Companies Act, with appropriate governance structures (board of directors being drawn from outstanding professionals/experts).

The National Commission for Enterprises in the Unorganized Sector (NCEUS): It has been set up as an advisory body for the informal sector to bring about improvement in the productivity of these enterprises and for generation of large scale employment opportunities on a sustainable basis, particularly in rural areas.

Public Private Partnership (PPP): Major emphasis has been given on the PPP mode in the Eleventh Five Year Plan. It focuses on the following:

- Private Investment in Skill Training.
- National framework for domain specific standards and common principles.
- National database for location wise availability (and shortage) of skilled personnel will be established.
- The system should provide the options of multiple entry and exit points and total mobility between vocational, general and technical streams.
- Special emphasis on economically weaker section.
- To overcome the regional disparities due to diverse socio-economic factors, VGF approach would be adopted to address regional imbalances through PPP.

The eleventh five year plan also envisions setting up an Apex skill development institute which will take initiatives on programme testing, certification, curriculum setting faculty development, introduction of new elective courses in IITs /IIMs etc.

State Govt. initiatives to be taken up in the 11th Five year plan are:

- Modernization of employment exchanges, which can act as career counselling centres.
- Modernization of existing it is.
- Giving institutes more autonomy.
- Execution of PPP mode.
- Personnel Policy to ensure accountability and outcomes.

Main focus of the 11th five year plan is to forge a joint collaboration between the States and the Centre and also boost private partnerships to create an estimated 58.6 million new jobs in the domestic economy and about 45 million jobs in the international economy.

World Bank also has taken initiative through its Millennium Development Goal to impart training and elementary education in India.

Points to focus on:

- The training courses lack focus on the changing job market. As a result it was seen from various reports that the number of students is declining for long term vocational courses, mainly in ITIs. The training policy should be focused on the changing job market in order to attract young people. More autonomy needs to be provided to institutes and they should have market linked infrastructure. For publicly funded training, equity distribution is also a problem. But job creation must be done regionally, not centrally; otherwise it will create regional imbalances of trained manpower. According to NSSO report (No. 470, 55th round) about 27 per cent of the Indian population were migrants. The proportion of migrants was higher (33 per cent) in urban areas than (24 per cent) in the rural areas. It was mainly in search of jobs. Creating job opportunities regionally can help 6maintain the equilibrium in future days.

- Funding for the public ITIs is very low compared to other countries like China and USA which have restructuring-funds, whose share goes for improvement of vocational training systems in order to achieve international quality. Although things have changed for the better in the 11th five year plan with the introduction of the National Skill Development Mission. But it is also desirable to have mechanisms to raise funds privately for up gradation of ITIs.
- ITIs must focus on low-literate youth and provide new vocational qualifications/training programmes and also on unorganised sector, otherwise it will cause long term losses. To take an example automobile industry is a technology intensive industry but most of the workshops are running without formally trained staff (we have currently no database of that). Sometimes, lack of training skills may harm the delicate instrument of vehicles. A vital challenge is to formally train workers for the crafts industry where a considerable number of informally trained craftsman work together.
- Lack of accountability and training/supply management are also major problems for ITI institutes.
- In our country different institutes impart vocational training but they do not have coordination among themselves. Information about this sector is not available from a single source. In fact we need to create a central database from where one can get full access on vocational training system right from school level to ITI/ITC institutes.
- In rural sector, radiographer and other trained para-medical persons are very less in comparison to the large number of the rural population. Policy makers should focus on the paramedical vocational studies, so that incremental change in number of trained paramedical worker can benefit rural masses.

- A central vocational training standardization system, accredited nationally and globally, for maintaining the quality of the vocational education can enhance credibility of vocationally trained persons in the industry.
- To attract more students from school level, reorientation of vocational courses is needed.
- There should be a bridge organization to relate R&D institutes and vocational education system. It would help the vocationally trained person to get the benefits of R&D.

Vocational Education in the United States

In the United States, vocational education varies from state to state. The majority of postsecondary technical and vocational training is provided by proprietary (privately owned) career schools. About 30 percent of all credentials in career training are provided by two-year community colleges, which also offer courses transferable to four-year universities; other programmes are offered through military technical training government-operated adult education centres. Several states operate their own institutes of technology which are on an equal accreditational footing with other state universities.

Historically, middle schools and high schools have offered vocational courses such as home economics, wood and metal shop, typing, business courses, drafting, and auto repair, though schools have put more emphasis on academics for all students because of standards based education reform. School-to-Work is a series of federal and state initiatives to link academics to work, sometimes including spending time during the day on a job site without pay.

National Programmes

Federal involvement is principally carried out through the Carl D. Perkins Career and Technical Education Act. Accountability requirements tied to the receipt of federal funds under this Act help provide some overall leadership. The Office of Vocational and Adult Education within the US Department of Education also supervises activities funded by the Act, along with grants to individual states and other local programmes.

The Association for Career and Technical Education (ACTE) is the largest private association dedicated to the advancement of education that prepares youth and adults for careers. Its members include CTE teachers, administrators, and researchers.

Accreditation

There is however an issue with vocational or "career" schools who have national accreditation instead of regional accreditation. Regionally accredited schools are predominantly academically oriented, non-profit institutions. Nationally accredited schools are predominantly for-profit and offer vocational, career or technical programmes. Every college has the right to set standards and refuse to accept transfer credits. However, if a student has gone to a nationally accredited school it may be particularly difficult to transfer credits (or even credit for a degree earned) if he or she then applies to a regionally accredited college. Some regionally accredited colleges have general policies against accepting any credits from nationally accredited schools, others are reluctant to because regional schools feel that national schools academic standards are lower than their own or they are unfamiliar with the particular school.

Students who are planning to transfer to a regionally accredited school after studying at a nationally accredited school should ensure that they will be able to transfer the credits before attending the nationally accredited school. There have been lawsuits regarding nationally accredited schools who led prospective students to believe that they would have no problem transferring their credits to regionally accredited schools, most notably Florida Metropolitan University and Crown College, Tacoma, Washington. The U.S. Department of Education has stated, however, that its criteria for recognition of accreditors "do not differentiate between types of accrediting agencies, so the recognition granted to all types of accrediting agencies — regional, institutional, specialized, and programmatic — is identical." However the same letter states that "the specific scope of recognition varies according to the type of agency recognized."

Job Retraining

In many states, vocational training is available to workers who have been previously laid off or whose previous employer is defunct; such training was expanded under the American Recovery and Reinvestment Act of 2009. Though results have been for the most part inconclusive, job retraining programmes have been noted to retain a positive effect on employee morale. Even in cases of displacement, those who underwent job retraining programmes exhibited a more positive outlook on their circumstances than those employees who did not partake in job retraining programmes. Several studies have also suggested that in cases of layoffs, employees who remain with the company exhibit positive morale and are more motivated in their work environment if the layoffs are handled effectively by the company. Job retraining programmes in the United States are often criticized for their lack of proper focus on skills that are required in existing jobs. A 2009 study by the United States Department of Labour showed that the difference in earnings and chances of being re-hired between those who had been trained and those who had not been was small.

History

In the early years of the twentieth century, a number of efforts were made to imitate German-style industrial education in the United States. Researchers such as Holmes Beckwith described the relationship between the apprenticeship and continuation school models in Germany, and suggested variants of the system that could be applied in an American context. The industrial education system evolved, after large-scale growth following World War I, into modern vocational education.

New York City's New CTE High Schools

In 2008, New York City's Department of Education began to rethink vocational training in high schools. Mayor Bloomberg in his State of the City 2008 address said, "This year, we're going to begin dramatically transforming how high school students prepare for technical careers in a number of growing fields. Traditionally, such career and technical education has been seen as an educational dead-end. We're going to change that. College isn't for everyone, but education is. Building on work by the State Education Department, we'll do what no other public school system in the nation has done- create rigorous career and technical programmes that start in high schools and continue in our community colleges" A hallmark of New York City public education is school choice. One category of schools students could choose since the early 20th Century has been the vocational high school. In recent years, several new CTE high schools have been started in New York City or reforged with a new perspective. The idea behind this reconfiguration of CTE is that vocational positions are becoming increasingly sophisticated and a high school degree will not be sufficient training. Future vocational technicians will need college training. The new CTE schools prepare students for success college in addition to providing a vocational certification. A new vocational high school, called City Polytechnic High School, will allow students to take college courses while still in high school. While many high schools in New York City offer college courses as part of their curriculum, City Poly, as the school is known, is the first to offer programmes in technical fields. Students will graduate in five years instead of the usual four, with a high school diploma and an associate's degree.

Some famous New York City CTE schools include—

- Aviation High School (New York), founded in 1925, known for supplying 12 percent of all of the workers on aircraft worldwide and sending several graduates to high level engineering programmes, such as Columbia School of Engineering and Applied Science and Massachusetts Institute of Technology. Famous alumni include Whitey Ford and Michael Bentt.
- High School of Art and Design, founded 1936, whose famous alumni include Tony Bennett, Lenny White, Tom Sito, and several others.
- Urban Assembly New York Harbor School, founded 2003, known for being the first non-U.S. Military organization to be housed on Governors Island in New York City Harbor since the Lenape. The school is also known for sending graduates to Cornell University and other prestigious schools in addition to supplying well-trained workers on New York City's 600 mile waterfront. This school has the second certified SCUBA training programme in a high school in the U.S.

Vocational School

A vocational school (or trade school or career school), providing vocational education, is a school in which students are taught the skills needed to perform a particular job. Traditionally, vocational schools have not existed to further education in the area of liberal arts, but rather to teach only job-specific skills, and as such have been better considered to be institutions devoted to training, and not liberal arts education. That purely vocational focus began changing in the 1990s "toward a broader preparation that develops the academic" and technical skills of students, as well as the vocational. Typically, most career colleges specifically design their curricula for fields that have the best current and future growth potential.

Australia

Vocational schools were called Technical Colleges in Australia and there were more than 20 schools specializing in Vocational Educational Training (VET). But, nowadays only four Technical Colleges remain and these are now referred to as Trade Colleges. At these colleges, students complete a modified Year 12 certificate and commence a school-based apprenticeship in a trade of their choice. There are two Trade Colleges in Queensland; Brisbane, Australian Trade College and the Gold Coast, Australian Industry Trade College and one in Adelaide, St Patrick's Technical College and another in Perth, Australian Trades College.

In Queensland, students can also undertake Vocational Educational Training at private and public high schools instead of studying for their OP or Overall Position which is a tertiary entrance score. However these students usually undertake more limited vocational education of one day per week whereas in the trade colleges the training is more time intensive.

Canada

Vocational schools are sometimes called colleges in Canada. However, a college may also refer to an institution that offers part of a university degree, or credits that may be transferred to a university.

In Ontario, secondary schools were separated into three streams: Technical Schools, Commercial/Business Schools and Collegiates (the academic schools). Those schools still exist; however, the curriculum has changed that no matter which type of school one attends, they can still attend any post-secondary institution and still study a variety of subjects (either academic or practical).

In Ontario, Ministry of Training, Colleges and Universities have divided postsecondary education into Universities, Community Colleges and Private Career Colleges.

In the province of Quebec, there are some vocational programmes offered at institutions called CEGEP's (*Collège d'enseignement général et professionnel*), but these too may function as an introduction to university. Generally students complete two years at a CEGEP directly out of high school, and then complete three years at a university (rather than the usual four), to earn an undergraduate degree. Alternatively some CEGEP's offer vocational training, but it is more likely that vocational training will be found at institutions separate from the academic institutions, though they may still be called colleges.

Central and Eastern Europe

In Central and Eastern Europe a vocational education is represented in forms of (professional) vocational technical schools often abbreviated as PTU and technical colleges (technikum).

PTU

PTU is usually a preparatory vocational education and is equivalent to the general education of the third degree in the former Soviet education, providing a lower level of vocational education (apprenticeship). It could be compared to a trade high school. In 1920-30s such PTUs were called as schools of factory and plant apprenticeship and later 1940s - vocational schools. Sometime after 1959 the name of PTU was established, however, with the reorganization of the Soviet educational system these vocational schools renamed into lyceums. There were several types of PTUs such as Middle City PTU and Rural PTU.

Technicum

Technical college (technicum) is becoming an obsolete term for a college in different parts of Central and Eastern Europe. Technicums provided a middle level of vocational education. Aside of technicums and PTU there also were vocational schools (Russian: Ïðîôåññèîíàëüíûå ó÷èëèùà) that also provided a middle level of vocational education. In Ukraine of 1920-30s technicums were a (technical) vocational institutes, however, during the 1930-32s Soviet educational reform they were degraded in their accreditation.

Institute

Institutes were considered a higher level of education, however, unlike universities they were more oriented to a particular trade. With the reorganization of the Soviet education system most institutes have been renamed into technical universities.

Finland

The Finnish system is divided between vocational and academic paths. Currently about 47 percent of Finnish students at age 15 go to vocational school. The vocational school is a secondary school for ages 16–21, and prepares the students for entering the workforce. The curriculum includes little academic general education, while the practical skills of each trade are stressed. The education is divided into eight main categories with a total of about 50 trades. The basic categories of education are

- Humanist and educational branch
- typical trade: youth- and free-time director
- Cultural branch
- typical trade: artisan, media-assistant
- The branch of social sciences, business and merchandise

- typical trade: Vocational Qualification in Business and Administration (Finnish: *merkonomi*)
- Natural Science
- typical trade: IT worker (Finnish: *datanomi*)
- Technology and traffic
- typical trades: machinist, electrician, process worker
- The branch of natural resources and environment
- typical trade: rural entrepreneur, forest worker
- The branch of social work, health care and physical exercise
- typical trade: paramedic (Finnish: *lähihoitaja*)
- The branch of travel, catering and domestic economics
- typical trade: institutional catering worker

In addition to these categories administered by the Ministry of Education, the Ministry of Interior provides vocational education in the security and rescue branch for policemen, prison guards and firefighters.

The vocational schools are usually owned by the municipalities, but in special cases, private or state vocational schools exist. The state grants aid to all vocational schools on the same basis, regardless of the owner. On the other hand, the vocational schools are not allowed to operate for profit. The Ministry of Education issues licences to provide vocational education. In the licence, the municipality or a private entity is given permission to train a yearly quota of students for specific trades. The licence also specifies the area where the school must be located and the languages used in the education.

The vocational school students are selected by the schools on the basis of criteria set by the Ministry of Education. The basic qualification for the study is completed nine-year comprehensive school. Anyone may seek admission in any vocational school regardless of their domicile. In certain trades, bad health or invalidity may be acceptable grounds for refusing admission. The students do not pay tuition and they must be provided with health care and a free daily school lunch. However, the students must pay for the books, although the tools and practice material are provided to the students for free.

In tertiary education, there are higher vocational schools (ammattikorkeakoulu which is translated to *polytechnic* or *university of applied sciences*), which give about 3-4 -year degrees in more involved fields, like engineering or nursing.

In contrast to the vocational school, an academically orientated upper secondary school, or senior high school (Finnish: *lukio*) teaches no vocational skills. It prepares for entering the university or a higher vocational school.

Ireland

A vocational school in Ireland is a type of secondary education school which places a large emphasis on vocational and technical education; this led to some conflict in the 1960s when the Regional Technical College system was in development. Since 2013 the schools have been managed by Education and Training Boards, which replaced Vocational Education Committees which were largely based on city or county boundaries. Establishment of the schools is largely provided by the state; funding is through block grant system providing about 90% of necessary funding requirements.

Vocational schools typically have further education courses in addition to the traditional courses at secondary level. For instance, *Post Leaving Certificate Courses* which are intended for school leavers and pre-third level education students.

Until the 1970s the vocational schools were seen as inferior to the other schools then available in Ireland. This was mainly because traditional courses such as the Leaving Certificate were not available at the schools, however this changed with the *Investment in Education* (1962) report which resulted in an upgrade in their status. Currently about 25% of secondary education students attend these schools.

Japan

In Japan vocational schools are known as *senmon gakkô*. There are part of Japan's higher education system. They are two-year schools that many students study at after finishing high school (although it is not always required that students graduate from high school). Some have a wide range of majors, others only a few majors. Some examples are computer technology, fashion and English.

Netherlands

In the Middle Ages boys learned a vocation through an apprenticeship. They were usually 10 years old when they entered service, and were first called *leerling* (apprentice), then *gezel* (journeyman) and after an exam - sometimes with an example of workmanship called a *meesterproef* (masterpiece) - they were called *meester* (master craftsman). In 1795 all of the guilds in the Netherlands were disbanded by Napoleon, and with them the guild vocational schooling system. After the French occupation, in the 1820s, the need for quality education caused more and more cities to form day and evening schools for various trades. In 1854, the society *Maatschappij tot verbetering van den werkenden stand* (Society to improve the working class) was founded in Amsterdam, that changed its name in 1861 to the *Maatschappij voor de Werkende Stand* (Society for the working class). This society started the first public vocational school (*De Ambachtsschool*) in Amsterdam, and many cities followed. At first only for boys, later the *Huishoudschool* (housekeeping) was introduced as vocational schooling for girls. Housekeeping education began in 1888 with the Haagsche Kookschool in The Hague.

In 1968 the law called the *Mammoetwet* changed all of this, effectively dissolving the Huishoudschool and the Ambachtsschool. The name was changed to *Lagere Technische School* (LTS) (lower technical school) where mainly boys went because of its technical nature. The other option, where most girls went was LBO (Lager Beroepsonderwijsl). In 1992 both LTS and LBO changed to VBO (Voorbereidend Middelbaar Beroepsonderwijs) and since 1999 VBO changed to the current VMBO.

United States

In the United States, there is a very large difference between career college and vocational college. The term *career college* is generally reserved for post-secondary for-profit institutions.

Conversely, vocational schools are Government-owned or at least Government-supported institutions, occupy two full years of study, their credits are by and large accepted elsewhere in the academic world and in some instances such as charter academies or magnet schools may take the place of the final years of high school. Career colleges on the other hand are generally not government supported in any capacity, occupy periods of study less than a year, their training and certifications are largely if not completely discredited by the larger academic world and are run more as a for-profit business than anything else. In addition, as most career colleges are private schools; this group may be further subdivided into non-profit schools and proprietary schools, operated for the sole economic benefit of their owners.

As a result of this emphasis on the commercialization of education, a widespread and well-deserved for the period poor reputation for quality was retained by a great number of career colleges for over promising what the job prospects for their graduates would actually be in their field of study upon completion of their programme, and for emphasizing the number of careers from which a student could choose. However, although this problem has been largely corrected in modern times due to more stringent regulation. careful research on the career college in question must be performed by the student prior to enrolling in order to get the best value.

Even though career colleges have exploded in recent years, true government-sponsored vocational schools on the other hand have decreased severely in the United States and have largely been replaced by the various alternative trade classes offered at either trade-specific schools or by being merged with their community college cousins, which in addition to offering associate degrees and core university curriculum courses, also offer vocational classes depending on the needs of the local community, all units of which are capable of transferring to four-year institutions.

The Association for Career and Technical Education (ACTE) is the largest American national education association dedicated to the advancement of career and technical education or vocational education that prepares youth and adults for careers, so the wise prospective student may wish to check with them to see if the school is in good standing with this and other trade organizations. Even though virtually none of the for-profit career colleges have distinguished themselves in any capacity, a great many true vocational schools have gone on to become some of the most prestigious universities in the world. The California Institute of Technology and Carnegie Mellon University are examples.

Retraining

Vocational rehabilitation or retraining is the process of learning a new skill or trade, often in response to a change in the economic environment. Generally it reflects changes in profession rather than an "upward" movement in the same field.

The need to retrain workers is often thought to apply to older members of the workforce, many of whom saw their occupations disappear and their skills lose value as technology, outsourcing and a weak economy combined to erode their ability to make a living. While older Americans do not face as high a rate of unemployment as the country's teenagers and young adults, when they do find themselves unemployed, they remain unemployed for more than twice as long as teenagers.

While the stereotype for retraining needs is the older worker, youth in the United States and across the European Community (OECD) and Africa suffer from the same problem. The gap between the skills they possess and those that employers are actively seeking is significant and stagnating to their employment prospects. Currently in the United States, psychology, history and the performing arts make up 22% of college degrees earned. Demand for skilled employees, however, is in the areas of technology and engineering, currently at 5% of conferred degrees. "In both Britain and the United States, many people with expensive liberal arts degrees are finding it impossible to get decent jobs," reports the Economist in its April 27, 2013 issue, adding that in northern Africa, job applicants with degrees face an unemployment level twice that of non-degreed candidates.

While technology anxiety and a nervousness about learning new processes and acquiring new skill sets has impacted older workers, younger job seekers are also facing a deficit of "applied soft skills" such as work ethic, social skills, communication and leadership.

The need for greater partnership and transfer of information between institutions of higher education is essential in reducing the skills gap for old and young people alike. Expanded internships and post-hiring training can help from the employers' perspective and upgraded and more authentic technical training will help close the gap on the side of educators.

There is some controversy surrounding the use of retraining to offset economic changes caused by free trade and automation. For example, most studies show that displaced factory workers in the United States on the average have lower wages after retraining to other positions when a factory is closed due to offshoring. A similar issue surrounds movement from technical jobs to liaison jobs due to offshore outsourcing. Such changes may also favour certain personality types over others, due to the changing tasks and skills required. Other research estimates that one academic year of such retraining at a community college increases the long-term earnings by about 8 percent for older males and by about 10 percent for older females.

Government policy may make a difference in employability and motivation for retraining and re-entry into the workforce for older workers. In economies with greater regulations surrounding the hiring, termination and wages, reductions in unemployment were difficult to achieve. The very groups harmed with continued higher unemployment were those that the regulations sought to protect.

Retraining is sometimes offered as part of workfare programmes, which may include support for transportation, childcare, or an internship. As difficult and controversial as it may seem, retraining older and younger workers alike to prepare them to be part of a changing workforce will have a lasting impact on workers across the globe. Unemployed workers are at significantly greater risk for poor physical health, greater stress, alcoholism, marital problems and even suicide. Among young workers, beginning their careers with extended bouts of joblessness results in lower overall earnings and more unemployment throughout their careers.

Life skills

Enumeration and categorization

UNICEF states "there is no definitive list" of life skills but enumerates many "psychosocial and interpersonal skills generally considered important." It asserts life skills are a synthesis: "many skills are used simultaneously in practice. For example, decision-making often involves critical thinking ("what are my options?") and values clarification ("what is important to me?"). Ultimately, the interplay between the skills is what produces powerful behavioural outcomes, especially where this approach is supported by other strategies..."

Life skills can vary from financial literacy, substance abuse prevention, to therapeutic techniques to deal with disabilities, such as autism. Life skills curricula designed for K-12 often emphasizes communications and practical skills needed for successful independent living for developmental disabilities/special education students with an Individualized Education Programme (IEP). However, some programmes are for general populations, such as the Overcoming Obstacles programme for middle schools and high schools.

Parenting 2.0 (P2.0), LinkedIn's largest parenting group with more than 2,700 members (as of March, 2013), defines Life Skills as all the non-academic foundational skills human beings learn and use to thrive individually and live optimally in community with others. P2.0's founder, Marlaine Paulsen Cover created a Life Skills Report Card that lists five basic skills categories:

- Personal care
- Organization
- Respect for self and others
- Communication
- Social skills

and proposes that life skills should be considered as important as academic skills.

Parenting

Life skills are often taught in the domain of parenting, either indirectly through the observation and experience of the child, or directly with the purpose of teaching a specific skill. Yet skills for dealing with pregnancy and parenting can be considered and taught as a set of life skills of themselves. Teaching these parenting life skills can also coincide with additional life skills development of the child. Many life skills programmes are offered when traditional family structures and healthy relationships have broken down, whether due to parental lapses, divorce or due to issues with the children (such as substance abuse or other risky behaviour). For example, the International Labour Organization is teaching life skills to ex-child labourers and risk children in Indonesia to help them avoid the worst forms of child labour.

Youth: Behaviour Prevention vs. Positive Development

While certain life skills programmes focus on teaching the prevention of certain behaviours the Search Institute has found those programmes can be relatively ineffective. Based upon their research The Family and Youth Services Bureau, a division of the U.S. Department of Health and Human Services advocates the theory of Positive Youth Development as a replacement for the less effective prevention programmes. Positive Youth Development, or PYD as it's come to be known as, focuses on the strengths of an individual as opposed to the older methods which tend to focus on the "potential" weaknesses that have yet to be shown. The Family and Youth Services Bureau has found that individuals who developed life skills in a positive, rather than preventive, manner feel a greater sense of competence, usefulness, power, and belonging.

Life Skill Development in Adults

Beyond the K-12 domain, other life skills programmes are focused on social welfare and social work programmes, such as Casey Life Skills. This programme covers diverse topics: career planning, communication, daily living, home life, housing and money management, self care, social relationships, work and study skills, work life, pregnancy and parenting.

Life skills are behaviours used appropriately and responsibly in the management of personal affairs. They are a set of human skills acquired via teaching or direct experience that are used to handle problems and questions commonly encountered in daily human life. The subject varies greatly depending on societal norms and community expectations.

The Role of Vocational Education in Economic Development in Malaysia

Ever since the Industrial Revolution in the late 18th century, progress and prosperity have been closely identified with economic development (Jomo, 1993). The economic competitiveness of a country depends on the skills of its work force. The skills and competencies of the work force, in turn, are dependent upon the quality of the country's education and training systems. Vocational education is perceived as one of the crucial elements in enhancing economic productivity (Min, 1995). Based on social efficiency theory, schools should prepare and supply future workers with appropriate knowledge and skills to enhance their productivity and, therefore, promote economic growth (Finch, 1993; Labaree, 1997).

Nevertheless, vocational education has sometimes become a tool for addressing the economic, political, and social crises that are threatening the political and economic stability of some nations. Rising unemployment, lack of skilled workers, high dropout rates, and the changing demographic nature of the work force have placed the issue of workforce education high on the educational reform agenda (Giroux, 1991). Traditionally, vocational education has prepared students for specific skills. However, in the post-Taylorist work environment, workers are expected to perform more broadly-defined jobs (Hirsch & Wagner, 1995). Therefore, a broad-based education is required. In the new economic environment, vocational education is expected to produce an educated, skilled, and motivated work force (Mustapha, 1999).

The economic argument in favour of vocational education is linked to the perceived need to orient the formal educational system to the needs of the world of work (Middleton, Ziderman, & Adams, 1993; Neuman & Ziderman, 1989). It is based on the assumption that economic growth and development are technology-driven and human capital-dependent. International comparisons show that employers in the U.S. and U.K. believe the present state of vocational education in their respective countries is inadequate to train students effectively for the changing demands of the work place (Brown & Keep, 1999; Distler, 1992). Australian employers, however, seem satisfied with their vocational education system (Fairweather, 1999). Research on educators' perceptions regarding vocational education generally reveals positive findings (Barnett, 1984; Matulis, 1989; Matthews, 1987; Pryor, 1984).

Despite vast research on employers' and educators' perspectives regarding the role of vocational education in the economic development of industrialized countries (e.g., Bishop, 1989; Carnevale & Schulz, 1990; Clouse, 1997; Harvey, 1998; Lewis, 1991; Lynch & Black, 1996; Mobley, 1998; Williams & Hornsby, 1989), minimal research exists in developing countries. Therefore, the purpose of this study was to investigate the perceptions of Malaysian employers and educators regarding the role of vocational education in the economic development of the country. Even though Malaysia was selected, some of the findings may be applicable to other countries with similar contexts.

Purpose of the Study

The purpose of this study was to investigate the perceptions of educators and employers regarding the role of vocational education in the economic development of Malaysia. Specifically, the research questions were:

1. To what extent does vocational education contribute to the economic development of Malaysia?
2. What are the perceptions of educators and employers regarding the employability of graduates of vocational programmes?
3. What are the factors that facilitate or inhibit the restructuring of vocational education in serving the needs of Malaysia's industrialization?
4. To what extent do educators and employers believe that government is responsive to the needs of vocational education and training systems?

Methodology

This was a descriptive study intended to examine the role of vocational education in the economic development of Malaysia. According to Gall, Borg, and Gall (1996), descriptive research involves providing careful descriptions of a phenomenon. Its purpose is to generate an accurate description of an event, attitude, or behaviour. The research design was based on the study's objectives. A survey questionnaire was constructed to collect the data for this study.

Population and Sample

There were two target populations in this study. The first population (N=4,316) included all vocational educators in public vocational schools and polytechnics (similar to community colleges in the United States) in Peninsular Malaysia as identified from a directory of vocational personnel obtained from the Technical and Vocational Division, Ministry of Education. A random sample of 300 subjects was selected. The second population was corporate management personnel from large and medium-size manufacturing companies in Klang Valley and Selangor. These areas were selected because of the concentration of large and medium-size manufacturing companies. The companies were limited to three categories: Fabricated Metal Products, Machinery Manufacturing, and Transport Equipment. The industrial categories were based on the classification used by the Malaysian Industrial Development Authority (MIDA).

The three industrial categories were chosen based on the assumption that the majority of vocational graduates were employed in these industries. The directory of these companies was obtained from MIDA. Management personnel surveyed in this study were limited to the Chief Executive Officer (CEO), Personnel Manager, Production Manager, and Head Supervisor. These management personnel were assumed to represent the employer perspectives. With the exception of the CEO, personnel and production managers and supervisors were assumed to have regular contact with the employees. Therefore, they were in a unique position to evaluate the employees. Of the 283 manufacturing companies in Klang Valley and Selangor, 30 (or approximately 10% of the companies) were randomly selected. In each selected company, four management personnel (i.e., CEOs, personnel and production managers, and supervisors) were requested to complete the survey, for a total sample of 120 employers.

Instrumentation

The purpose of the survey questionnaire was to identify the role of vocational education in the economic development of Malaysia. The items were generated based on the research questions posited for this study. The instrument items, format, and procedures were constructed based on existing research studies and literature related to vocational education and training, educational reform, economics of education, employability, school and business partnerships, technology-preparation (tech-prep), school-to-work, and current trends in education.

The first section of the survey contained a purpose statement, directions, and demographic information. A code number was assigned to each instrument to maintain the anonymity of the respondents. The demographic items for educators and employers included gender, ethnicity, present position, and highest qualification. The educator survey also included primary programme area, type of institution, location of institution, years of teaching and/or administrative experience, and the number of in-service courses attended. Additional demographic information included in the employer survey were years of management experience, company size, and type of ownership

The second section of the instrument contained directions and 26 five-point Likert-scale items. The following scale ranges were constructed: 4.50 - 5.00 Strongly Agree; 3.50 - 4.49 Agree; 2.50 - 3.49 Uncertain; 1.50 - 2.49 Disagree; and 1.00 - 1.49 Strongly Disagree. Several drafts of the instrument were reviewed by a panel of experts, which consisted of four professors in the field of vocational and technical education. Revisions were made based on their comments and recommendations. The instrument was also pilot-tested on a small group (n=12) of vocational and technical educators. The internal consistency reliability for the instrument using Cronbach's Coefficient Alpha was estimated to be á = 0.94. Therefore, the final version of the instrument was considered to possess an adequate degree of content and face validity and internal consistency reliability.

Data Collection and Data Analysis

Survey instruments were mailed to the 300 educators and 120 employers. The cover letter explained the purpose and importance of the study and requested their assistance and cooperation. Three follow-up mailings were conducted at three, six, and nine week intervals after the initial mailing. A total of 276 educator instruments (92%) and 53 employer instruments (44%) were returned. The data were coded and analyzed using Statistical Analysis Software (SAS) version 6.12. Descriptive and inferential statistics were used to organize, analyze, and interpret the data. Descriptive statistics included frequencies, percentages, rank-orders, means, and standard deviations. Confidence intervals and margins of error were the inferential statistics used in this study. The information was then summarized and described.

Results

Demographics of Educators: Of the 276 educators, 69% were male and 31% were female. The majority of the respondents were Malay (85.7%), followed by Chinese (12.5%), and Indian (1.5%). Most (89%) were teachers and the remainder (11%) was administrators. Two-thirds (66%) of the respondents were educators in vocational schools and 34 % were polytechnic educators. More than one-fourth

(26%) of the sample had 6 to 10 years teaching experience. The majority (60.8%) of the participants had no administrative experience. The top three programme areas were electrical engineering, represented by 13% of the respondents, followed by mechanical engineering (10.1%) and civil engineering (9.1%).

Demographics of Employers

The respondents were 91% male and 9% female. The majority were Malay (76%) followed by Chinese (15%), and Indian (9%). Over one-half (59%) of the respondents were managers, and the remainder were supervisors (32%) and CEOs (9%). Half of the respondents (51%) indicated the Bachelor's degree as their highest level of education. Approximately one-third (30.2%) of the respondents had management experience between 6 to 10 years. Respondents were management personnel in locally owned companies (68%), joint-ventures (17%), or multi-national corporations (15%).

The second section of the survey contained 26 Likert-scale items. The findings were organized around the study's four research questions. For each research question, the data showed no significant differences among demographic variables, with the exception of programmes areas. Thus, the data were fairly consistent across the demographic data.

Items 1 through 5 addressed research question 1: To what extent does vocational education and training contribute to the economic development of Malaysia? The means, margins of error, and standard deviations for items 1 through 5. Regarding item 1, the educators (M=4.64, SD=.53) strongly agreed and employers (M=4.38, SD=.69) agreed that vocational education and training has contributed to the economic development of Malaysia.

For item 2, the educators agreed (M=3.78, SD=1.07) that vocational institutions have prepared sufficient numbers of skilled workers, but the relatively large standard deviation suggests that the responses were dispersed. Employers (M=3.02, SD=.97) indicated that they were uncertain.

For item 3, educators (M=4.26, SD=.75) and employers (M=3.91, SD=.77) agreed that polytechnics and vocational programmes were more suitable than academic programmes in preparing for new skills and use of technology.

For item 4, educators (M=3.60, SD=.97) agreed that public vocational institutions had produced higher quality graduates than their private counterparts, while the employers (M=3.06, SD=.73) were less certain. Interestingly, both educators (M=4.02, SD=.73) and employers (M=3.85, SD=.79) agreed that a substantial financial investment in vocational education and training was justified (item 5). For items 1 through 5, the margins of error for the educators' data (.06 to .12) were much lower than the margins of error for the employers' data (.19 to .27) at the 95 % confidence level. One possible explanation is that the educator sample size was much larger (n=276) than the employer sample size (n=53). Overall, educators (M=4.06, SD=.46) seemed to agree more than employers (M=3.64, SD=.51) regarding the positive effect of vocational education on the economic development of Malaysia.

Items 6 through 14 were formulated to address research question 2: What are the perceptions of educators and employers regarding the employability of graduates of vocational programmes? Regarding employment opportunities (item 6), both educators (M=4.44, SD=.72) and employers (M=4.08, SD=.65) agreed that completers of vocational programmes have better employment opportunities than completers of academic programmes.

For item 7, educators (M=4.12, SD=.74) and employers (M=3.57, SD=.79) agreed that vocational graduates were well prepared to enter the work force. With regard to communication skills of the graduates (item 8), both educators (M=3.46, SD=.88) and employers (M=2.70, SD=.85) were uncertain regarding the communication skills of vocational and technical graduates. Variability was relatively large for both groups.

With respect to interpersonal skills (item 9), the educators (M=3.70, SD=.83) agreed that their graduates possessed interpersonal skills but the employers (M=2.89, SD=.89) were unsure. Again, the standard deviations were relatively large which shows dispersed responses. For item 10, employers (M=3.02, SD=.75) were uncertain regarding the self-motivation of vocational graduates, while the educators (M=3.64, SD=.84) agreed that their graduates were self-motivated.

Both educators (M=3.72, SD=.82) and employers (M=3.70, SD=.80) agreed that completers of vocational programmes possessed technical skills (item 11). However, educators (M=3.38, SD=.91) and employers (M=2.70, SD=.95) were uncertain regarding the critical thinking and problem-solving skills of vocational graduates (item 12). In terms of entrepreneurial skills (item 13), educators (M=3.54, SD=.83) agreed but employers (M=2.26, SD=.92) disagreed that vocational graduates possessed entrepreneurial skills.

The standard deviations on items 8 through 13 for both groups were relatively large, suggesting a lack of consensus among educators and employers regarding the employability skills of vocational graduates. With regard to positive attitudes toward work (item 14), educators (M=3.98, SD=.67) agreed while the employers (M=3.39, SD=.72) were uncertain whether graduates of vocational programmes possessed positive attitudes toward work. At a 95 % confidence level, the margins of error for items 6 through 14 ranged from .08 to .11 for educators and .18 to .26 for employers. The total for research question 2 indicates that educators (M=3.77, SD=.55) possessed more favourable attitudes toward the employability of vocational graduates than the employers (M=3.14, SD=.52).

Items 15 through 19 addressed research question 3: What are the factors that facilitate or inhibit the restructuring of vocational education and training in serving the needs of Malaysia's industrialization? These items identified the factors that facilitate or inhibit the restructuring of vocational programmes to serve the needs of the labour force. On item 15, educators (M=4.00, SD=.81) and employers (M=3.68, SD=.80) agreed that government is committed to restructuring vocational programmes. With respect to business and school partnerships (item 16), educators (M=3.63, SD=.87) agreed but employers (M=3.04, SD=1.09) were unsure about the government's initiatives to link vocational institutions with business and industry. The standard deviations for items 15 and 16 were relatively large, indicating that the responses were dispersed. In terms of the relevancy of the vocational curriculum to the needs of the labour market (item 17), educators agreed (M=3.69, SD=.85) but employers (M=3.43, SD=.82) were uncertain about its relevance.

On item 18, both educators (M=3.65, SD=.81) and employers (M=3.52, SD=.63) agreed that the structure of vocational education has become more flexible. Interestingly, both educators (M=4.01, SD=.82) and employers (M=4.11, SD=.93) agreed that public vocational institutions would achieve greater efficiency if they were managed similar to businesses (item 19). The margins of error for items 15 through 19 ranged from .09 to .10 for educators and .17 to .30 for employers. Overall, both educators (M=3.80, SD=.56) and employers (M=3.56, SD=.52) agreed with regard to the role of government in restructuring vocational programmes.

The means, margins of error, and standard deviations for items 20 through 26, which addressed research question 4: To what extent do educators and employers believe that government is responsive to the needs of vocational education and training systems? Regarding item 20, both educators (M=3.82, SD=.81) and employers (M=3.55, SD=.70) agreed that the government is responsive to the needs of vocational education and training. On item 21, both educators (M=3.88, SD=.77) and employers (M=3.57, SD=.60) also agreed that the government's policy was focusing on the expansion of vocational education and training.

With respect to public funding (item 22), educators (M=3.57, SD=.98) agreed that the government had allocated sufficient funding to upgrade vocational programmes while employers (M=3.34, SD=.68) were uncertain. Regarding the provision of adequate facilities and resources for vocational institutions (item 23), educators (M=3.49, SD=.97) and employers (M=3.21, SD=.69) were less certain. For item 24, the educators (M=3.80, SD=.94) agreed that the government is committed to maintaining the high quality of vocational education and training while the employers (M=3.26, SD=.86) were uncertain. Large standard deviations for both groups suggest a relatively large variability of responses.

On item 25, educators (M=4.07, SD=.75) and employers (M=4.30, SD=.72) agreed that input from joint public and private sector advisory committees is crucial for the improvement of vocational education and training systems. Employers (M=4.51, SD=.58) strongly agreed and the educators (M=4.26, SD=.75) agreed regarding the perceived positive benefits of technical exchanges between vocational institutions and business/industry (item 26). The relatively small standard deviations for items 25 and 26 indicated strong agreement among respondents. The margins of error for items 20 through 26 ranged from .09 to .12 for educators and from .15 to .24 for employers. The total for research question 4 indicates that both educators (M=3.84, SD=.55) and employers (M=3.68, SD=.43) agreed that the government was responsive to the needs of vocational education and training in Malaysia.

Implications and Conclusions

Role of Vocational Education and Training: The results reveal that educators and employers believed that vocational education and training contributed to the economic development of Malaysia. In addition, educators and employers believed that a substantial financial investment in vocational education and training is justified. Further, they believed that vocational programmes were more appropriate than academic programmes for developing new skills and the ability to use contemporary technologies. This implies that the government and private sector should invest in vocational education and training in Malaysia.

Employability of Vocational Graduates: In terms of the employability of vocational graduates, educators and employers in Malaysia believed that the completers of vocational programmes had better employment opportunities than completers of academic programmes. Further, educators and employers indicated that vocational graduates possessed more than adequate technical skills. However, both groups were less satisfied regarding the motivation, communication, interpersonal, critical thinking, problem solving, and entrepreneurial skills of the vocational graduates. This clearly suggests that employability and generalizable skills should be integrated into vocational programmes.

Government's Commitment toward Restructuring Vocational Education and Training: Educators and employers perceived that the government of Malaysia is committed to restructuring vocational programmes. However, both educators and employers favoured a business approach to the management of public vocational education and training. This suggests the need to reduce bureaucracy and to increase the efficiency and effectiveness of vocational institutions at the secondary and post-secondary levels. In addition, the government should seriously consider decentralizing the management of public vocational institutions and encourage the expansion of private and community-supported vocational training institutions, as suggested by Psacharopoulos, Tan, and Jimenez (1986).

Furthermore, employers perceived that vocational curricula had questionable relevance to the contemporary needs of business and industry. Employers' participation in school-business partnerships was minimal. This suggests that vocational education and training institutions should conduct continuous needs assessments to create relevant curriculum. Governmental agencies should also initiate outreach programmes to establish school-business partnerships and collaboration with the private sector.

Government's Responsiveness to the Needs of Vocational Education and Training: In general, educators and employers believed that the government responded less than satisfactorily to the management of human resource needs. Employers were not aware of government initiatives to seek input from business and industry. The implication is that government and its agencies need to be more proactive rather than reactive in responding to human resource needs. This can be accomplished by eliciting input from business and industry and creating meaningful partnerships with the private sector. With limited financial resources, government must identify alternatives to encourage the private sector to invest in upgrading vocational education and training. This is only feasible if the private sector is convinced that there are mutual benefits and favourable returns.

In general, educators and employers believed that government was responsive to the needs of vocational training and was focusing on the expansion of vocational education and training. However, educators and employers also believed that the government's Ministry of Education, in particular, had not allocated adequate funds to upgrade and expand vocational programmes. Similarly, inadequate facilities and resources inhibited efforts to maintain high quality standards for vocational education and training.

Government should seek employers and private sector involvement in financing and expanding vocational education and training. The issue of quality and standards is another area that needs to be addressed. In this study, employers indicated that to improve vocational education, emphasis should be focused on establishing and maintaining quality standards for vocational programmes. Quality standards include entrance requirements, teacher certification, accreditation, and standardized assessment.

As expected, educators and employers believed that input from the public and private sector advisory committees is crucial for the improvement of vocational education and training systems. Similarly, educators and employers were in support of technical exchanges between vocational institutions and business/industry. This implies that a paradigm shift is needed, in which collaboration and partnerships between schools and business/industry are viewed as the vehicles that will advance the industrialization agenda.

2

The Role of Career and Technical Education in High School

America's attempts to revitalize education have been steeped in controversy and have resulted in the initiation of multiple reform policies over several decades. Too often schools have tried to implement what is tantamount to the reform policy *du jour*, at times focused on targeted populations and specific programmes, then just as quickly refocused on whole school reform. The result has been confusion and consternation across all aspects of public education, negatively affecting many stakeholders in the system.

Defining what educational content is necessary for all youth has become both vexing and contentious. The focus of American education has been debated throughout the past century. The debate on whether the focus of schooling is to be academic, vocational, or a mixture of the two, continues today. Faced with the stagnant and lackluster achievement of comprehensive schooling and a vocational education system that has too often been considered a warehouse for low-achieving students, the call for transforming all education has gained support from all levels of government. High standards, high-stake assessments, and greater relevance to the world of work are the central tenets of current reform.

Beginning with the Improving America's Schools Act of 1994 (P.L. 103-382) and Goals 2000 (P.L. 103-227), through the recently passed Leave No Child Behind Act of 2001 (P.L. 107-110), federal funding of elementary and secondary education programmes require state assessments to be aligned to state content and performance standards as a condition of funding eligibility.

In addition to these standards and accountability reforms, two initiatives currently playing a major role in education reform activities are School-to-work (STW), or School-to-Careers (STC), and whole school reform. Both STW and whole school reform are driving much of the current curriculum redevelopment and education restructuring.

School to Work

As business and education leaders widely concurred that American students are inadequately prepared, not only for further education, but for successful careers, high schools in the early 1990's began to organize all or parts of their curricula around career training and preparation. The Carl D. Perkins Vocational and Applied Technology Education Act of 1990 spurred renewed interest and experimentation in this area. Four years later, career focused education became the cornerstone of federal education reform policy.

Congress passed the School-to-Work Opportunities Act of 1994 (STWOA, P.L. 103–239) to address the failure of America's primary, secondary, and vocational education systems to produce graduates with marketable knowledge and skills. This legislation was designed to provide an umbrella philosophy for many activities that were intended to systematically restructure all education for all students. The STWOA centred education restructuring around school-based learning and work-based learning. Vocational education was no longer to be a stand alone programme. All education at all levels would now take on attributes of career training and preparation.

Embodied in the STWOA are the central concepts of the School-to-Work philosophy – integration of academic and vocational education, workplace competencies, and explicit connection of learning with careers. Contextual, or applied learning, is the hallmark of this philosophy. Proponents of STW argue that students will attain higher levels of academic achievement when learning is placed within the context of the workplace. It is believed that education must be relevant to the real world, particularly the world of work, to foster in students a desire to achieve greater levels of learning. Proponents assert that integrating academic and vocational education in every discipline, across all subjects, at all grade levels, in all schools will produce higher achievement.

To varying degrees, the defining features of STW have been absorbed in other education reform efforts including state academic standards, Title I grants to local educational agencies, New American High Schools, Small Learning Communities and whole school reform models. Many of these activities encourage teaching and learning in the context of real-life applications and careers. The infusion of career based education throughout the curriculum as academic and technical curricula are integrated across all subject areas and grade levels is substantially changing the delivery and focus of K-12 education despite the lack of evidence substantiating the need for such dramatic reform.

Whole School Reform

Since the passage of Goals 2000, many major educational programmes targeted to specific populations have been replaced by whole school reform measures. Designers of reform models recognized the capability of whole school reform to act as a vehicle to expand delivery of contextual learning and career focused education to more schools through federally funded programmes. While whole school reform is not the only means by which education can be altered to deliver contextual or career focused education, STW proponents viewed it as an advantageous opportunity to combine STW principles with other reform practices in one model. STW concepts continue to be sustained through inclusion in whole school reform models despite the sunsetting of the STWOA. For example, the Comprehensive School Reform Demonstration Act (CSRD) provides increased federal funding for whole school reform and specifically lists reform models that meet federal funding criteria, many which incorporate STW principles.

Many questions and concerns surround the effectiveness and necessity of both STW and whole school reform. Whole school reform models, even absent STW principles, are problematic in practice. The majority of whole school reform models, endorsed through federal legislation and funding, reflect the prevailing wisdom of modern educators, many of whose ideas are rooted in questionable pedagogical practices.

Historically, progressive education has rarely lived up to its promise. Its main features, student centred learning, teacher as facilitator, thematic learning, the project method, discovery learning, authentic assessments, and emphasis on developing higher order thinking skills have yet to prove effective in consistently raising academic achievement. Progressive methodologies have successfully impacted achievement levels in only a small number of schools – affluent schools attended by highly motivated students. Traditional schools have experienced greater success in raising student achievement, especially among children from disadvantaged backgrounds.

Beyond their ineffectiveness to impact achievement levels, whole school reform models are often expensive to implement and maintain. Teachers, whose time is limited, are typically overwhelmed by training, committee requirements, and curriculum development. Resource allocation and staffing needs over several years of implementation result in burdensome costs to districts. Furthermore, reform models are often implemented piecemeal due to many factors including conflict with existing district policies and teacher practices.

Some districts, dissatisfied with results, are totally abandoning whole school reform for a more traditional approach to education despite having made the major investments of time, money, and effort needed to implement whole school reform. A prominent example of a district discarding whole school reform is the Memphis City Schools. After six years and $12 million, Memphis City Schools abandoned whole school reform in June of 2001 due to stagnant or declining test scores on state tests in mathematics, reading, and English. Other districts nationwide are also abandoning whole school reform on a large scale, including San Antonio and Miami-Dade County.

These examples are important because it is seemingly assumed that there exists a core set of well proven, comprehensive whole school reform initiatives. That simply does not agree with observable data. The majority of whole school reform initiatives can not provide substantial evidence of effectiveness in improving student achievement. A 2001 RAND report notes that only about half of schools involved in a study of whole school reform made gains relative to their district. Incorporating STW principles into whole school reform does not make whole school reform any more effective. Neither does linking STW to whole school reform make STW any more effective.

Economic Considerations

STW has been a business driven education reform for the past two decades. Proponents perceive a growing lack of American skilled labour capable of meeting the demands of the 21st century workplace. Labour market inefficiencies are faulted for producing a mismatch of job openings and worker skill level.

Guided by the influential Commission on the Skills of the American Workforce (CSAW) 1990 report, *America's Choice: high skills or low wages!*, business is ardently promoting education reform, steeped in STW principles, that entails integration of academic and technical education at all grade levels, work-based learning, national skill standards, and skill certification.

It is argued that the United States possesses "the worst school-to-work transition system of any advanced industrial country... Education is rarely connected to training and both are rarely connected to an effective job service function." (CSAW, 1990, p. 4). Proponents of STW contend that not everyone will or should go on to college, as census numbers indicate that the majority of jobs in America do not, and will not, require a college education. They point out that while only 20 percent of jobs in the future will require a four year degree or higher, our educational system has in the past been fixated on providing academic curricula aimed at college preparation for all students. The majority of future jobs are projected to be in the professional and technical degree professions requiring only two years of post-secondary work or apprenticeships.

It is also argued that American businesses are transitioning to high performance workplaces requiring high skills related to a flexible technologically based organization where decisions are forced down to empowered front line workers.

In light of these arguments, the current American system of education has come to be portrayed as inefficient, uneconomical, and out of date:

- Inefficient – Labour trends and needs are ignored in the education of students.
- Uneconomical – Public dollars are wasted by providing unnecessary education to those who are unlikely to need a college education. Moreover, U.S. labour markets are perceived as chaotic as well as uneconomical. Job shopping and searching is viewed as wasteful, while the marked churning and instability of the U.S. youth labour market is considered costly.
- Out of date – Business is transitioning to high performance work organizations requiring workers skilled in problem solving and decision making, skills which the current American education system is incapable of producing.

Therefore, according to STW proponents, American education must be restructured to provide a smooth transition from school to work and equip students with the skills directly applicable to their career interest. Education and economics must meld in order to ensure U.S. competitiveness worldwide.

This is a questionable course at best, for market realities do not support the underlying arguments of STW reform. First, STW initiatives, including work-based learning and the explicit connection of students to business, are heavily influenced by Northern European systems of education, in particular the German education and training model. However, such initiatives are based on speculation and questionable interpretations of existing evidence (Heckman, Roselius, Smith, 1994):

- There is no evidence that the German apprenticeship system is any more effective in promoting skill formation. (p. 84)
- Lower youth unemployment in Germany is a result of regulations that compel German youth to stay in school or participate in apprenticeship programmes until age 18. (p. 84)
- German apprentices leave the firms that train them at very high rates and often take jobs in occupations different from those in which they are trained. (p. 84, 99)
- Wage growth rates for German apprentices are comparable to American youth. (p. 117)
- The assertion that German labour is more productive than U.S. labour is a myth. (p. 84)
- Proponents have failed to demonstrate that high performance workplaces actually increase productivity. (p. 85)
- Very few American businesses are participating in the new high performance workplace revolution. (p. 92)

Secondly, characterizing the U.S. youth labour market as uneconomical and wasteful denies the value of job searching and shopping. Job shopping permits youth to learn more about their own skills, aptitudes, interests, and suitability to careers while moving through a series of jobs. It is an activity that requires thought and effort, while promoting individual growth.

Thirdly, the perceived economic value of career and technical education is not substantiated. Research shows that education oriented to specific workplace skills and job training produces graduates who are less versatile and unable to change occupations without substantial retraining. By contrast, graduates of a rigorous academic education can readily learn new skills and adjust to new jobs. STW programmes may have greater impact on securing entry-level positions at higher wages, but do not lend to improved future labour market outcomes. There is little positive evidence to date that STW programmes positively impact adult labour market outcomes.

As American educators, business leaders, and policy makers look abroad for solutions, the education and training systems of Northern

Europe are increasingly criticized for their narrow training that limits future individual growth and life options. Critics of STW have correctly warned of the limiting effects of education directly linked to perceived skill needs of a particular labour market at a certain point in time.

Finally, academic education does have economic value and translates to improved future labour market outcomes. It has been demonstrated that higher educational attainment is positively related to earnings. More years of schooling result in better jobs, higher earnings, and greater potential for occupational achievement. Although education in and of itself does not guarantee higher income, the benefits accrue with time. Academic education nurtures cognitive abilities essential to post-secondary education success and occupational advancement. For the non-college bound student, an academic education maintains the individual's options for future post-secondary education. On the job, academic skills provide opportunity for advancement and enhanced productivity in the workplace. Often upward mobility is dependent on educational attainment. A comprehensive academic education opens doors to opportunities far in the future, including avenues not considered at a younger age.

Though education has always had economic implications, there are other benefits implicit to an academic education beyond securing gainful employment or occupational advancement. Knowledge of history, science, mathematics, and literature is valuable regardless of whether it leads directly to a job. Academic education exposes students to the great thoughts and ideas of every age and discipline which enlightens minds, and civilizes mankind. It is considered to be the type of education that is necessary for a person to be free.

Businessmen, as well as college professors, regularly point to the lack of academic skills in today's high school graduates.

- According to a 1998 report by the National Association of Manufacturers (Carnevale, 1998), "40 percent of all 17-year-olds do not have the necessary math skills—and more than 60 percent do not have the necessary reading skills—to work in a $33,000 per annum production job at a modern auto plant." (p. 17)
- More recently, the American Management Association reported that 38.3 percent of job applicants tested in 1999 lacked sufficient skills for the positions they sought. (p. 1)
- Both the 1998 and 2001 Public Agenda polls of employers and professors revealed that the greatest dissatisfaction with recent high school graduates' skill levels lies in basic academic

knowledge and skills – math, writing, spelling and grammar.

- A 1997 Investor's Business Daily poll queried business leaders from the top ten percent of publicly-traded U.S. companies on the skill set they favoured in applicants; 79.2% stated general skills (reasoning, analytical, broad knowledge) while only 17% stated specific skills (task-specific skills such as computer programming).

Curiously, education reformers have responded to this academic skills shortfall by redefining the issue as a lack of workplace skills. Disguising academic deficits as work skills deficits cheats students and society alike. The fact that many job applicants lack the literacy and math skills necessary to perform anything but rudimentary job assignments is not the result of the schools' failure to teach workplace skills; rather, it is the result of their failure to teach literacy skills and essential academic knowledge.

The Hudson Institute's landmark report on workforce development, *Workforce 2020: Work & Workers in the 21st Century*, correctly relates:

If America could increase the number of traditional high school graduates with the appropriate reading, writing, math, reasoning, and computer skills, it could go a long way toward filling available jobs and laying a suitable foundation on which workers could upgrade their skills once in the workforce. (p. 134)

Reform Impact: School to Work

Due to STW's major impact on the current delivery and focus of K-12 education, serious consideration must be given to its effectiveness and impact on academic achievement. If the principles of STW are to be applied to all students and its defining features applied in current education reform nationwide, contextual learning, career majors, and work-based learning must be capable of raising academic achievement apart from conveying occupational competencies and skills. If it does not, then this reform is merely advancing the academic mediocrity of the current vocational system throughout all public education. Transforming all education to vocational education is surely not the desired goal. All students, including vocational and technical, must be challenged by higher academic standards.

Early STW research was mainly focused on the implementation and process of reform. But a high degree of completion of the reform implementation cannot be employed as a proxy for the actual results of the programme. However, more recent studies are assessing the impact of STW on student engagement as well as academic achievement. Many studies do conclude that STW programmes support youth development and career preparation; that employers are enthusiastic about STW; that teachers see value in STW; and that STW improves attendance, grades, and graduation rates (Hughes, Bailey, Mechur, 2001).

However, there is very little evidence that student participation in STW improves learning. To date STW has not proven to increase the academic achievement of students as measured by standardized test scores.

- A study of 100 students participating in the Cornell Youth Apprenticeship Demonstration Project found that the youths did gain job-related skills and knowledge, but there were no effects on academic achievement (Hamilton & Hamilton, 1997).
- A random-assignment study found that participation in a career academy had no effect, either positive or negative, on standardized test scores (Kemple, Snipes, 2000).
- A report produced by the Institute on Education and the Economy concluded that "research regarding STW students' achievement on standardized tests is inconclusive. The few existing studies indicate that there is little, if any, effect on test scores." (Hughes, et. al., 2001).

These studies reaffirm the conclusion reached in a 1996 U.S. Department of Education study that, while "most [STW] programmes are reported to be effectively teaching occupational skills at a sufficient level...less commonly, gains in academic skills are reported." (U.S. Department of Education, 1996, p. 40).

According to the largest study of STW conducted to date, Mathematica Policy Research's National Evaluation of School-to-Work Implementation, many schools experience a tension between the priority to raise academic standards and the interests of STW implementation (Hershey, Silverberg, Haimson, 1999):

- It has been difficult in evaluation site visits to identify clear plans for promoting [academic] skills in workplace activities that STW partnerships have arranged. (p. 141).
- Efforts by states to raise academic standards are occurring independently of STW. (p. 141).
- In some cases, [STW] activities can occur only in ways that intrude on academic class time. Even when they are part of

special courses, they consume time that students could otherwise devote to elective academic courses. (p. 142-143).

- Despite the theory that STW-type activities can contribute to academic attainment, the absence of rigorous evidence applicable to their own schools often leaves frontline staff feeling caught between the pressures of competing priorities. Moreover, when academic teachers embrace [STW] ideas about making learning more applied and contextual, their early efforts sometimes appear to retreat from high standards. (p. 142-143).
- Teachers are often concerned that incorporating more practical and hands-on learning will detract from the more traditionally defined academic skills they consider critical to their students' success in standardized testing, college admissions, and more advanced study. (p. 73).
- Students often face a trade-off between taking the time to pursue electives with career content and using their elective options to take more advanced traditional academic classes. (p. 144).

Reform Impact: Work-Based Learning

Questions surround another fundamental component of STW – work-based learning. As a result of STW, and in particular the STWOA, the number of high schools offering work-based learning experiences such as internships, school-based enterprises, cooperative education, and other programmes that directly link school and work has increased nationwide. It is assumed that student learning is reinforced through both the application of academic knowledge in the workplace and workplace activities reinforcing school-based knowledge.

However, work-based learning has not been proven to reinforce academic learning. Research evidence provides no strong support for the academic reinforcement claim.

- More often than not interns' tasks were productive for the work of the office or site. (Hughes, et. al., p. 32).
- Except for students who were taking courses in clerical skills and data entry in school, the academic reinforcement functions were minimal. Thus, in general, the work of the internships was functional to the organization, as would be expected, but hardly academic. (Hughes, et. al., p. 32).
- Students who participated in structured work-based learning worked more hours than students who just had jobs, were less

likely to take a mathematics and science course during their senior year, and had lower achievement than students who just had jobs. (Bottoms, Presson, 1997).

- The richer learning experiences of school-sponsored, work-based learning do not offset the loss of learning that occurs when students leave school early and fail to take high-level mathematics and science courses in their senior year. Data from the 1996 *HSTW* Assessment offer little evidence that work-based learning experiences are an acceptable substitute for chemistry, Algebra II and demanding language arts courses. (Bottoms, Presson, 1997).

Other studies conducted by the National Centre for Research in Vocational Education (Stasz, Kaganoff, 1997) and Mathematica Policy Research, Inc. (Haimson, Bellotti, 2001) also point out the lack of rigor and academic application in work-based learning experiences.

- Students are rarely assigned challenging tasks unless they receive substantial amounts of training. (Haimson, Bellotti, 2001, p.19).
- Even when internships are connected to the school curriculum, many opportunities to practice or reinforce academic skills are not provided. (Haimson, Bellotti, 2001, p.38).
- Student tasks tend to be primarily clerical, requiring little creativity. (Stasz, Kaganoff, 1997, p. vi).
- Problem solving skills centred around procedural aspects of work not substantive, technical matters. (Stasz, Kaganoff, 1997, p. vii).

David Stern of the National Centre for Research in Vocational Education observes that most evidence claiming improved academic achievement through work-based learning is anecdotal – interviews and surveys of participating students and employers. He comments that:

All of these studies, however, rely on reports by participants themselves about what they are learning. Objective measures, and comparisons with non-participants, are lacking.

We cannot tell whether the positive reports indicate a true effect of [work-based learning], as opposed to the effect of recruiting participants who are enthusiastic about [work-based learning] to begin with, or the Hawthorne effect of participating in something innovative that attracts attention. (Stern, 1997).

"[W]ork-based learning proponents who stand on the reinforcement claim as a way to convince skeptics of the programme's value are standing on thin ice." (Hughes, Moore, Bailey, 1999, p.36).

Reform Impact: Career Academies

Career Academies are growing rapidly across the nation due to the impetus of STWOA. Over 1,500 high schools have implemented the approach as a response to the many problems they face. Established over 30 years ago, the Career Academy initiative was originally designed as a vocational training programme targeted at students considered to be at high risk of dropping out of school.

Over the past decade the primary goals and target populations of many Career Academies have changed. Today it is widely accepted that the Career Academy initiative should no longer be distinctly vocational but should seek to prepare a broad range of students, from high-performing to high-risk students, for both work and college. It is specifically identified as a "preferred approach" by the STWOA. Only recently has research attempted to determine the relative effectiveness of Career Academies on the educational outcomes for the broad cross-section of students it seeks to serve.

Manpower Demonstration Research Corporation's (MDRC) Career Academies Evaluation (Kemple, Snipes, 2000) provides new evidence on engagement, performance, and initial transitions to post-secondary education and employment for Career Academy students. Their findings reveal Career Academies:

- Increase the level of interpersonal support students experience. (p. ES-2).
- Increase participation in career awareness and work-based learning activities. (p. ES-2).
- Reduce dropout rates, improve attendance, increase academic course-taking, and increase the likelihood of earning enough credits to graduate on time for students at high risk of dropping out. (p. ES-2).
- Had little or no impact on most indicators of students' engagement and performance for low risk sub-groups. (p. 44).
- On average produced little or no change in outcomes for medium-risk subgroups. (p. 44).
- Do not improve standardized math and reading achievement test scores. (p. ES-3).

- When the findings are averaged across diverse groups of students in the full study sample, it appears that the Career Academies produced only slight reductions in dropout rates and modest increases in other measures of school engagement. These aggregated findings, however, mask the high degree of variation in effectiveness among different groups of students and across different programme contexts. (p. ES-3).
- When data are averaged across the diverse groups of students and sites participating in the evaluation, it appears the Career Academies produced only modest improvements in students' engagement and performance during high school. (p. 44).

MDRC does stress the importance of recognizing that Career Academies affect groups of students differently depending on the background characteristics students bring with them into the programme (Kemple, Snipes, 2000, p. 43).

The most recent MDRC evaluation (Kemple, 2001), released December of 2001, gives further insights into the effectiveness and impact of a Career Academy's career-focused education. Career Academies:

- Had little influence on course content and classroom instructional practices.
- Left standardized test scores unchanged.
- Relative to similar students nationally, both the Academy and non-Academy groups had high rates of high school graduation, college enrollment, and employment.
- Had little or no impact on high school graduation rates and initial post-secondary education and employment outcomes. The Academy group's relatively high outcome levels were matched by those of the non-Academy group. This was true for subgroups of students at high, medium, and low dropout risk.

STW's inability to impact standardized test scores is a serious concern. Widely considered an effective measure of student learning, standardized tests are envisioned to play a greater role due to the standards and accountability requirements of the No Child Left Behind Act of 2001. In an era of high-stakes testing, STW may be viewed as more of an impediment to student and school academic success.

Contextual Learning

The underlying learning theory on which STW initiatives rest is contextual or applied learning. The integration of academic and vocational curricula is said to be necessary in order to connect the work students do in school to the demands of the 21st century workplace. The assumption that this type of active learning will raise student achievement while providing the economically necessary skills sought after by employers is more theoretical than empirically based.

The most common form of integration is the infusion of work tasks and examples into academic courses – making academic courses more applied. Despite its wide appeal, relatively little evidence exists that supports contextual learning and curricula integration's actual ability to improve student achievement. A review of several studies of applied academics by Stern, Kaganoff, and Eden (1994) found:

- Little hard evidence that participation in an integrated programme affects student learning. (p. 42).
- Nearly every study had serious methodological or conceptual flaws that cast doubt on reported findings. (p. 42).
- No study could link integrated programme participation to economic competitiveness. (p. 41).

Lauren Resnick of the University of Pittsburgh, a leading theorist and proponent of constructivist and contextual learning, notes that, "Despite broad interest in contextualized learning programmes, there is little systematic evidence about their effectiveness, especially with respect to meeting academic standards in math, science, and English/ communications." (Resnick, Jury, 2000).

Some of the foremost cognitive psychologists in the United States, John Anderson, Lynn Reder, and Herbert Simon of Carnegie Mellon University, are among those whose work refutes current education policy. They conclude that both constructivist education theory and contextual learning claims are unproven and, in several respects, at odds with well-known scientific findings. In fact, such methods may be detrimental to learning as knowledge becomes situation-bound and context-specific, leaving the student unable to generalize and transfer his knowledge to new and different situations.

Youth who learn contextually do not perform well when basic knowledge and theoretical thought are required. What is known of contextual learning demonstrates it is likely to be highly variable and uncertain. It does not instill knowledge and skill effectively, securely, or universally. What students remember remains uncontrolled, contingent, and largely irrelevant to definite and responsible learning goals (Hirsch, 1996, p. 218).

Contrary to the more commonly implemented contextual/applied learning integration, findings do suggest that making vocational courses more academic improves student academic achievement. Vocational students who completed a challenging curriculum comparable to college-preparatory courses, including English, mathematics and science, obtained higher achievement test scores (Rock & Pollack, 1995; Bottoms, Fox, New; Bottoms).

In spite of weak results, STW maintains prominence because federal policy has too long relied on accepted educational research and theory that has conformed to the constructivist and contextual philosophy. Too often education research is dominated by ideological conformity and anti-empiricism. A body of scientific research exists that counters current dogma, but is seldom acknowledged, let alone applied in the education community. It is time to open the forum for discussion so that all evidence and empirical research can contribute to formulating sound education policy and practice.

Reform Impact: What Works

To determine what, if any, STW education reform concepts produce positive results, it is necessary to sift through the many elements. Often concurrent reforms are implemented in conjunction with career-focused education. A perceived success of STW may not be attributable to career-focused education or integrated curricula. Rather, success may arise from the concurrent implementation of other reforms. Strategies that have shown evidence of being more likely to raise student achievement are as follows:

- All students complete a challenging curriculum that includes college preparatory courses in English, mathematics, and science.
- Increased graduation requirements.
- All students complete either algebra or pre-algebra by the end of eighth grade.
- Teachers set high expectations for all students through challenging lessons and rigorous assignments.
- Students are taught by teachers who are knowledgeable in their subject.
- Early and continual guidance and advisement concerning post-secondary options and choice of high school courses.
- Creation of small learning environments, including smaller high schools and schools within a school.

All of the above strategies can be implemented without a career focus and absent contextual or work-based learning requirements. Optional career-focused and work-based learning programmes must be offered to provide flexibility and alternative education paths for those students who voluntarily choose such.

Aside from providing opportunities for students to gain occupational skills and work related attitudes, the strongest argument for many STW initiatives is higher student motivation and engagement. Though early studies point to higher completion rates for graduation requirements and lower dropout rates, these findings were not substantiated by the latest MDRC study. Evidence does suggest, however, that many STW programmes have a positive impact on keeping high risk students in school by providing an alternative option that engages and motivates them to complete their education.

These outcomes cannot be dismissed. Increasing the likelihood that high risk students remain in school and graduate is significant when considering the societal and economic penalties faced by high school dropouts.

However, caution must be taken in assessing these findings, for at this time only students who elect to participate in STW programmes are enrolled. This self-selecting process likely skews the resulting programme outcomes. Students who take the initiative to enroll are pre-motivated and it is this motivation that may account for these positive effects. An initiative that benefits self-selected students does not necessarily benefit all students. Career and technical education must not be the focal point of all high school education. Rather, it must be one of many options open to all students. The current dramatic move to restructure high schools around a series of career fields is accelerating and unwarranted.

Many districts and schools, including Minneapolis; Boston; Chicago; Denver; Houston; Prince George's County, MD; Lancaster County, PA, and others have moved in this direction. The Minneapolis school district provides an pertinent example of restructuring the high school curriculum wholly around specific career areas. Students' career choice requires approval based on teacher recommendations, test scores or grade point averages, and writing samples as condition of acceptance. The approved career area will determine the classes each student will take as well as the school they will attend. Changes of a student's career choice requires process and approval and is not guaranteed. If approval is given, the student may need to transfer to a new school and begin again earning credits towards the new career interest.

These dramatic changes are unwarranted. Unsupported by research and unsuccessful in meeting all students' needs, reformers have merely exchanged one "one size fits all" approach for another. There is a built in systemic rigidity that restricts the student who has a change of mind concerning their chosen career (which is a likely scenario for a teenager).

Further, research findings on enrollment and attrition rates for Career Academies from recent MDRC studies do not support the current expansion of career-focused education. Students voluntarily chose to participate in the Career Academies, yet less than 60 percent of the students remained in the programmes throughout high school. Many leave due to loss of interest in the occupational area. The demand for career focused education may not be at the level proponents project. More importantly, research findings highlight the importance of individual choice. Parents and students must be afforded the opportunity to freely pursue the educational options that best suit their needs and interests. If the "one size fits all" academic education is not adequate for all students, neither is the "one size fits all" career-focused education.

Requiring all students to be immersed in career-focused education blindly ignores the fundamental right of individual choice and the realities of adolescence. Ninth and tenth grade students should not be required to concentrate their education on one career interest. Any degree of specialization in the curriculum narrows the focus of education and limits individual flexibility and opportunity for the future. Career focus and decision choices should remain open as long as possible. All students must be given a solid academic grounding (preferably college preparatory) that is essential for keeping open many life choices and options. Driving career focused education into ever younger grades exacerbates the problems already noted. Most students are simply not prepared to make such weighty life decisions at the beginning of high school, much less in junior high or even elementary school.

Students can be better prepared for life choices through informed and thoughtful counselling. The need for quality guidance and career awareness to help guide students through the expected times of youthful indecisiveness cannot be overstated. Sadly, studies suggest that few students receive adequate guidance counselling, particularly urban students who are especially in need of support.

Providing students and parents with early and continued assistance in setting goals and encouragement to complete challenging academic courses leads to higher achievement and post-secondary enrollment. Too often students do not even know they lack the necessary academic skills and knowledge needed to meet their personal goals. Over three-fourths of urban career and technical students desire to continue their education after high school, but few are prepared to succeed in college, and fewer still realize it.

Guidance must begin earnestly in the middle school years so that all students are apprised of the critical necessity to complete core academic courses through the junior and senior years. The use of career fairs, field trips, skills and interest inventories, and elective career interest courses provides exposure to the world of work, allowing all students to gain valuable information regarding future options. Career awareness is distinct from career focused education and does not include work-based learning, internships, and job shadowing although these types of programmes should be available to all students who have a desire to participate. No student should be required to centre courses around a particular career focus.

Policy Implications

Educational reform should not be about the integration of technical and academic education for the purpose of ensuring high school graduates possess occupational skills relevant to certain careers. Rather, reform should be about improving academic requirements for all students, college and non-college bound, to ensure that their future life options are not constrained. A continued emphasis on high academic standards with challenging coursework in core academic subject areas must be required of all students.

Though it is difficult to mandate reform through legislation as local capacity and will cannot be controlled from the federal or state level, federal policy should strongly encourage the following:

- Policymakers must be cautioned against "one size fits all" legislation. Educational initiatives that are smaller in scope can yield great gains in achievement. It is not necessary to package various initiatives into one model to produce results. The emphasis on whole school reform in federal policy is costly and meeting with growing resistance. More emphasis must be given to encouraging educational initiatives smaller in scope, more affordable, and proven to positively impact student achievement. In so doing, local districts and schools will find the flexibility needed to implement policy that is applicable to conditions existing in individual schools and is best suited to their unique student needs.

- Halt funding of education reforms that utilize contextual learning for all students and all subjects. Define core academic courses as free of contextual and applied learning elements. Federal policy must prevent the infusion of workplace competencies in academic subjects, particularly in elementary and middle school curriculum.
- Utilize federal funding not just for failing schools, but for failing students. Provide funding grants directly to parents and students for remedial and tutorial services through both public and private providers.
- Encourage locally developed accelerated learning schedules aimed at bringing failing students up to grade level.
- Teacher quality must be improved to support higher academic expectations. Teacher preparation and development that requires teachers be qualified in their subject area and promotes higher expectations for all students must be supported. Initiate funding for teacher development to improve content knowledge and performance so to better support students in meeting higher standards. Vocational teacher preparation should include training on how to incorporate academic skills into vocational courses.
- Teacher development must incorporate higher expectations for all students, particularly for career and technical education students. Funding for training in the design of more challenging assignments and incorporation of more literacy skills in technical education is required.
- Alternative certification routes that bypass teacher education and training programmes will open the door to a vast pool of potential applicants from the professional and retired ranks, as well as liberal arts majors. Compressed classroom management training and mentoring controlled at the district level is but one way to provide alternative teacher training to applicants already qualified in the subject matter.
- Technical and career education must not ignore the elementary and middle school years. Promotion of proven reading and mathematics instruction in the elementary grades will ensure that students are prepared when entering ninth grade to do

high school work. The lack of basic reading and math literacy skills often results in student failure and lack of engagement in the high school years.

Federal policy initiatives that encourage and demand stronger academic requirements during the middle school years will have enormous impact on the success of all students to meet post-secondary and occupational goals. Requirements can include: all students complete pre-Algebra or Algebra I by the end of eighth grade and increasing the number of students who complete honours English or a comparable English course.

- Policy promoting increased core academic requirements for graduation for all students will not only improve post high school opportunities, but better prepare students for high-stakes tests and improve achievement levels for all sub-groups nationwide.
- Policy promotion of improved guidance and career awareness beginning in the middle school years and continuing throughout high school and focusing on academic requirements must occur. Funding for guidance staff development and resources for effective awareness programmes must be a priority.
- Federal policy must encourage and fund initiatives that provide options for all students at multiple stages of their high school careers – including job shadowing, internships, apprenticeships, and work-based learning. A vibrant, voluntary vocational education should allow free movement in and out of career and technical education with no penalty. Such a system will attract both career and college-bound students while complementing, not supplanting, academic education.
- Implement federal tax credit legislation to encourage corporations and individuals to contribute to education initiatives that have been shown to be effective.

The Role of Vocational Education and Training in Transition Countries: The Case of Central and Eastern Europe and the New Independent States

'Transition' indicates the act of passing from one stage of development to another. Societies, even 'established' ones, are undergoing continuous review and change. As regards vocational education and training, this implies a permanent adaptation of the system to technological and social change.

The notion of 'transition countries' is not new. History has seen many examples of countries trying to adapt to a new economic and social order. We also refer to 'transition countries' when we speak about Central and East European countries and the New Independent States, whose developments in the field of vocational education and training shall be reviewed in this paper.

The region in question includes in principle all former 'Eastern bloc' countries that have, in the context of their transition to a market economy and a democratic society, undergone tremendous political, economic and social change after the collapse of the socialist system in 1989.

In comparison with the context in which reforms usually take place, the current vocational education and training reforms in Central and Eastern Europe and in the New Independent States (particularly in the more advanced Central and East European countries), have two very unusual aspects. Firstly, the breadth, range and depth of education and training reforms proposed or already started is extraordinarily large. They concern all levels and sectors of vocational education and training: legislation, management and administration, the financing of the system, vocational education and training institutions, programmes and personnel.

They also include the creation of new vocational education and training institutions and the design of completely new types of curricula.

Secondly, the speed of the reform process is also quite exceptional. Conceiving educational reforms in established systems usually takes a relatively long time. Vocational education and training reforms in Central and Eastern Europe and in the New Independent States have been designed, adopted and launched in a matter of months rather than years.

This process is, of course, not isolated from the overall transition process in Central and Eastern Europe and the New Independent States. The global nature and speed of vocational education and training reforms have their roots in the general climate of rapid and radical change which those societies are undergoing and which aim at the transition to a market economy and a pluralistic democracy.

The past nine years have shown that the process of modernisation can be started quickly. However, deeper, systematic reforms in vocational education and training will take time. It will be a matter of a whole generation rather than a couple of years.

European Union Programmes to Support Reforms in Central and Eastern Europe and in the New Independent States

Financial aid and technical assistance to support Central and Eastern European countries and the New Independent States in their reform efforts is provided by multilateral organisations such as the World Bank or the European Union, as well as bilateral donors including individual Member States of the European Union and other OECD countries.

The European Union Grants Financial Support Through two Programmes: The Phare Programme is a European Union initiative which was launched in 1990. Countries eligible for Phare support include Albania, Bulgaria, Bosnia-Herzegovina, the Czech Republic, Estonia, Hungary, Latvia, Lithuania, Poland, Romania, the Slovak Republic, Slovenia and the former Yugoslav Republic of Macedonia. The main aim is to support these countries in the process of economic transformation and the strengthening of democracy. For those countries which have applied to join the European Union, special effort is being made to assist them to reach the stage where they are ready to assume the obligations of membership. The Phare budget available between 2000 and 2006 is expected to amount to ECU 10.5 billion. Some ECU 6 billion was allocated between 1993 and 1999, making Phare the largest assistance programme of its kind.

The Tacis Programme which was launched in 1991 is a European Union initiative for the New Independent States of: Armenia, Azerbaijan, Belarus, Georgia, Kazakhstan, Kyrgyzstan, Moldova, the Russian Federation, Tajikistan, Turkmenistan, Ukraine and Uzbekistan. This programme fosters the development of harmonious and prosperous economic and political links between the European Union and its partner countries. Its aim is to support partner country initiatives to develop societies based on political freedom and economic prosperity. It provides funds for know-how to support the process of transformation to market economies and democratic societies.

Staff development, in particular through training, has always played a central part in Phare and Tacis sector reform programmes. In addition, vocational education and training has been acknowledged by the Phare Programme as a sector in its own right. Amounts ranging from ECU 3 to 25 million have been allocated to each of the countries eligible to participate in the programme. However, vocational education and training has only recently become a priority sector for Tacis funding. To date programmes have been endorsed for Moldova, the Russian Federation and Uzbekistan.

The Socio-Economic Context of Vocational Education and Training Reforms in Central and Eastern Europe and in the New Independent States. Before 1989, education and training in Central and Eastern Europe and the New Independent States was designed to meet the needs of centrally planned economies. Under the Comecon (1) arrangements, there was a division of labour whereby one country would provide the other countries with supplies of particular commodities. This led to an over-concentration of certain industries and the complete neglect of others. Furthermore, areas such as crafts, commerce, banking, accountancy, financial control, insurance and entrepreneurship remained underdeveloped.

Under the former system, vocational education and training was tailored to the needs of large companies employing excessive numbers of staff, with low levels of innovation and productivity, following a tayloristic scheme of work organisation and offering menial jobs. Training was very often directed towards a life-time job. As mentioned above, crafts, trades and service professions were seriously neglected. Standards of equipment in vocational education institutions reflected the poor technological standard of industry itself. Ministries of Education or sector ministries in charge of vocational education and training were traditionally strongly involved in defining the scope, contents and length of vocational education programmes, thus encouraging high rigidity and fragmentation within the system.

From 1989, the countries of Central and Eastern Europe and the New Independent States have undergone political and economic changes which are fundamental and more far-reaching than any in the past. These changes encompass all aspects of life, from the democratic structure of society, to the privatisation of enterprises, to the subjects studied by young people and adults at educational establishments. Since 1989/90 the economies in most of these countries have experienced deep adjustment crises. Land reform and privatisation have, on paper, been completed in a number of countries. However, the definitive settlement of property rights, the establishment of functioning land markets and the restructuring of industries are still on-going processes which are far from completion. In particular the absorption of surplus labour from both the farm sector and the previously labour-intensive industrial sectors such as coal mining and the steel industry which are now in decline and pose a major challenge. Traditional established links between schools and large state enterprises were dismantled as the latter closed down their training facilities due to a lack of resources.

The countries in question are seeking trade links and export opportunities in their neighbouring Western countries where standards are particularly high. New investors enforce new strategies and require skills, which are currently in short supply. To add to the burden, a large number of local enterprises are facing serious financial crises. The restructuring or closing down of companies will inevitably lead to increasing unemployment - a phenomenon largely unknown in former times. The above-described tendencies, alongside the enormous pressure on companies to raise their level of competitiveness, result in an increased demand for training and retraining of the labour force. Short and long-term training programmes will need to be carried out to equip people with the new skills required by industry and the developing service sector, to prevent them from being socially excluded.

The Vocational Education and Training Situation in Central and Eastern Europe and the New Independent States at the Start of Reforms. Given the similarity of the political and economic systems, Central and Eastern European countries and the New Independent States shared a common starting base for reforms in 1989/90. Education and training systems were characterised by common structures and underlying organisational patterns.

Responsibilities

While the Ministry of Education was responsible for the majority of vocational education institutions and for the overall education policies, other ministries were and still are in charge of schools within their sector. This division of responsibilities was an obstacle to both the design of an overall reform policy framework at the start of reforms and the major restructuring of the school network. All decisions over budgets, staff allocations, curricula, textbooks, etc. were traditionally taken by the ministries, while regional and/or local education authorities, as well as school directors were mainly 'implementers' of these decisions. Initiative and individual responsibilities were not encouraged. Social partners, i.e. employers' and employees' representatives, and other key stakeholders were not involved in policy discussions and decision-making.

The Vocational Education Model

In most countries there were two distinct types of curricula in the system of vocational education: the curriculum offered in vocational schools (for skilled workers) and that provided in post-secondary technical schools (for technicians). Vocational schools provided education and training for grades 9 or 10 to 12. Post-secondary technical schools - the higher level of vocational institutes - offered programmes of between 2.5 and 4 years duration.

As vocational education was always perceived as a continuation of general education, there was a predominance of general gymnasium subjects in vocational education programmes which left little space for special theoretical subjects. Graduate students had therefore limited vocational knowledge and skills when they sought employment.

Legislation and Distribution of Students

The education sector was regulated as a whole. Education legislation did not usually take the specific aspects of vocational education and training into account. The distribution of secondary level students between general and vocational education paths varied in the individual countries and represented between one and two thirds of the overall age group. In view of the permanent shortage of skilled workers in the enterprises of the socialist states resulting from inefficient work organisation and the 'hoarding' of human resources, one of the main tasks of upper secondary education was to direct the large majority of young people into the various paths of vocational education. However, a common feature among these countries was the relatively low social status of vocational education.

Funding of the System

Traditionally, costs for vocational education and training were shared between the state and the big (state) enterprises. Before 1990 state investment in education in relation to the countries' GDPs was relatively high. This education investment still paid off in the first years of reform. However, the proportion of the budget earmarked for vocational education and training was traditionally quite low. An additional financial burden was added when the economic restructuring processes started and most employers withdrew from their former involvement in training. Funds were, by and large, sufficient to cover the running costs of the system (teacher salaries, operational and maintenance costs of schools, etc.). However, only a very small budget was available for actual investment.

The need to establish a social benefit system coupled with rising unemployment and increased demand, on a massive scale, for training and retraining to cope with the economic adaptation and restructuring processes added another financial burden on the state budget. As a result, a major reshuffling of funds earmarked for training is required. Given the numerous reform tasks in these countries after 1989/90, a major increase in funding for the vocational education and training sector could not be expected. Assistance from external donors was needed without which most of the countries would not have been able to kick-start reforms.

Role of the Companies and Human Resources Planning

State-run enterprises had an important role in providing practical training for students in school-based vocational education and training. Training took place within a dual system where the vocational school was often part of a state-owned company. The utilization of labour resources was centrally planned on the basis of the manpower resources requirements of individual enterprises. The school became an agent of the company helping to train a workforce according to the needs of the latter. With the breakdown of the centrally planned system, the former well established links between schools and companies vanished. This was a serious problem as specific vocational training had been carried out for the last 50 years in companies, while schools catered for general subjects and the basic introduction to working life. The contact with companies ceased, and the state did not have the resources needed to compensate for this loss. The result was that schools were left with out-dated and poor quality equipment, and became uncertain of their new role.

Vocational Education Qualifications and Examinations

Under the former system vocational schools provided education and training for strictly defined specialisations. A curriculum pre-defined in terms of content and lesson/hours was the main feature of the system. There was a restrictive and inflexible 'input' control, and at the same time there was a widely different school-based 'output' quality system with arbitrary examinations.

With the collapse of the central planning system after 1989/90, there was a great uncertainty as to which qualifications should be selected. The situation was complicated by an absence of overall government economic policies indicating priority economic sectors for development. Industry representatives and new entrepreneurs lacked the essential methodology to identify their training needs based on business plans which could have provided valuable input to ministries and schools on the skills requirements of the labour market.

Schools had to predict themselves which qualification profiles the companies may require. As a result, they often had to build their programmes on a conceptual world and concentrated on increasing the 'academisation' of technical vocational education.

The Teaching Staff

There were three different types of teachers in the vocational schools and the differences were significant. The teachers of general education subjects were educated at some university and highly specialised. They had, in parallel to their subject, learned pedagogy at the university. These general education teachers lacked essential practical knowledge and skills and were, of course, not trained in new technologies. The 'academisation' of vocational education was due in particular to this group of teachers.

The vocational subject theory teachers comprised a middle group: they received a technical education (e.g. engineering) and some of them had taken in-service training courses in pedagogy from universities or other institutions. A large group of workshop instructors, i.e. supervisors of practical training in workshops or companies, had skilled worker qualifications but no pedagogical education at all.

The qualifications of the three groups of teachers and trainers/ instructors represented a significant barrier to the development of the vocational education system. The main challenge was to integrate these teaching groups and create a more holistic system of pre-service and in-service teacher and instructor training.

The Present Change Process

Since the beginning of the reforms in 1989/90 the individual Central and East European countries and the New Independent States have developed in different directions. There are huge differences as to the state of play of vocational education and training reforms between the Central European countries on the one hand and the New Independent States and Mongolia on the other. In general, one can say that reforms in the New Independent States and Mongolia are much slower given the extreme scarcity of resources, the high degree of central control and the lack of efficient management structures. Reforms in Central and Eastern Europe were often initiated from the grassroots level. This difference in development is the reason why the nature of vocational education and training reforms and related challenges will hereinafter be reviewed separately by geographical region.

However, it is important to note that even within these two groups of countries the picture is anything but homogenous, depending on the time when reforms started, overall economic and political dynamics, legislative frameworks, history, culture and ideologies, the importance attached to education and training compared to other sectors and the extent of external support.

Central and Eastern Europe

Since the beginning of the economic and social reform process, Central and Eastern European countries (Bulgaria, the Czech Republic, Estonia, Hungary, Latvia, Lithuania, Poland, Romania, the Slovak Republic and Slovenia), have undertaken reforms to adapt vocational education and training provision to the new challenges of the labour market. As mentioned before, funds from many donors, in particular the European Union's Phare budget, were used initially to address the most urgent needs of the system after the collapse of the centrally planned economies. At a later stage more substantial reforms began.

Initial activities concentrated on:

- the revision of existing, and the development of new curricula with the aim of providing training for a range of rather broad-based occupations, partly within new sectors of economic activity, such as banking, finance, etc.;
- staff development on a wider scale, including training for policy-makers, education administrators at all levels, representatives from employers' and employees' organisations, school managers, curriculum authors and teachers;
- the upgrading of school equipment;
- the establishment of partnerships with training institutions in European Union Member States, and
- the drafting of policy papers on the main directions of vocational education and training reforms and the adoption, in most countries of the region, of new laws regulating specific aspects of the work of vocational education institutions.
- Policy papers that have been or are being developed in most countries of the region provide for the following objectives of vocational education and training reforms:
- new principles of decentralised management, involving tripartite decision-making processes;
- new, more flexible funding mechanisms to give more freedom for decision making and room for innovations to institutions;
- the development of an integrated initial and continuing training system, making maximum use of resources and exerting a reduced level of control over the quality of vocational education and training provision;
- a diversification of the vocational education and training structure, comprising applied higher professional institutions

at pre-university level and aiming at an increased horizontal and lateral mobility of students in the system; and,

- a re-orientation of the focus of vocational education and training on employers' current and future needs and the involvement of social partners in decision-making processes through the setting-up of structured communication mechanisms.

Vocational education and training reforms were kick-started through a pilot school approach, empowering staff at a local level to develop new curricula and methodologies of work. This approach reflects both the change of mentality and the democratic nature of the reforms in Central and Eastern Europe. One weakness of this approach was the partial lack of guidance from the central level, especially in the start-up phase of reforms when overall education and training reform policies were still absent, support institutions did not exist or were unsure of their role, when neither a revised curriculum development model nor new industry-based qualification standards had been adopted at national level, etc. Schools acted mostly on their own to develop new vocational education models. Bilateral donors supported different curriculum models through technical know-how, although in some cases these took little or no account of the prevailing needs or scope for replicability in other schools.

Another weakness of the pilot schools approach may also be the fact that they are likely to become elitist and isolated from mainstream education and training provision, if national authorities do not accept and back up reform initiatives - legally, but also financially - and disseminate reform outputs over the entire country. In conclusion, reform efforts were especially successful in those countries where both the national, regional and local levels had worked to common targets in a complementary top-down and bottom-up approach. While it is too soon to draw firm conclusions concerning the sustainability of the initiated reforms in Central and Eastern European countries, the main impacts to date of these 'pilot school' initiatives include the following:

- the partial change of pedagogic attitude of teachers (and students) both towards curricula more oriented to new labour market needs and new active learning styles, which ultimately increase the employment prospects of graduates;
- a change in the schools' management style;
- new syllabuses, equipment and materials which have been developed to a coherent design;

- improved communication between the Ministries of Education and Labour and sector ministries still retaining a degree of responsibility for vocational education and training, regional & local administrations, central employers' and employees' organisations, training institutions and individual employers in the region;
- a positive attitude towards the opportunities that greater decentralisation of the management of education and training offers both to training institutions and local/regional authorities, and,
- new approaches to assessment and quality assurance.

The main drawbacks of the first phase of vocational education and training reforms in some of the Central and Eastern European countries include the fact that reform programmes were generally launched on the basis of insufficient labour market information. Countries are only now gradually changing the nature of curricula reforms from being education-driven to more demand-driven, involving industry representatives in a systematic way. In addition, most countries have yet to integrate their different reform initiatives into an overall education and training policy framework and to determine the roles and functions assigned to different players in the system.

The New Independent States and Mongolia

The enormous economic and social pressure faced by the New Independent States and Mongolia has also had an impact on the vocational education and training sector. Regular cuts in state allocations of funds for education, and a reduction in the contributions formerly paid by enterprises resulted in difficulties to cover even basic costs like teacher salaries, students grants or school maintenance. Moreover, learning is further hampered by a lack of textbooks. Furthermore, the extreme shortage of funds has had a detrimental effect on the range of activities that the Ministries of Education are able to undertake. Whatever reform ideas are conceived, such as the revision of qualification standards, the guarantee of a basic budget for schools or the access to education and training for all, their implementation has been slow and difficult. In addition, the decentralisation of responsibilities for the management of the vocational education and training to regional authorities will not have a positive impact if it is not accompanied by the allocation of funds or possibilities for income generation. Schools must increasingly cope with crisis management. In order to survive they have to identify additional sources of income. This is frequently achieved by selling products manufactured or services provided by the students in a 'production school' setting. For both employers and trade unions, vocational education and training does not currently rank among the highest priorities. The Ministries of Social Affairs or Labour have become aware of the immense adult training needs to underpin economic restructuring processes. However, the resources of these ministries are also scarce and, for the most part are being utilized for the payment of unemployment benefits.

There are hardly any state funds available to invest in school infrastructure or for the upgrading of vocational education and training. Neither are there funds available for the badly needed teacher (re)-training. All these create a difficult climate for innovation.

Some reform projects with international or bilateral donor support were launched in pilot institutions in agreement with the national authorities. European Union Tacis programmes to reform the vocational education and training sector have started in Moldova, the Russian Federation and Uzbekistan in 1998. The European Training Foundation co-ordinates a project in the Northwest Russian region which is co-financed by five different donors. The project's overall objective is to pilot-test an innovative vocational education and training model. Major components of all the above projects include curricular reforms and institutional developments both at school and administrative levels. This is a promising start, which has to be continued. In the forthcoming years the New Independent States and Mongolia will have to face the challenge of initiating substantial vocational education and training reforms in the same way as their Central and Eastern European neighbours did. A prerequisite for achieving major change is, however, political and economic stability.

The Main Functions of Training in the Transition Period and Resulting Challenges

Vocational education and training in countries in transition have remedial, adaptive and pro-active functions. These are interlinked and indicate the significance of the role of vocational education and training:

- to underpin and motivate the economic and social transformation process;
- to prevent and combat the social exclusion of people disadvantaged in the labour market; and,
- to cope with constant technological changes and labour market uncertainty.

As a follow-up to the reforms already initiated, Central and Eastern European countries and the New Independent States are facing the following challenges which will have a major impact on their vocational education and training systems:

Anticipation

Anticipating future skills and market changes are key priorities for countries in transition, if they want their training systems to be responsive and their companies to become and/or remain competitive. Well-structured institutional arrangements have to be established to anticipate shifts in employment and vocational qualifications. Co-ordination mechanisms have to be set up to ensure the use of forecasts in initial and continuing vocational training, vocational guidance and the work of employment agencies. In addition, individual companies' capacities need to be strengthened to identify their own skill requirements and training needs.

In this context the need to understand the labour market and predict its evolution and the need to understand skill trends and structures resulting from changes in products, technology and forms of work organization are even more important.

Successful anticipation requires the existence of:

- bipartite and tripartite social partnership in actions to anticipate and react to change,
- a credible research base to help vocational education and training institutions respond to changes in the structure of jobs and skills, and
- institutions capable of incorporating anticipation into industrial policies and the management of the companies themselves.

In the absence of clear economic development guidelines, the vocational education and training sector may consult the Ministries of Economy, Labour and other related sector ministries and launch, on its own initiative, sector-related and/or regional analyses to assess economic development and employment perspectives, as well as training capacities and needs.

Management Training

"The key to growth are experienced entrepreneurs."(2) A case study undertaken in the Czech Republic revealed that companies in which foreign shareholders had also invested in the training of managers performed much better than local companies whose managers had not been trained.

Companies in Central and Eastern Europe and the New Independent States require a revolutionary change in management thinking and the development of related management skills to enable them to raise the competitiveness of their companies, as they adapt to new economic conditions.

The reorganisation of companies demands that managers and entrepreneurs operating in a context of continual change have the ability to play roles distinct from those of autocratic controllers. This leads inevitably to the development of new entrepreneurial and managerial cultures.

To integrate and operate new organisational structures, managers need to be trained to:

- decentralise decision-making, place wider responsibilities on workers (especially in relation to quality assurance), and encourage innovation;
- flatten hierarchical structures, bringing in new moderating, coaching and guidance roles for management; and
- integrate functions of 'brain and hand' in the workplace by forming multi-task teams of multi-skilled workers responsible for their own work.

Managers need to overcome their reluctance to invest in new training, organisational and human resource systems. Training should be reviewed as a long-term investment and as a means to implement business development strategies. Major training and tutoring programmes for new managers are still needed particularly in the case of SME's.

Improved Initial Vocational Education and Training

In order to improve the responsiveness of vocational education and training to new labour market requirements, reforms have to be sustained and extended with a particular view to:

- adjusting existing school infrastructures and programmes to the new economic priorities;
- further reforming qualifications so that they correspond more closely to the needs of the labour market;
- increasing investment in vocational education and training to promote innovation and to ensure higher levels of both participation and attainment;
- re-establishing links between education and training institutions and the world of work and enterprises; and

- placing greater emphasis on the acquisition of transversal competencies ("core competencies"), including technological, social, organisational, linguistic, cultural and entrepreneurial skills, through active types of learning.

All the above aim to improve the employability of young people.

Continuing Training

Mayor transformations in society and the employment situation have profoundly increased the importance of continuing training. Much larger scale continuing training programmes are required than are currently provided in order to underpin and stimulate processes of economic recovery, conversion and diversification.

The economic objectives of continuing training in the transition context concern:

- increasing efficiency and growth;
- avoiding skill shortages that might hamper growth;
- improving considerably productivity and competitiveness; and
- attracting external investment.

In the context of major structural adjustments, continuing training can provide a link between past and future economic activity, ensuring that knowledge and skills of the labour force are adapted to the changes that have already occurred or are likely to occur in the labour market. In this context, continuing training should not only guarantee the updating of qualifications and skills improvement on a larger scale, but also prepare workers for newly evolving jobs in new areas of economic activity. In this context, continuing training has to take account of the fact that societies in Central and Eastern European countries and the New Independent States are likely to move away from the concentration on heavy, environmentally dangerous and labour-intensive industries and the provision of raw materials or semi-finished products.

The emphasis will be shifted towards high-quality, high-tech products and services. The countries in question are also likely to develop as service economies, as have other industrialised countries. This includes the production sector where a higher emphasis will be placed on services dedicated to the distribution and maintenance of products and the design or research and development of new products.

In addition, companies will, like those in other industrial societies, be confronted with demands to meet ever-changing and continually rising technical and quality standards. Experience from Western countries shows that expected increases in productivity can only be achieved if sufficient investment has been made to prepare the labour force or to reorganise production within companies. SME's require special support in this respect as they find it particularly difficult to incorporate the latest technology or best practice in their working processes and methods.

Training to Combat Social Exclusion

Reforms have so far mainly focused on mainstream developments and students. However, given the projected high levels of unemployment, it is important that those who are long-term unemployed or disadvantaged in some other way, including young people with or without sufficient qualifications, older people, women, ethnic minorities and others are given special assistance to improve their labour market performance and help them find their place in the new society. It is anticipated that without such assistance these groups would become even more removed from the labour market and increasingly socially excluded.

The range of measures need to be tailored to meet individual circumstances and allow each person to follow a planned set of training modules, education, temporary work and work experience. Labour market measures should be linked to local community development and the provision of social, health and welfare services. The individual may participate in a number of activities, including advice, vocational educational and training and work experience facilitated by different providers, but planned in an integrated and co-ordinated way.

Supporting Measures

Supporting measures to enhance the effectiveness of the above described training measures would need to concentrate on the training of trainers and teachers, assessment and certification arrangements, infrastructure development and the ongoing evaluation of human resource development activities. They also require that access to qualifications is opened up by building progression routes horizontally and vertically through the education and training systems, removing barriers to higher level education and training, and creating bridging routes in-between different pathways.

Conclusion

Training can no longer be reserved just for the young. We must equip and train the whole of the potential workforce. This statement holds especially true for the transition countries.

There is a dialectic interaction between the economy and vocational education and training provision: economic reforms and the general liberalisation of the system are not only paralleled, but largely motivated and triggered by vocational education and training reform and vice versa. In order to master the transition process and achieve economic and social progress, which is balanced and sustainable, skilful, adaptable and innovative, people have to be prepared through training or retraining measures.

Fundamental changes are required in the behaviour of the main players of the system, i.e. the state, the institutions, the teachers and 'clients', including students, parents, employers and employees.

Policies need to be balanced, aiming at:

- macro-economic stability through targeting resources;
- containing costs and mobilising additional financial resources;
- promoting educational choices for young people and adults;
- introducing incentives and competition among providers of education and training services;
- regulating labour markets by maintaining qualification standards;
- ensuring access to education and training services for all, including groups who are presently excluded; and
- strengthening institutional capacity to implement the reforms.

The development of the vocational education and training system does not primarily depend on new laws being passed, but first and foremost on new processes being started which are open and where all available national and international knowledge can be used to solve specific problems. Modernisation can be started through experiments and learning processes for all those participating. However, as in other learning processes, desired changes do not occur spontaneously but require careful guidance and support by all partners concerned.

3

Tertiary Education

Tertiary education, also referred to as third stage, third level, and post-secondary education, is the educational level following the completion of a school providing a secondary education. The World Bank, for example, defines tertiary education as including universities as well as institutions that teach specific capacities of higher learning such as colleges, technical training institutes, community colleges, nursing schools, research laboratories, centres of excellence, and distance learning centres.

Higher education is taken to include undergraduate and postgraduate education, while vocational education and training beyond secondary education is known as *further education* in the United Kingdom, or *continuing education* in the United States.

Tertiary education generally culminates in the receipt of certificates, diplomas, or academic degrees.

Transition From a Secondary Education Into a Tertiary Study

University students who undergo their first years in tertiary education face new challenges as university life is a learning environment where independent study is central to education. Interaction between the students and lecturers is limited. In tertiary education, analytical skills take precedence over the ability to memorize. Hence, for a successful academic result, students must strive hard and utilize all possible resources. This includes writing down all the major points from lectures and taking advantage of all available materials – using the supportive mediums provided by institutions such as online lecture notes and PowerPoint presentations.

In the United Kingdom

"Tertiary education" includes further education (FE), as well as higher education (HE). Since the 1970s specialized FE colleges called "tertiary colleges" have been set up to offer courses such as A Levels, that allow progression to HE, alongside vocational courses. An early example of this which expanded in September 1982 as part of a reorganization of education in the Halesowen area which also saw three-tier education axed after just 10 years in force.

In some areas where schools do not universally offer sixth forms, tertiary colleges function as a sixth form college as well as a general FE college. Unlike sixth form colleges, the staff join lecturers' rather than teachers' unions.

Tertiary Education in India

Tertiary education in India is accessible to 1 in 10 young Indians. Nevertheless, India's higher education system is the third largest in the world, after China and the United States. Out of those who reach higher level education, Mercer Consulting estimates that only a quarter of graduates are employable.

Higher Education

Higher education in India has evolved in divergent streams with each stream monitored by an apex body, indirectly controlled by the Ministry of Human Resource Development and funded jointly by the state governments. Most universities are administered by the States, however, there are 18 important universities called Central Universities, which are maintained by the Union Government. The increased funding of the central universities give them an advantage over their state competitors.

Apart from the several hundred state universities, there is a network of research institutions that provide opportunities for advanced learning and research leading up to a PhD in branches of science, technology and agriculture. Several have won international recognition. 25 of these institutions come under the umbrella of the CSIR - Council of Scientific and Industrial Research and over 60 fall under the ICAR - Indian Council of Agricultural Research. In addition, the DAE - Department of Atomic Energy, and other ministries support various research laboratories.

The Indian Institutes of Technology were placed 50th in the world and 2nd in the field of Engineering (next only to MIT) by Times Higher

World University Rankings. Earlier, an Asia Week study had ranked them (Along with Birla Institute of Technology and Science - Pilani), among the top 20 technical universities in Asia. Indian Institute of Science is the premier research institute in the field of science and engineering. There are several thousand colleges (affiliated to different universities) that provide undergraduate science, agriculture, commerce and humanities courses in India. Amongst these, the best also offer post graduate courses while some also offer facilities for research and PhD studies.

Technical education has grown rapidly in recent years. With recent capacity additions, it now appears that the nation has the capability to graduate over 500,000 engineers (with 4-yr undergraduate degrees) annually, and there is also a corresponding increase in the graduation of computer scientists (roughly 50,000 with post-graduate degree). In addition, the nation graduates over 1.2 million scientists. Furthermore, each year, the nation is enrolling at least 350,000 in its engineering diploma programmes (with plans to increase this by about 50,000). Thus, India's annual enrollment of scientists, engineers and technicians now exceeds 2 million.

2008 data from Maharashtra's Higher Secondary Board reveals that .87 million passed the school leaving exam and enrolled in college for undergraduate studies. Adding enrolment in polytechnic programmes and graduates from other boards puts Maharashtra's total at close to a million and its college enrolment ratio at roughly 39%. States like Tamil Nadu, Haryana and Kerala also have comparably high tertiary enrollment ratios. In Andhra Pradesh, the tertiary enrolment rate is now approaching 25%.

Across the country, tertiary enrollment rates have been increasing at a rate between 5-10% in the last decade, which has led to a doubling of the tertiary enrolment rate to near 20%. (However, outdated government data does not yet capture this trend, which can be seen from analyzing individual state data.)

International league tables produced in 2006 by the London-based Times Higher Education Supplement(THES) confirmed Jawaharlal Nehru University (JNU)'s place among the world's top 200 universities. Likewise, THES 2006 ranked JNU's School of Social Sciences at the 57th position among the world's top 100 institutes for social sciences.

The University of Calcutta was the first multi-disciplinary university of modern India. According to The Times Higher Education

Supplement's survey of the world's top arts and humanities universities, dated November 10, 2005, this university, ranked 39, was the only Indian university to make it to the top 50 list in that year. Other research institutes are the Saha Institute of Nuclear Physics, the Asiatic Society, and the Indian Statistical Institute.

The National Law School of India University is highly regarded, with some of its students being awarded Rhodes Scholarships to Oxford University, and the All India Institute of Medical Sciences is consistently rated the top medical school in the country. Indian Institutes of Management (IIMs) are the top management institutes in India.

The private sector is strong in Indian higher education. This has been partly as a result of the decision by the Government to divert spending to the goal of universalisation of elementary education. Within a decade different state assemblies has passed bills for private universities, including Birla Institute of Technology and Science, Amity University, Xavier Labour Relations Institute and many more.

Accreditation

Accreditation for universities in India is required by law unless it was created through an act of Parliament. Without accreditation, the government notes "these fake institutions have no legal entity to call themselves as University/Vishwvidyalaya and to award 'degree' which are not treated as valid for academic/employment purposes". The University Grants Commission Act 1956 explains,

> *"the right of conferring or granting degrees shall be exercised only by a University established or incorporated by or under a Central Act carlo bon tempo, or a State Act, or an Institution deemed to be University or an institution specially empowered by an Act of the Parliament to confer or grant degrees. Thus, any institution which has not been created by an enactment of Parliament or a State Legislature or has not been granted the status of a Deemed to be University, is not entitled to award a degree."*

Accreditation for higher learning is overseen by autonomous institutions established by the University Grants Commission:

- All India Council for Technical Education (AICTE)
- Distance Education Council (DEC)
- Indian Council of Agricultural Research (ICAR)

- Bar Council of India (BCI)
- National Assessment and Accreditation Council (NAAC)
- National Council for Teacher Education (NCTE)
- Rehabilitation Council of India (RCI)
- Medical Council of India (MCI)
- Pharmacy Council of India (PCI)
- Indian Nursing Council (INC)
- Dental Council of India (DCI)
- Central Council of Homeopathy (CCH)
- Central Council of Indian Medicine (CCIM)
- Veterinary Council of India (VCI)

Graduation Market

This is a chart of India as per Census 2001.

Degree	*Holders*
Total	37,670,147
Post-graduate degree other than technical degree	6,949,707
Graduate degree other than technical degree	25,666,044
Engineering and technology	2,588,405
Teaching	1,547,671
Medicine	768,964****
Agriculture and dairying	100,126
Veterinary	99,999
Other	22,588

Quality Improvement in the Vocational Education and Training Industry

Concern about the quality of services provided to students and other clients, and focus on outcomes rather that processes are emerging as imperatives for the Australian vocational education and training systems in the 1990s. This is increasingly evident as such state system as part of an explicit reform agenda. This paper will examine the role of the technical and further education (TAFE) system in the national vocational education and training reform agenda: specifically, the impact of introducing competency-based training and establishing quality assurance systems within devolved operation structures. It will be argued that the TAFE systems, as part of the vocational education and training sector, need to put in place quality assurance policies and processes if agreements such as the National Framework for Recognition of Training are to work in practice.

Let us consider first the Australian national reform agenda. The major elements are neatly summarised in the recently agreed national goals for vocational education and training. Overall, the national system of vocational education and training is intended to:

- Be effective, efficient and collaborative;
- Improve the quality of outcomes;
- Improve opportunities and outcomes for individuals;
- Be more responsive to industry;
- Improve access and outcomes for disadvantaged groups;
- Increase contribution from industry and individuals as training is to be seen as an investment (MOVEET 1992).

Fundamentally then, the national reform agenda is about expanding education and training on the one hand, and reducing rigidities within current awards and education and training practices on the other.

These goals, which merely signpost to foreshadow the direction of reform, were endorsed be VEETAC, the Vocational Education, Employment and Training Advisory Committee, at its meeting in June 1992. VEETAC comprises senior state officers of the TAFE and training systems and representatives of the industry partners, that is the Australian Council of Trade Unions (ACTU) and the Confederation of Australian Industries (CAI), and is chaired by the commonwealth. VEETAC then, given its membership, can be seen as the policy arm of the reform agenda in operation.

In brief, the reform agenda in policy and practical terms is far reaching, not merely because it is national in scope but because it has tripartite and cross-sectoral support which transcends party politics. Its origins lie in economic and social considerations which find expression first in the industrial relations arena and which are, we will see, being reflected in a new pedagogical base for vocational education training. The mission statement of the 'Business/Higher Education Round Table' captures the duality of the rationale well:

A prerequisite for more prosperous and equitable society in Australia is more highly-educated community. In material terms it fosters economic growth and improved living standards through improved productivity and competitiveness with other countries. In terms of equity, individual Australians should have the opportunity to realise their full social, cultural, political and economic potential.

In other words the rationale for change stems from Australia's weak position by comparison to other OECD counties which is indicated in general terms by:

- Our lack of productive and severe balance of trade deficit;
- The apparent low skill levels of much of our current workforce and the segment nature of it which is particularly in case with respect to gender.

So, reform of education and training is seen as an urgent priority if Australia is to improve its economic position by the 21st century.

It is in Industrial relations context to the reform agenda which is of particular interest to TAFE systems. This is so because of the way in which the core business of TAFE-vocational education training-has been fundamentally shifted, since the starting point for all major curriculum development is now not educational issues *per se* but industry competency standards. Unless an industry sector has developed competency standards which have been endorsed by the National Training Board, there is no agreed outcome basis by which the corresponding nation curriculum development work can proceed. To date only a few industry sectors have developed their standards and still less have their standards endorsed (*NTB Network* 1992). In practise, however, significant national curriculum development has occurred over the last two to three years in competency format in the absence of endorsed standards because of pressure from particular industry sectors which, as part if restructuring, have been keen for workers to benefit from more flexible forms of training in line with new awards.

The most notable example is that of Metals and Engineering Industry. Significant funds, in excess of A$2 million, have been expended through ACTRAC, Australian Committee on Training Curriculum, in developing the so called national 'metals modules' which form the new trade-based course that replaces some 14 separate trade certificates. In addition, a new operative-level form of training that provides an alternative to the trade route, particularly for existing, unqualified but experienced employees, the Engineering Production Certificate (EPC), has also been developed. It is currently being offered together with the modular trade courses through most TAFE systems. Despite massive curriculum development, all of which has been modular and in a competency-based format, there is still no agreement by the industry partners to the competency standards *per se*. This is now expected to be achieved by early 1993.

To pursue the case study, the question has to be asked: Has this competency-based approach been of benefit to students training to enter the metals industry? The cursory answer is that it is too early to tell in terms of long-term outcomes. A fuller analysis reveals, however, that there are a number of apparent benefits:

- Students who complete the modular-based metals trade course will be more skilled than those previously because they will have acquired competencies across the fabrication, electrical and mechanical streams.
- The outcomes approach means that students have more opportunity to control and place their own learning.
- The EPC offers an alternate form of training not previously available to those at operation level without formal qualifications.

It is fair to acknowledge that the decision to re-focus curriculum development, delivery and assessment of training in this direction did not necessarily arise from an evaluation of available options by educators but rather from the industrial relations context which demands a pedagogy that could provide a more equitable means of accessing and recognising training. The curriculum expression of award restructuring is an outcome-based model of education and training which is designed so as to provide for multiple entry and exit points, recognition of prior learning, including that derived informally from life experiences, and credit transfer. In this sense competency-based training contributes am important equity orientation towards vocation education and training.

In development the model, competency-based training has become both a system of linked processes an a approach to teaching and learning. As a system of linked processes, competency-based training involves:

- Development of industry standards;
- Development of the corresponding curriculum for courses and training programmes;
- Establishing mechanisms for accreditation and national recognition;
- Provision for flexible methods of delivery and outcomes-based assessment;
- Certification of student achievement.

As an approach to learning, competency-based training:

- Places primary emphasis on what the learner can actually do;
- In focus on outcomes rather than learning processes or time spent on engaged in these processes;
- Is concerned with the attainment and demonstration of acknowledge and skills and their application;
- Is concerned with achieving flexibility in the use and adoption of national industry standards while still enabling the consistency essential for national requirements.

There has been criticism of competency-based training from some quarters partly because we have seen, it has arisen to meet demands of award restructuring and as such has not been subject to scrutiny or debate by educators. This is not to say, however, that competency-based training does not have educational potential. Concepts such as flexible learning, multiple entry points, pathways and recognition of prior learning are essentially emancipator in character and when fully implemented will provide a better deal for young people and existing workforces. Notwithstanding this, competency-based training has been characterised by some in such a way that at first glance it appears to be anti-educationist. As Hager and Gonzi (1992) have argued, however, many of the myths associated with competency-based training can be debunked. In brief, competency-based training is not necessarily behaviourist, complex, only about training which is centrally controlled or developed, nor is it focused only on the lowest common denominator in terms of performance, or impractical to assess.

Clearly, competency-based training, like all other pedagogies, is either wholly deleterious nor a panacea to all our educational problems. It is simply a tool. And yes, it is a tool which we as educators have used and misused before. But like any tool in the kit of educators or trainers it has the potential to make a difference. If competency-based training provides a means of promoting alternate pathways to higher education, training or employment, is used as the basis for granting credit where none has been granted before, and contributes to the breaking down of existing rigidities in the way we often draw and reinforce boundaries around the various sectors of education and training, then it is an approach that I endorse as a valuable step forward. It is a step forward because of the potential to add the value to student learning.

The work of the Mayer Community in developing a set of key, generic, employment-related competencies is further evidence of a step forward. The cross-sectoral educational work has demonstrated that competency can be viewed holistically and developed to integrate knowledge and skills, and their application. Competencies of this kind apply to work generally rather than being specific to work in particular occupations and industries. In this sense it is possible to describe knowledge and skills richly enough to be able to identify discrimination variable which may be used to distinguish between performance standards at arbitrary points or levels. Preliminary field testing undertaken with employers and trainees in industry during the consultation phase in the development of key competencies makes sense in real work situations (Mayer Committee 1992). More research, however, needs to be done to validated and establish as benchmarks the current level descriptions.

In practical terms, the implementation of competency-based training certainly does create difficulties for TAFE systems. A few, as yet unresolved, questions illustrate the point:

- What was the role of workplace assessors and who determines their suitability for assessing on-the-job competencies *vis-á-vis* the off-the-job assessment which will be conducted typically by qualified TAFE teachers or their equivalent in private training organisation?
- To what extent can vocational skills be satisfactorily demonstrated and performed to the requisite industry standard outside an actual work situation?
- How are competencies to be recorded now that the critical; issue is no longer 'who is the best apprentice?' but 'which competencies has this apprentice required?''

By the end of 1992 the following mechanisms are likely to be in place which will assist TAFE systems and other providers to implement competency-based training. The National Framework for Recognition of Training (NFROT) came to existence in August, 1992. It has been endorsed by MOVEET as a means of ensuring that accredited training is recognised nationally and that there is consistency in the application of the principles which characterise a competency-based system of vocational education and training namely:

- Assessment will be measured against clearly defined competency standards set by industry and endorsed by the National Training Board.
- Prior learning will be recognised and credit transfer arrangements will be promoted.

- Consistency will derive from a focus on outcomes.
- Common criteria will apply for registration of providers and accreditation of courses.

A common format for t he development of modular, competency-based curriculum has been recently developed by ACTRAC and endorsed by other key stakeholders. This means that there will be greater consistency in curriculum design and that more attention will be paid to the difficult task of deriving units of competency and learning outcomes of industry standards. Currently staff development train-the-trainer package and strategy is being developed which will provide opportunities for key personnel such as TAFE teachers, curriculum writers and industry trainers to become familiar with the pedagogical issues involved in undertaking such tasks.

Notwithstanding these national agreements there are a number o important 'quality' questions which have to be addressed, including: 'How the TAFE system is responding to the national reform agenda assured students of the quality and vocational relevancy to there courses?' Traditionally TAFE systems have dealt with quality assurance through their accreditation systems. In some cases the past, courses have been largely internally developed and did not involve or allow for very much industry input or scrutiny. In other cases, as in New South Wales (NSW, there has been a long tradition of industry involvement, and external review panels have always been a feature of the accreditation system. Irrespective of these differences in the past, in line with a key tenet of the national reform agenda, 'the level playing field', all TAFE systems have lost their monopoly in respect of course accreditation and correspondingly, registration of providers. Accordingly, in all states and territories there is now an independent accrediting authority, often created by a specific piece of legislation. This is the case in NSW, where the Vocational Education and Training Accreditation has been established since mid-1991. In line with the provisions of the legislation, the NSW TAFE Commission has negotiated self-accrediting status and has now established a TAFE Accreditation Council to manage its accreditation processes.

At the same time as TAFE systems have been responding to the National training reform agenda, they have also been restructuring in their own right. In NSW the former Department of Technical and Further Education was subject, long with the Department of Education (schools sector), to a major management review, the Scott Review, which resulted in significant organisational changes. In summary,

TAFE NSW became a commission with an independent board; the teaching schools became training divisions with an explicit industry or educational focus; colleges were clustered into networks and later into larger groupings as institutes; head office functions such as teacher recruitment, budgeting, planning, quality control and other related operations were developed or out-sourced, with a corresponding reduction in staff numbers.

In 1992 there were a small number of central support divisions and 11 institutes: three are institutes of technology and eight are institutes of TAFE. Each of the metropolitan institutes are significant state-wide functions in addition to their delivery responsibilities through the college/campus structure. All 13 training divisions, which are jointly responsible for the development and maintenance of TAFE curriculum, examinations, and the setting of quality assurance standards for recruitment of staff, provision of facilities and equipment, sections of students and course delivery, have been developed to relevant institutes. Responsibilities for the development of corporate policies and frameworks in critical customer service areas such as marketing and quality assurance including accreditation, remain a central function. Thus there is a quality assurance and customer service group which includes division on marketing (corporate and international), educational quality assurance and student services (examinations and enrolments).

The challenge, then, is to improve quality while developing the majority of the operational functions, which determine whether a particular service, such as the enrolment process, actually meet students needs. As with industry generally, the vocational education and training industry, including TAFE systems, are under increasing pressure to more visibly and credibility implement quality assurance measures. The pressure is from internal and external sources:

- Internally, students and teacher need assurance of the quality and consistency of the education services provided irrespective of the location or circumstances where by these are offered.
- Externally, industry expects a timely response in the development of new courses, and relevance in terms of the vocational content and technological context,

To respond to these internal and external pressures, the approach adopted by NSW TAFE has been drawn from the Australian Standard for Quality Management Systems. Many in industry will already be familiar with the application of Australian Standards to various products. A standard also exists for Quality Management Systems (AS 3901). Its purpose is to define a system for 'all those planned and systematic actions necessary to provide adequate confidence that a product or service will satisfy given requirements for quality'. The standard consists of separate elements which describe the kind of procedures and records that must be established and maintained to ensure confidence in the quality of a system.

At thios stage NSW TAFE has undertaken preliminary work to group and translate these elements into an educational service delivery context. It is no easy task. What follows is an outline of what this translation might look like in terms of a major education and training system such as NSW TAFE.

Management Responsibility for Maintaining Quality,

- TAFE management has the responsibility to develop, implement and maintain policies and procedures to achieve a quality education service to its customers which includes students, staff, as well as external clients.
- Management must support personnel with responsibility for quality assurance by providing adequate resources.
- Management must review its quality system at appropriate intervals.

Meeting the Needs of Industry, the Community and Individual Students

- Procedures must be established and maintained to ensure that the requirements of customers are known and can be met, and that individual students have been enrolled in the correct and agreed course/subject/module.
- The design, both of course content (curriculum) and of the programme of courses offered in a particular institute/college must reflect student needs, industry requirements and be soundly based in educational terms.
- Current courses and other curriculum documents must by readily identified and obsolete ones destroyed as a part of a review and maintenance cycle.

Delivery of Quality Courses, with Appropriate Staff, and Provision of Student Services

- The college/campus must maintain procedures for delivering and reviewing courses to the standards set down in course documentation for content, teacher qualifications, assessment and physical resource.

- All resources which TAFE purchases to provide educational services-including staff recruitment-must be chosen by selection procedures that ensure that they meet specific requirements.
- Students must have access to services such as counselling, course information advice, or tutorial support to support them in their studies, and appropriate student and course records must be maintained.

Maintenance of Appropriate Assessment and Testing, and Conferring of Awards

- Procedures must be established and followed to ensure that initial, ongoing ad final assessment occurs as necessary, and that assessment is valid, and consistently applied.
- Records of students' enrolment, attendance, assessment and examination results and final awards must be maintained
- Student outcomes must be reviewed in a regular basis, problems identified and improvements made, with the aim of increasing student success.

Support and Teaching and Learning through Maintenance of the Physical Environment and Human Resource Development

- The college/campus must provide a physical environment appropriate for learning, and occupational health and safety requirements must be met
- Human resource development needs staff who are responsible for developing or delivering courses to students must be identified so that priorities can be set and training planned and delivered

Maintain Checks on the System Through Educational Quality Audits

- All aspect of the quality system must be audited to ensure that activities comply with set procedures
- Auditors undertaking such review and monitoring must be trained appropriately

What would the operation of a quality management system mean in practice? Put simply it would mean that meeting students needs would be seen as am important value and would therefore become the prime focus of *all* activities in practice. Also, all functions within the TAFE system would be carried out by staff in a manner consistent with the value of 'continuous improvement'. TAFE NSW believes that changing the internal culture of the TAFE system to embrace these values is necessary, particularly in the context of a developing structure. It is easy for consistency to be lost under the guise of autonomy unless there are clearly articulate and understood standards. If value is to be added to student learning then clearly essential, for example, that all students enrolled in a particular course have the same chance, subject their ability, or satisfactorily completing the course irrespective of the place or time or mode of delivery, or the specific teacher involved.

Gaining executive and staff commitment to reorient existing operations so that students come first is not a single-event process. Nor can it be done in an isolated or piecemeal fashion. It requires an integrated and system-wide strategy which has been developed through collaborative processes so there is ownership and recognition of the need for change. TAFE NSW has set itself such an agenda, but over a two to three year time frame. As a billion dollar enterprise with more than 400 000 students and 20 000 staff, there is a significant amount of work to do in reshaping existing policies and procedures to achieve a more explicit customer focus consistent with our vocational education and training charter.

Currently the Queensland TAFE system has made a similar commitment to establish quality management systems. It is likely that all other TAFE systems will soon begin to define quality in customer service terms. It is interesting to note that the university sector has been responding to the quality imperative in some respects, at least, in a similar way.

Arising from the employment, education and training minister's 'quality' reference to the National Board of Employment, Education and Training (NBEET) (Baldwin 1991) each Australian university in the next three years will need to construct a system of quality management appropriate to its context and mission. As we have seen, there are three preliminary questions to consider:

- Who are the customers?
- What are the product and/or services?
- How is it intended to achieve congruence between these, that is, fitness for purpose?

As recent commentators have noted, there are in fact numbers of measures already in place in universities which are used to assure the quality of academic experience. These can be summed up as:

- Designing for quality through procedures;
- Attaining quality through attainment of conformance to design, that is, continuous improvement.

It can be argued that many of the concepts associated with equal theory-continuous improvement through feedback, use of collaborative processes including team work, and teacher rather than management input into the curriculum and course design-are essentially educational in character and so are compatible with the core function of universities. The same situation, of course, also applies in the case of TAFE sector.

So, there is no reason why the TAFE systems cannot continue to pursue those quality assurance measures which are likely to add value to student learning on the one hand and to resulting higher levels of customer satisfaction on the other.

The Contribution of IGNOU in North East India

Vocational training is about "imparting of specialized skills and knowledge, instilling social and political attitudes and behaviour patterns for successful economic activities by people engaged in dependent employment, self-employment in both Formal as well as Non-formal trainings". In its 'Formal training' all training courses are held in state or private (but state-certified) institutions and are regulated by state guidelines where as in the 'Non-formal training' it takes place without being subject to state guidelines and provides skills-upgrading for those who wish to extend their competencies. Vocational training, in its non-formal form, upgrades the skills, helps in capacity building, expands livelihood opportunities for the underprivileged, unreached informal sector workers and plays a key role in the national development.

This paper enumerates the non-formal vocational training being imparted by the Indira Gandhi National Open University (IGNOU) to the underprivileged and unreached people in the North East Region (NER) .It underlines the university's two channels i.e Regional Centres and Institutes through which these training programmes are imparted. The paper highlights the university's contribution towards the national development by conducting these training programmes in the N E R.

Ignou

The Indira Gandhi National Open University, established by an Act of Parliament in 1985, is the largest University in terms of its enrolment. Today, nearly 3 million learners from India and 36 other countries are enrolled in IGNOU. There are 21 schools of study, 61 Regional Centres, approximately 3000 learner support centres in India and 60 overseas centres. The university offers nearly 350 Certificate, Diploma, Degree and Doctoral Programmes and has 420 faculty members and academic staff at the Head Quarters and Regional Centres. About 36, 000 academic counsellors from the conventional institutions of higher learning and professionals from various organizations conduct the face-to-face sessions and contribute to continuous evaluation of the learners' performance. The Commonwealth of Learning (COL), Canada, has conferred on the University the 'Centre of Excellence Award' in Distance Education and the 'Award of Excellence for Distance Education Materials'. As an open learning institution, IGNOU provides flexibility in entry level in terms of age, place, pace and duration of study.

The university uses multimedia teaching-learning packages which include self-instructional print and audio-video materials, radio and television broadcasts, face-to-face counselling, laboratory, hands-on experience, teleconferencing, video-conferencing, interactive radio counselling, interactive multimedia CD-Roms, Internet- based learning, the use of mobile phone for instant messaging and practical / practice teaching at selected programme centres.

Non-formal Vocational Training Programmes in Ner

As per the National Skills Commission Report , Ministry of Labour , 2008, IGNOU is giving a new connotation to the term 'Vocation'. With a mandate to create a work force among the youth in both the organized and the unorganized sector, the university is imparting the Non-Formal Vocational Training programmes in the NER. The university, through the Educational Development of North East Region Unit (EDNERU) , has created the educational access in the region by cutting across physical and geographical barriers. Its inherent flexibility of Open and Distance Learning (ODL) helps in equalising opportunities of education to the hitherto 'unreached' in the region. A wide network of Regional Centres, learning centres, tele-learning centres and institutes have been established to overcome geographical constraints and to provide the best resources available through Information and Communication Technology (ICT) and Open and Distance Learning . Need-based vocational and entrepreneurship programmes have been planned and implemented in collaboration with other State/Central agencies to increase employment opportunities in the region.

The Channels

Through its various educational activities, the university has been constantly striving for the development of human resource in the region by contributing to a holistic planning of education and vocational skills. This is being undertaken in consonance with the regional ethos and the requirements of the region. Initiatives have been taken to develop value added, tailor made courses which have demand in the job market. The University conducts several skill development, entrepreneurship and vocational training programmes in different states of the region through its regional centres and institutes to enhance the employability and self-reliance of the youth of the region in various sectors of the region's economy. One of the foremost initiatives undertaken by the university has been the operationalization of the following institutes in the NE region for the professional development of the people of the region:

The IGNOU Institute for Vocational Education and Training (IIVET), Shillong

The IGNOU Institute For Vocational Education And Training (IIVET), Shillong identifies and develops need-based relevant vocational programmes. It trains the educated youth of the region in various skills to enhance their opportunities for gainful employment in collaboration with 60 Common Service Centres in Meghalaya and Sikkim adopting the tele-centre model.

Institute for Professional Competency Advancement of Teachers Through ODL (IPCAT), Guwahati

The institute provides training for the untrained teachers and continuous training for the in-service teachers through ODL mode using multi-media technology. The Institute organizes orientation programme for Madarsa Teachers of Assam and workshop on Teacher Training Strategies for elementary level in the context of Right to Education Act 2009 assisted by UNICEF

IGNOU Centre for ODL in Research & Training in Agriculture (ICRTA), Agartala

The centre studies the socio-economic aspects, gaps and challenges in imparting knowledge and skills to farmers. Its objective is to develop an action model for using Information and Communication Technology (ICT) in Agriculture Extension and Education and Information System; to develop human resources for Agriculture and Agriculture based industries; and to capacity building and competency upgradation of the professionals in agriculture and allied sectors through ODL system. At present the ICRTA is conducting training programmes for farmers and extension personnel of Assam, Mizoram, Arunachal Pradesh, Nagaland, Manipur, Meghalaya, Sikkim and Tripura.

Modes of Training

The training programmes conducted in the NER are imparted by the following modes:

- Lectures by experts
- Field-visits
- Practical field experience
- School screening
- Diagnostic camps
- Practical counselling
- Collaboration Centres
- Hands—on training
- E-Learning portal - Information Systems Services and Networking for North East Agriculture (KISSAN -NE)
- Video studios
- Call-centre system

These training programmes are imparting the following technical and general vocational skills:

Vocational Training Programmes

a) *Technical Vocational Skills*
   - Auto Mobile Repair,
   - Weaving,
   - Repair of Gadgets and Instruments(Mobile Phones and Computers)
   - Electrical Repairs
   - Tailoring
   - Printing

b) *General Vocational Skills*
   - Public Speaking
   - Personality Development
   - Writing skills

- Vocational Skills for Domestic Workers
- Vocational Skills for Dropouts
- Plastic Engineering Technology for the Educated Unemployed
- Low Cost House making with Bamboos
- Communication / Soft Skills

c) *Vocational skills in Agriculture*

- Watershed Management
- Rain Water Harvesting

d) Vocational Skills in Information & Technology

- Use of multimedia packages
- Operation of Information Systems Services in a Call-Centre system

Methods of Training

Outlined below are the methods being used in the non-formal vocational training programmes for imparting the technical and general vocational skills:

Barefoot Technicians/ Grass root Level Workers Course in the Hearing Disability

- Practical
- School screening
- Awareness and diagnostic camps in the villages
- Family visit and counselling
- Maintenance of Record books

Marketing of Agricultural Produces

- Practical Training by experts from ICAR, National Research Centre for Orchid, ICRTA, IGNOURegional Centre Agartala, SIMFED, NERAMAC, & MEVEDIR
- Lectures
- Colourful slide , diagrams & photographs
- Face to face interaction with the scientists

Bamboo Based Handicraft Training

- Division in four sessions
- Sessions on teaching and learning skills to make utility items having local demand.

- Sessions devoted to teaching making of decorative items having substantial demand outside state.
- Experts from IITs

Dairy Farming

- Technical session with practical demonstration on scientific dairy farming technology.
- Theory classes by experts from the Agricultural Science Centre, Central Agricultural University and the Animal Husbandry Department
- Colourful slide show, photograph & diagrams
- Practical classes on different aspect of preparation of rations, demonstration on fodder production and preservation, artificial insemination, care & management of dairy animals
- Field visits to the Research Complex and Milk Cooperative to demonstrate the practical aspects.

Watershed Management

- Specialists/ experts from Indian Council of Agricultural Research (ICAR), State Agriculture University, Forest Department, Ground Water Board, National Bank for Agriculture and Rural Development (NABARD)
- Survey and demonstration of topography of land
- Preparation of inventory of resources, soil erosion and its management, rainwater conservation and its reutilization, people participation and financial avenues from the banks .

Water Harvesting and Watershed Management

- Experts from Assam Agricultural University (AAU), the ICAR Research complex for the North Eastern region and the Agriculture Science Centre (KVK), and School of Agriculture, IGNOU
- Lectures on topics pertaining to water storage, conservation and utilization.
- Local field visit to a place where a 'Watershed Society' actively involved in water harvesting during rainy season
- Collecting rainwater in ponds constructed at particular points in the fields for utilizing conserved water for irrigation and fish and duck culturing.

Integrated Farming System

- Experts from Assam Agricultural University (AAU), State government, Assam and ICAR
- Lectures on various aspects of an Integrated Farming System. (IFS), Organic farming, farm composting, marketing, economics and fish production.
- Organization of exhibition showing the models of IFS, new crop varieties, animal health care approaches (vaccines), improved farm implements and handicraft items
- Field trip to village.

Vocational skills Development programme in Advanced Auto Cad

- Collaboration with Tool Room & Training Centre
- Field visits
- Hands –on -Training

Vocational Training for Women Domestic Workers in Basic Computer Skills and Communication Skills.

- Collaboration with the North East Domestic Workers Association.
- Computer Skills in typing, word processing, browsing the internet
- Communication in English language pronunciation and Conversation

Vocational Training Programme of Hardware and Software Repairing

- Knowledge of Hardware and Software
- Fault finding, trouble shooting,
- PCB identification .
- Division of group in 4 batches
- Group discussion

Career Counselling on Mobile Repair.

In these training programmes, the trainees were evaluated by testing their basic knowledge prior to (pre-test) and after completion (post-test). A questionnaire developed and used for pre- and post-tests consisted of objective -type questions on various aspects of the training programme. Most of the candidates scored 3 to 10 marks in the pre-test and 11 to 19 marks in the post-test, result which revealed that the training had significantly improved their knowledge and skills.

Feedback

The feedback from the participants about the training programme was collected by the IGNOU officials . It revealed the following observations of the participants :

- The training programme was quite useful for helping them to gain technical skills;
- They can utilize the technical skills for improving their existing management;
- They gained knowledge about new scientific techniques;
- The programme inspired them to take up entrepreneurship on a large scale.
- The knowledge gained can improve their performance
- They had learned many technical skills which can be utilized for improving their existing agricultural / horticultural and soil and water conservation practices
- They had gained knowledge about new scientific techniques used in rainwater- harvesting, soil conservation
- The knowledge gained can improve their watershed and water-harvesting management skills
- They wouldl adopt the new techniques to manage their agro-wastes and apply them to raise their crops
- They are inspired to become entrepreneurs
- They learnt many technical skills through these training programmes which would help in their capacity- building and improving their socio-economic condition
- They were willing to undergo an advance training programme to acquire the skill of designing in weaving and expressed their willingness to undergo further training to sharpen their skills.
- The Programme built their capacity to earn and made them self dependent financially.
- The Programme was very useful for poor and unemployed youth to earn a

living without any big capital investment

- It had a tremendous impact
- It really benefited the disadvantaged and under-privileged
- Most of the trainees got sponsorship from Sans Cellular Concept, to be later absorbed in the company for further mobile repair training.

- It revived the art of weaving and inspired the women association to take it up on commercial scale.
- They formed Self Help Groups in villages.
- Supplied mini tool kits speeded up the production process.
- Such vocational training programmes must be organized regularly.

The participants expressed their satisfaction and offered thanks to the IGNOU authorities for conducting such useful vocational training programmes for upgrading their skills, for their capacity building and expandingtheir livelihood opportunities and boosting the economic growth and development of the NER.

National Development

The university is contributing towards the national development in a big way by adopting successful models of training and capacity building. Following the National Skills Mission and the National Scheme of Enhancement of Gross Enrolment Ratio (GER) and Skill Development in the economically backward districts, the university is developing and implementing a skill development action plan which evolves around the possibilities of optimal utilization of the training infrastructure and the intellectual capabilities available both in the formal sector of education and in other public and private sectors. The short-term vocational training programmes of the university through effective partnerships with Small and Medium Scale industries, Corporate Houses and both public and private training centres are showing encouraging results in the employment generation .

At present the vocational training programmes are being diversified, considering the social needs of the people. The university has ventured into the socio economic development programmes with a view to train the village artisans and rural entrepreneurs in taking up self employment. Its approach and system of functioning, being people oriented, has resulted into formulation of several programmes and schemes and collaboration with various agencies in order to provide assistance in getting bank loan, familiarization with self employment schemes, identification of technical collaboration and providing of help in setting up infrastructure. Such training programmes enable the local youth to form Self Help Groups ,analyse the emerging problems and take corrective action accordingly. Through these training programmes they learn to produce the items at affordable price in bigger quantity to meet the market demands and exposes them to the skills of using the modern tools and equipments and skills of ensuring the survival and sustainability and thereby enhancing their confidence.

Conclusion

Vocational training, in its non-formal form, upgrades the skills, helps in capacity building, expands livelihood opportunities for the underprivileged, unreached informal sector workers and plays a key role in the national development . The Indira Gandhi National Open University (IGNOU) is imparting the vocational training to the underprivileged and unreached people across the country. The university's unit Educational Development of North East Region (EDNERU) is promoting the non-formal vocational training programmes in the North East Region (NER) through the channels of Regional Centres and Institutes and collaboration with the relevant institutions and organizations. Various vocational training programmes are being imparted to develop the technical vocational skills like Auto Mobile Repair, Weaving, Repair of Gadgets and Instruments, Electrical Repairs, Tailoring, Printing, Barefoot Technicians/ Grassroot level workers course in the Hearing Disability ; general vocational skills like Public Speaking, Personality Development, Writing skills, Vocational Skills for Domestic Workers, Vocational Skills for Dropouts, Plastic Engineering Technology for the Educated Unemployed, Low Cost House Making with Bamboos, Food Processing and Candle Making, Basket Making and Flower Making, Bamboo based Handicraft product for the Village Artisans, Communication / Soft Skills; vocational skills in Agriculture like Watershed Management, Rain Water Harvesting Marketing of Agricultural produces , Integrated Farming System, Dairy Farming and vocational skills in Information & Technology like development and use of multimedia packages, Operation of Information Systems Services and Call-Centre system. Different modes like lectures by experts, field-visits, practical field experience, school screening, diagnostic camps, practical counselling, collaboration centres, hands—on training,E-Learning portal, Information Systems Services and Networking for North East Agriculture, video studios and call-centre system etc. are being used for imparting the training programmes effectively.

The feedback collected from the participants of the training programmes outlines the university's models of vocational training and capacity building. It also highlights the university's successful implementation of skill development action plan which has an optimal utilization of the training infrastructure and intellectual capabilities from the formal sector of education and public and private sectors along with effective partnerships with small and medium scale industries and corporate houses. The promising results after the conduct of these non-formal vocational training programmes are showcasing the university's contribution towards the employment generation and socio-economic development of the NER .

A Road Map For the Success of India

Vocational Education and training means that one acquires some skill which will help in some economic activity and generate wealth for the person. VET also improves SQ and EQ. The present education system concentrates mostly on IQ improvement. In India nearly 58% of the work force of 509 million is self employed.

Human Resource Development in India

In Germany and the Central European countries, nearly 80 to 75% of the children entering the age of 14 and beyond go in for vocational education & training. About 20 to 25% go ahead for higher studies. The same is also true for the 'Asian Tigers' and USA. People in India between the ages of 15 to 30 are nearly 300 million. There are 550 million people in India, who are less than 30 years of age and 770 million who are less than 35 years of age. The average Indian is only 25 years old. *Indians are very young.* This is a big strength and advantage of India which needs to be fully energized and strengthened.

The total unemployed, in India, are estimated at about 300 million, out of these only 41 million are registered with the employment exchanges. Most of these so called educated youth are not employable as they have no relevant skills! About 450 million are illiterate. About 260 million live below the Poverty Line. Sectors overlap. They have no 'net' to fall back upon least of all a 'safety net'. The 'organized sector' constantly complains about the unavailability of a 'safety net', not realizing that they are living in India and not in USA or Europe.

About 29 million are born every year and enter the present educational system at different stages. We notice that nearly 92% drop out at different stages, between classes 1st to 12th, only 3 million make it through the present educational system, which lays emphasis and seems to guide and direct the youth for higher education. The drop-outs are left to fend for themselves or may get some help from Central & State aided programs! *To us the present system seems to be very elitist in nature.*

The above is also reflected in the number of institutions in India. We have 1,200,000 primary schools, 130,000 secondary schools, 37,000 colleges and 7,000 ITI's (for vocational education & training). China has 500,000 VET centres, while Germany has 100,000 VET centres and a small country like Austria has 5,000 VET centres.

In India the civil society, the parents and most of the youth want to be an engineer or a doctor or do an MBA. As if no other skill is required to run the Indian Economy? You can get a doctor but not the hundreds of Para-medical support staff who are required for our healthcare sector? You can get an engineer but not a plumber, electrician or carpenter. You can get an MBA but not a person who understands import-export and understands the procedures and paper work of a simple letter of credit document? India's external trade, imports and exports is nearly 35% of the economy, but we do not have qualified people to strengthen this infrastructure? India needs 300,000 urban planners but we hardly have 3,000. Mumbai has three urban planners while Singapore with a population 25% of the Mumbai Region has one hundred urban planners. You can buy a fancy and world class car in India, but can you get a world class driver? Similar situation is in other sectors of the economy like banking, retail, construction, insurance, agriculture, horticulture, animal husbandry, forestry, mining, manufacturing and hundreds of other sectors of the world economy.

Employment in the 'Organized Sector'

Out of the total 509 million employed, about 29 million, or 6%, work in the *organized sector* (3m in PSU's + 17m with Central & State Governments + 10m, with the 'organized private sector'). This sector is 'high cost' and 'overstaffed' leading to high cost and inefficiency, in the Indian context. We could do with lower cost with higher quality and efficiency. This also hampers India's export potential in world markets. The present education system seems to be preparing the youth for this sector alone. This is the *rich or elite* sector of India and needs no form of subsidy whatsoever.

In India, Poverty line is at Rs. 330 per month per person for rural India and Rs. 520 per month per person in urban India. The old World Bank definition for 'Poverty Line' was about Rs.50 per day per person (US$ 1 per day). Minimum wages in India are approximately at Rs. 1,250/1,500 per month or Rs 50 per day. The average GDP of an Indian is about US$2.5 per day or about Rs 125 per day. Recently the World Bank has raised the poverty line definition to US$ 2 per day or about Rs. 100 per day. To improve its cost competitiveness, the Indian business sector needs to empower its work force with enterprise skills development (ESD) and vocational education & training (VET).

Labour or *employee* reforms are also needed in this sector, as explained in our *Manufacturing Policy for India*. The present 'Labour Laws' seem to protect the 'organized Public sector' and also the 'organized Private sector'. Work Ethics and Work Culture Standards also seem to emanate from this sector, which indirectly are reflected on the behaviour of the entire 'unorganized sector', some political parties and the youth of India.

Employment in the 'Unorganized Sector'

480 million, or 94%, work force is in the 'unorganized sector', in agriculture, construction and with SME's. They are the ones who need help in primary & secondary education (P&SE), enterprise skills development (ESD) and also vocational education & training (VET)

Funding of P&SE, ESD and VET

In various seminars and studies conducted within the country, we understand that the present funds are inadequate, since the GDP spend on education was hardly 3.0 %. In a country like India we need to spend at least 6% to 9% of GDP on education.

In the EU, USA, Japan & S. Korea the total expenditure on Primary and Secondary education is about 6% of GDP. Additional 3% for VET and additional 3% for Higher & Technical Education and R&D. Human development and human empowerment is the key driver. China and the Asian Tigers follow the same path. India, Pakistan, Nepal, Bangladesh, Burma, Afghanistan, Sri Lanka are lagging behind and the results speak for themselves. *The importance of human infrastructure has not been generally understood by civil society*. Most of the chambers of commerce mostly concentrate on financial infrastructure or material and physical infrastructure. Political parties understand education only as far as higher, medical and technical education is concerned; the number of colleges being run by politicians in Maharashtra and Karnataka is a case to point.

As the central as well as the state governments are in huge deficits of nearly 10 to 12 % of GDP, we suggest that private funding, either from domestic private parties or from NRI's should be encouraged with tax benefits and suitable tax breaks for the next 30 years. No questions should be asked of the source of funds. In Germany this was done after the war to spur investments in buildings, infrastructure, plant and machinery and other assets which were destroyed and were badly needed for the economy. Even after 62 years India lags far behind. We also suggest that all higher education should be privatized, i.e. after the 10th or 12th. Any funds being spent presently for higher education should be funneled back to the primary and secondary sectors by the Central and State governments. We need to strengthen the 94% of the work force as our 1st priority.

Maximize use of Existing Infrastructure in the Country

India is a poor country. The existing land, building and other infrastructure should be upgraded and used, as far as possible. Operating two or more shifts in metropolitan towns and cities should be encouraged, so that the existing workforce could also have an opportunity to upgrade its skills and competency. In most countries, VET is an ongoing and continuous life long process of learning. People develop multiple skills with time.

Marketing the Benefits for Vocational Education & Training

There are 14 stake holders, please see paragraph 11, within the Indian Economy, who are connected with the need and use of Vocational education & training skills. We, who are outside the PSSCIVE, NCERT, MHRD, AICTE, UGC and the Ministry of Labour & Employment, feel that very little has been done to inform and educate the citizens and these 14 stake holders about the benefits and need for vocational education & training.

India's Future lies in Becoming a Resource Base in Manufacturing, Trading and Services.

India has 2.2% of the land mass, 17% of the world population but hardly 1.8% of the world GDP. It is all the more important that we need world class vocational education and training as well as entrepreneurship skills development for a major part of our workforce. Only a world class work force can generate wealth for the nation and make us a world class economy. Germany, Japan, S. Korea and others are examples of countries, much smaller than India in area and having no mineral wealth or energy, but with very powerful economies.

With 17% of the World Population - India Should be a Powerhouse for Human Resources.

Excepting in information technology and software, which is only 2.5% of world GDP, we do not train Indians to world class standards. We do export engineers, doctors and chartered accountants, but this number is very small. There is no planned effort for the balance 97.5% of economic activity, such as for healthcare, foreign languages, engineering and skilled craftsmen in about 1100 sectors of the world economy.

India has no known manpower plans which are relevant for the present and future world markets or a national plan for the onslaught and opportunities because of globalization and aging population in Japan, the EU and the USA.

We do not know the international manpower requirements for the next 10 to 20 years, country by country and where Indians could play a role.

Entrepreneurs are Mostly People who are Skilled in Some Trade or Competency.

From the above data it is quite clear that government cannot provide jobs to the 29 million who enter the workforce every year. Otherwise we would need one 'NEW' India every year, just for this. Since most of the employment generation would come from 'export led organized sector activities' or from the 'unorganized sector', which accounts for nearly 94% of the work force, the empowerment of the people of India with vocational education & training can only be overemphasized time and time again.

10. Restrictive Economic practices, *which restrict employment generation, such as*

- Reservation of some Industry under Small Scale sector. The size of a manufacturing unit cannot be decided by some official in New Delhi. It is decided by International market forces and by the cutting edge technology and processes which would be required to produce the product with the best quality and lowest cost, to be able to make it world class. A case in point is the 'Mini Steel Plants' where thousands of crores of Indian tax payer's money was invested in about 100 mini steel plants! In today's context a steel plant should be of 5 to 10 million tons capacity per year. It will produce low cost steel which could trigger off many down stream units, using this steel as a raw material.
- Restrictive Labour Laws. Indian companies are migrating to high Capital Cost Technologies since Indian Labour Laws encourage Indian business to employ the lowest number employees and use very expensive technologies, rather than have the freedom to use the lowest cost technology and use the largest number of employees. This is the saddest testimony of what we have achieved in the last 62 years and how we have systematically 'deformed' our manufacturing and service sectors.

- Not recognizing that Enterprises means all types of business and not only Industry! In USA, Europe, Japan and most countries of the world, SME's account for nearly 80% of economic activity and employment. This has been elaborated in our book – Transforming INDIA through education. In India, sadly, this fact is also here but it is not fully recognized. For example banks will lend to an Industry but not to a firm in trading, agriculture, services or non-industrial activity. An Enterprise *means all types of economic activity and not only Industry.* A SME in USA, Japan, Taiwan, Europe means enterprises with about Rs.150 to Rs.250 crores turnover and about Rs 80 to 100 crores investment. How can an Indian small unit ever compete with such an enterprise?

It is estimated that the 480 million who work in the 'unorganized sector' are mostly in the SME's, who number about 100 million organizations. 80% are in agriculture and plantations and about 20 million in the manufacturing and services sector. This is where we need 100% Functional Literacy and 100% Vocational Education & Training.

Central and State Boards of Education

The boards of education seem to consist of employees of government departments and people from the field of teaching, with practically very few or no representatives from the other 14 stake holders, as mentioned in item 4 above. These stake holders are from business, chambers of commerce, labour unions, youth organizations, parent organizations, media, think tanks, NGO's, NRI organizations, PSU's, CSIR & R&D organizations, Local Corporator, Local MLA and Local MP.

Inadequate use of the Internet to Enhance Productivity

India is doing a fine job the area of software and Information Technology. Most of this benefit goes to countries where our I.T. services and solutions are exported. Very little is being used to improve India. Only 6 to 7 % of Indians understand English, yet we do not have central government or state wise websites in the state languages so to provide transparent information about the Vocational Institutions and the courses offered by them, in each State, city wise, village wise and district wise.

The sites must be hosted in *dynamic fonts* so that the regional media, schools, colleges, trade, politicians and all citizens, can down load the information, where ever they may be located, since most Indian PC's do not have Indian software loaded on their systems.

The NRI world is very strong, and estimated at about 25 million people in all the 5 continents. Their GDP, gross domestic product, is estimated to be as nearly 35% of India. Many of them would like to help, participate and invest for education in India. This is the only way they can reach us, yet we have not planned for internet sites, as explained above!

Mapping of Economic Activity in India

In spite of 62 years of Independence, we have not mapped and continue to update, on a yearly basis, all forms of economic activity in each state,

- road wise
- Village wise
- town or city wise
- district wise

By economic activity we mean:-

- Agriculture
- Industry, (Large and MSME's)
- Trading
- Services
- NGO's
- Religious Organizations

This is a very important aspect of information, since it is the area where apprentices can work and learn on-the-job. In Central Europe, at any given time, nearly 8% to 10% of the country's work force population is under some sort of vocational education & training or skills development programmes.

In India this would mean about 50 million people, at any given time. Since we are a developing country and need to use a lot of labour intensive technology for our economic activity. Presently it is just about 1 to 3 million per year.

Conclusion

As per Prof. C. K. Prahlad, who is working on the vision of India@75 Project with CII, gives maximum importance to education and skills. Out of the 74 National Committees in CII, he has narrowed down his vision of transformation of India only to three National Committees, viz. on education on skills & HR and the youth wing called Yi or young Indians. This study was jointly undertaken by CII & BCG.

The major emphasis is on the following four broad objectives for the Nation. The importance of vocational education and training for skills development has been clearly defined:

- India achieves 100% functional literacy
- India builds 700 million globally employable workforce, comprising 200 million university graduates and 500 million vocationally skilled people
- India develops world-class infrastructure to become a global hub for knowledge creation, talent development and entrepreneurial incubation
- India meets its own unique domestic demand while setting global standards and become a scale provider of value based learner-centric education, skills development and professional educators through industry partnerships

Teacher Education

Context and Concerns

Teacher education is an integral component of the educational system. It is intimately connected with society and is conditioned by the ethos, culture and character of a nation. The constitutional goals, the directive principles of the state policy, the socio-economic problems and the growth of knowledge, the emerging expectations and the changes operating in education, etc. call for an appropriate response from a futuristic education system and provide the perspective within which teacher education programmes need to be viewed.

When India attained freedom, the then existing educational system was accepted as such because it was thought that an abrupt departure from the same would be disturbing and destabilising. Thus a predisposition to retain the system acquired preponderance and all that was envisaged by way of changes was its rearrangement. Consequently, education including teacher education largely remained isolated from the needs and aspirations of the people. During the last five decades certain efforts have been made to indigenize the system. The gaps, however, are still wide and visible. The imperatives for building the bridges may be as follows:

- to build a national system of teacher education based on India's cultural ethos, its unity and diversity synchronising with change and continuity.
- to facilitate the realization of the constitutional goals and emergence of the new social order.

- to prepare professionally competent teachers to perform their roles effectively as per needs of the society.
- to upgrade the standard of teacher education, enhance the professional and social status of teachers and develop amongst them a sense of commitment.

These are but a few of the major concerns which call for an immediate action. A comprehensive, dynamic and responsive system of teacher education needs to be continually evolved keeping the overall scenario in view.

Scenario of Teacher Education

The need for improved levels of educational participation for overall progress is well recognised. The key role of educational institutions in realising it is reflected in a variety of initiatives taken to transform the nature and function of education — both formal as well as non-formal. Universal accessibility to quality education is considered essential for development. This has necessitated improvement in the system of teacher education so as to prepare quality teachers.

Various Commissions and Committees appointed by the Central and the State Governments in recent decades have invariably emphasised the need for quality teacher education suited to the needs of the educational system. The Secondary Education Commission (1953) observed that a major factor responsible for the educational reconstruction at the secondary stage is teachers' professional training. The Education Commission (1964-66) stressed that 'in a world based on science and technology it is education that determines the level of prosperity, welfare and security of the people' and that 'a sound programme of professional education of teachers is essential for the qualitative improvement of education.'

India has a large system of education. There are nearly 5.98 lakh Primary Schools, 1.76 lakh Elementary Schools and 98 thousand High / Higher Secondary Schools in the country, about 1300 teacher education institutions for elementary teachers and nearly 700 colleges of education / university departments preparing teachers for secondary and higher secondary schools. Out of about 4.52 million teachers in the country nearly 3 million are teaching at the primary/ elementary level*. A sizeable number of them are untrained or under-trained. In certain regions, like the North-East, there are even under- qualified teachers. As far as in-service education is concerned the situation is not very encouraging. It is estimated that on an average 40% of the teachers are provided in-service teacher education once over a period of five years. Regarding non-formal education, though a number of models are in vogue in various states in the country, much more needs to be done to prepare teachers and other functionaries for the system.

The Programme of Action (POA 1992) has emphasised teacher education as a continuous process, its pre-service and in-service components being inseparable. The POA, among others, has pointed out the following in respect of teacher education :

a) Professional commitment and overall competencies of teachers leave much to be desired ;
b) The quality of pre-service education has not only not improved with recent developments in pedagogical science, but has actually shown signs of deterioration;
c) Teacher education programmes consist mainly of pre-service teacher training, with practically no systematic programmes of inservice training, facilities for which are lacking.
d) There has been an increase in sub-standard institutions of teacher education and there are numerous reports of gross malpractices; and
e) The support system provided by the State Councils of Educational Research and Training (SCERTs) and the University Departments of Education has been insufficient and there is no support system below the state level.

In pursuance of the NPE 1986 a major step was taken by the Central Government to enhance the professional capacity of a large number of teacher education institutions. Nearly 430 District Institutes of Education and Training (DIETs) have already been established by 1997-98. The DIETs are charged with the responsibility of organising pre-service and in-service programmes in addition to being the nodal resource centres for elementary education at district level. Likewise, Colleges of Teacher Education (CTEs) and Institutions of Advanced Study in Education (IASEs) have been given the responsibility of introducing innovations in teacher education programmes at the secondary and higher secondary stages and in vocational education.

The National Council for Teacher Education (NCTE) as a non-statutory body (1973-1993) took several steps as regards quality improvement in teacher education. Its major contribution was to prepare Teacher Education Curriculum Framework in 1978. Consequently, teacher education curricula witnessed changes in teacher preparation programmes in various universities and boards in the country. A similar effort was made in 1988. During the last decade, new thrusts have been posed due to rapid changes in the educational, political, social and economic contexts at the national and international levels. Curriculum reconstruction has also become imperative in the light of some perceptible gaps in teacher education. Teacher education by and large, is conventional in its nature and purpose.

The integration of theory and practice and consequent curricular response to the requirements of the school system still remains inadequate. Teachers are prepared in competencies and skills which do not necessarily equip them for becoming professionally effective. Their familiarity with latest educational developments remains insufficient. Organised and stipulatory learning experiences whenever available, rarely contribute to enhancing teachers' capacities for self-directed life long learning. The system still prepares teachers who do not necessarily become professionally competent and committed at the completion of initial teacher preparation programmes. A large number of teacher training institutions do not practice what they preach. Several of the skills acquired and methodologies learnt are seldom practiced in actual school system. This highlights the need to bring realism and dynamism in the curriculum.

Constitutional Goals

The Constitution of India solemnly resolves "to constitute India into a sovereign, socialist, secular and democratic republic and secure to all its citizens: justice-social, economic and political; liberty of thought, expression, faith, belief and worship; equality of status and of opportunity; and to promote among them all fraternity assuring the dignity of the individual and the integrity of the nation." These are the main goals which the nation expects to be realised through education. Teacher preparation must not lose sight of this basic thrust so as to empower teachers to inculcate the same among the students.

In order to reinforce faith in democratic socialism, secularism, justice, liberty, freedom etc. the role of education needs to be understood in its true perspective. Democracy is a process of building consensus among the citizens on matters of common concern. It expects high morality from them, protects the interest and preserves their uniqueness, dignity and individuality. Quality of democracy depends on its citizens willing to discharge their responsibilities towards the self, the family, the community, the nation and humanity at large. Democracy is a way of life and its values need to be imbibed through education and practised in the day-to-day life. Democratic socialism attempts to achieve a synthesis between individual freedom and social compulsion and combines liberty with responsibility and authority with accountability. The Indian situation demands citizens capable of making conscious and purposive efforts directed towards social cohesion and living together harmoniously.

Indian Society is plural and heterogeneous with an underlying current of unity. The imposition of a homogeneous and uniform curriculum of teacher education may prove counter productive under this situation. Except for identifying certain basics and essentials, regional autonomy must be exercised for developing region/culture specific curriculum of teacher education. Indian reality demands that plurality should be used for strengthening national solidarity and social cohesion.

The Indian state is secular. The Indian society, however, is religious. To resolve this dichotomy between the state and polity, the principle of equal respect for all the religions* has been accepted. This is the essence of Indian secularism. The teachers themselves have to internalise the imperatives of secularism in national context and interpret the same effectively to the learners. That alone would develop the right attitudes among all citizens irrespective of their own backgrounds. In India religion is also the source of value and morality. The teachers have to develop values and morality in a different context. Teacher education has to respond to this reality.

Justice, liberty, equality of status and of opportunity and promoting fraternity constitute another set of inter-related goals. Justice protects the rights of the weak and ensures impartiality. To ensure justice and fulfil the constitutional commitments in this regard, certain positive and legal provisions have been made by the state. Special measures such as reservation in educational institutions, financial support, scholarships, hostel facilities, etc. have been extended to the under-privileged groups like Scheduled Castes, Scheduled Tribes, Other Backward Classes etc. It implies change in attitudes and values through education, in which the role of teachers needs to be stressed. Liberty of thought, expression, faith, belief and worship is another constitutional goal which education is expected to help realise. Indian Constitution ensures equality of status and opportunity to all its citizens. The objective is to minimise social and economic disparities, inequality of power and life chances by positive discrimination in favour of the weak. The education of teachers should equip them with the competencies needed to deal with discrimination, disparities and inequalities. Fraternity stands for acceptance of universal brotherhood, respect for human personality and feeling of oneness irrespective of linguistic, racial, cultural and religious diversities.

Teacher Education and Problems of the Nation

It is universally acknowledged that education is an effective means for social reconstruction and to a great extent it offers solutions to the problems a society is faced with. These problems may be economic, social, cultural, political, moral, ecological and educational. Since the teachers play a major role in education of children, their own education becomes a matter of vital concern. Teacher education must, therefore, create necessary awareness among teachers about their new roles and responsibilities.

Education of teachers needs to strengthen and stress upon the main attributes of a profession, such as, the systematic theory, rigourous training over a specified duration, authority, community sanction, ethical code and culture, generating knowledge through research and specialisation. It is acknowledged that formal professional training on continuous basis is necessary for becoming a good teacher as it caters to the development of one's personality and sharpening of communication skills and commitment to a code of conduct.

Economic Problems: Poverty, unemployment, and low rate of growth and productivity are some of the major economic problems of the country which have led to the compulsions of the backward economy. These problems seek immediate solution and demand a realistic co-ordination between economic planning and manpower planning. Education can help find solutions if it is properly coordinated with manpower needs. Introduction of work education and vocationalisation of education in secondary schools will have to be given a modern and meaningful direction. The attitude towards the work culture needs a transformation. The Indian society needs education with special emphasis on science and technology, vocational inputs and realistic work experiences. Teacher education curriculum, therefore, has to promote such attitudes as are necessary for the emergence of a new economic order. Alongwith the vocational competencies and skills a new work culture will have to be created which necessarily involves the inculcation of dignity of work, the spirit of self-reliance and scientific temper among students. The courses of teacher education need to be enriched to enable teachers to understand the attributes of modernity and development.

Social Problems: Casteism, communalism and regionalism are some of the problems in the body politic of the society which misguide the youth. Increasing delinquency, violence, terrorism and fissiparous tendencies and use of inappropriate means to get one's ends served are threats to the national integration and social cohesion. Democracy, violence and terrorism cannot coexist. Education has to develop a peace loving personality and the programme of teacher education has to contribute in this regard.

The explosion of population with all its allied disturbing trends is not only neutralising the economic gains but also creating many problems for the country. Indian society still suffers from evils like child labour, child marriage, untouchability, discriminatory treatment to women, violation of human rights, etc. and most of the people are unaware of their legal rights.

Modern model of development which puts man against nature by making it an object of exploitation has disturbed the harmony and equilibrium between the two. Its consequences are visible in serious environmental degradation, pollution and ecological imbalances.

Strengthening national and social cohesion in a diverse and plural society, accelerating the process of economic growth, improving the life of the downtrodden and the people living below the poverty line, removing the widely prevalent ignorance, superstition and prejudices from the masses, inculcating scientific temper and developing a critical awareness about the social realities of Indian life are some of the issues which call for immediate attention. Teachers and the teacher educators have a special role to play in such efforts.

Problems of Cultural Reconstruction: Education is the process of transmission of dynamic and responsive components of cultural heritage and its continuous enrichment. There is a need to reinterpret the Indian culture in its distinct identity and composite strength. Its capacity to absorb the sublime from the other cultures needs to be highlighted. The teachers will have to play their role in cultural transmission and reconstruction.

Crises of Values and Morality: There has been a persistent erosion of values in the society. In the present day context certain values need to be redefined and reinstalled. There are situations when the values imparted and inculcated in schools are not generally practised in society. Value education demands a planned and purposive approach. It is through education and as of necessity through teacher education programmes that the task of inculcating values can be substantially accomplished. Whereas values are emotive, the other related significant dimension is that of moral education which is essentially conative in character. Morals are situation-specific and demand immediate decision and action and yet there are morals which are considered to be eternal and universal. Through committed teachers, the art of ensuring moral development in a secular, multi-religious and multi-ethnic society needs to be cultivated.

Problems Within Education System

The nation has yet to fulfil the constitutional commitment to provide free and compulsory education to all children till they attain 14 years of age. India is also a party to the global commitment for achieving the goal of Education for All by the year 2000. The education system however, has to respond to several major issues and problems which have hindered the progress in this regard. Maintenance of educational standards against the pressure of increasing enrolment, relevance and quality of school education, efficacy of school functioning under the decentralized role of political power through the enactment of Panchayati Raj Act are some of the pertinent issues. In addition, specific requirements and need of social and economical groups of the society and of the minority communities, vocationalization of education, scientific and technological literacy, alienation of youth, rush for urbanisation, perceived urban orientation of educational system and its inflexibility to respond to rural, tribal and regional requirements are some of the dominant issues. These would determine the nature and shape of teacher education programmes and the efficacy and functioning of teachers in their new and emerging multifaceted roles.

Isolation of Teacher Education: Teacher education institutions which were considered 'islands of isolation' have gradually developed linkages with schools, peer institutions, universities and other institutions of higher learning as also the community. However, much remains to be done in this direction. The curriculum of the school, its actual transactional modalities, examination system, management processes and its ethos need to be the main thrust areas of teacher education programmes. To achieve these ends, teacher educators need to be made conversant with various aspects of school experiences. It is observed in day-to-day functioning that teacher educators often tend to lose contact with content areas relevant to their own disciplines resulting into gaps in communication and latest information. It is, therefore, a felt need in the present-day context that teacher education institutions keep in continuous touch with institutions of higher learning and peer institutions for effective transmission of knowledge and its upgradation.

The breaking of isolation from the community is essential for enabling teachers and teacher educators to reconstruct pedagogical and educational principles and practices in the light of experiences gained from mutually beneficial community interactions. Teacher as a professional and intellectual cannot remain indifferent to the events that are taking place in society. The academic and social issues are inter-related and inter-dependent. In contemporary context, the role of the teacher is no longer confined to teaching alone. The teachers are expected to play an active role in the developmental activities responding to progress of the community.

Expanding Scope of Teacher Education: Education of teachers is not an end in itself. Its target is the school. Any change in the nature, purpose, quality and character of the school demands a concomitant change in teacher education, specially in its curriculum. The implementation of the 10 + 2 scheme at the school level has transformed the complexion of education to a considerable extent from the pre-primary to the + 2 stage. There has been an increase not only in the quantum of knowledge, but also in its nature and purpose. In addition, new transactional techniques and strategies have also been evolved. Certain new subjects have replaced the old ones whereas some others have changed their context, content, orientation, theme and philosophy. These changes at the school level, out of necessity, demand a new pedagogy and evaluation techniques. But the changes at the level of teacher education have not adequately responded to the emerging realities at the school level. All that the teachers are expected to do in their work places need to be reflected in the teacher education activities and programmes.

The teaching community has to face the challenges thrown by science and technology. There has been an explosion not only of scientific and technological knowledge but also in the means and techniques of acquiring knowledge. The scientific researches and developments related to theories of heredity, learning, mental health, neurology, attention, motivation etc. can no longer be treated alien to teacher education programmes.

Evolving a Culture-Specific Pedagogy: Every region and state has its typical cultural identity, and there is a need to utilise the same as a basis for developing meaningful, relevant pedagogies. Since there is no one universal way in which the children learn, there is a strong need for looking into the cultural context in which a child is placed. A child in a tribal society may process information in an altogether different manner as compared to the one from the urban area and high socio-economic stratum. Pedagogy, therefore, should be culture-specific. Cultural practices such as story-telling, dramatics, puppetry, folk-play, community living, etc. should become a strong basis of pedagogy instead of using one uniform, mechanistic way of student learning. Cultural specificity should get embedded in the pedagogical practices which should be evolved for tribal, rural, urban communities and other ethnic groups.

Inseparability of Pre-service and In-service Education

A learning society visualises education as a continuing activity. This is equally applicable to teacher education. The policy stipulation on inseparability of the pre-service and in-service education of teachers and emphasis on continuing education need to be given pragmatic shape at the implementation stage. The curriculum of pre-service and in-service teacher education has to be redesigned to maintain continuity between the two. Teachers who are being educated today will have to devote major part of their life to education during the twentyfirst century. If the present rate of explosion of knowledge continues, in a few years the teachers will find themselves in a world where their present knowledge and teaching skills to an extent would become obsolete. They will have to face the challenge of electronic media and information technology.

Research and Innovation

One of the major inputs towards enhancing the quality of teaching and learning in schools as well as the teacher education institutions would be the extent to which research outputs and the outcomes of innovations are utilized by the system. Researches on teacher education have been and are being conducted in universities, national level institutions and other establishments but their utility for the teacher educator or the classroom teacher remains rather low. Majority of the researches are undertaken to obtain a degree and hence the focus on its possible utility and relevance gets misplaced. The situation is compounded by non-availability of appropriate dissemination mechanisms, like journals, publication of findings in different forms and opportunities to the target group to get an access to these. Institutional capabilities and resources need to be augmented, enabling them to undertake relevant researches.

There is a definite requirement of bringing in research methods and methodologies in appropriate form in teacher education at preservice and inservice programmes. To an extent, it finds a place in master level courses in education though in some universities the same is not insisted upon. The structure and design of future courses and programmes need to take this aspect into account. Preparation of teacher educators can no longer be completed without adequate grounding in various aspects of research. Researches must respond to policy issues, curriculum issues, evaluative procedures and practices, training strategies, classroom practices etc.

The areas of teacher preparation for children with special needs, gifted children and children from groups with specific cultural, social and economic needs can no longer be ignored. Surveys and studies also need to be encouraged. These may be exploratory or diagnostic in nature. The new initiatives and innovations need to be encouraged and studied. Wherever considered appropriate, these could be brought into the system of teacher education for wider and gainful use.

The concept of field interaction and laboratory area approach in the context of establishment of DIETs is indeed timely. Researches, innovations and surveys must become an integral part of the training programmes of teacher education institutions irrespective of the stages. The trainees need to be familiarised with innovations in general and innovative practices in teacher education in particular.

Other Critical Concerns

The factors and forces influencing teacher education are many, some of which have been discussed in the preceding sections, certain others are being mentioned hereunder:

- gradual change-over from conventional programmes of teacher education to integrated courses to ensure greater professionalism.
- increased duration of teacher education programmes to accommodate for proper assimilation of emerging professional inputs.
- stage-specific theoretical and practical components, transactional strategies and evaluation
- plans and programmes of teacher education to respond to the expectated role performance of teacher.
- flexible and pragmatic approach to plans and programmes of teacher education.
- proper planning and orientation of education of teacher educators.

Spectrum of Institutional Functions

In the light of context and concerns teacher education institutions will acquire a wider spectrum of functions and greater responsibilities.

Resolution of specific functions from the spectrum will have to be made depending upon the institutional capabilities. It is visualised that the following institutional functions will have to be undertaken by different institutions according to availability of resources :-

- develop capability to provide for both pre-service and in-service education.
- provide training and orientation programmes to the functionaries of alternative educational strategies aimed at achieving universal elementary education and eradication of illiteracy.
- organise programmes for heads of schools and school complexes and supervisory staff.
- offer courses for community leaders, voluntary agencies and parents.
- provide academic support to schools and other agencies engaged in education of children and adults.
- undertake research and experiments with innovative educational ideas.
- act as a resource centre for education for a specific area.
- offer counselling and guidance services.
- organise need-based programmes for educational administrators, planners, curriculum designers, evaluators etc.
- impart training for other areas of education, like physical education and special education.
- act as a link between the school and the university system.

Commitment and Performance in Teacher Education

A major concern in school education is the quality and relevance of education being imparted to young learners. Every learner is supposed to acquire mastery level learning in identified competency areas. NCTE has analysed the existing curriculum of teacher education from the point of view of competency areas. It has emerged that to enhance the quality of school education equal emphasis needs to be given to competencies, commitment and willingness to perform. A curriculum framework based upon competencies, commitments and performance has been developed. Competency areas namely, contextual competencies, conceptual, content, transactional, related to other educational activities, developing teaching learning material, evaluation, management, working with parents and working with community and other agencies, have been identified as critical to teacher preparation at elementary stage.

Acquisition of competencies alone will not be sufficient until and unless the teacher is fully committed. Teacher commitment areas identified include commitment to the learner, commitment to the society, commitment to the profession, commitment to attaining excellence for professional actions and commitment to basic values.

Alongwith competency and commitment areas, performance areas have also been identified. These include classroom performance, school level performance, performance in the out-of school educational activities, parents related performance and community related performance. Teacher education institutions could identify details in each of the three major categories. For each competency, commitment and performance area, the existing curriculum needs to be analyzed. Whenever certain unit of curriculum is taken up for transaction, its relationship to commitment and performance has to be examined. Such an approach would provide an opportunity to the training institutions to prepare teachers who are not only competent but also committed and both these aspects are reflected in their performance leading to higher learning attainments by all children.

Breaking the Barriers

The critical analyses of the context and concerns presented in the preceding sections help in developing a vision for teacher education in future. In the Indian situation basic character of the framework must provide for adequate and inbuilt flexibility for incorporating the regional and local specificities. Total trust in the capabilities of institutions and organisations to develop an indigenous, comparable and area-specific curriculum has to be the guiding principle.

Teacher education has to be conceived as an integral part of educational and social system and must primarily respond to the requirements of the school system. It can no longer remain conventional and static but should transform itself to a progressive dynamic and responsive system. National values and goals need to be meaningfully reflected and their inculcation attempted with care and caution. The theoretical and practical components need to be balanced appropriately. The theory and practice of education has to be enriched with the latest research findings not only in the field of education but also in the allied disciplines and areas. While it is essential to develop identified competencies to prepare effective teachers it is equally necessary to develop commitment and build capacity to perform as integral part of teacher preparation. The teachers have to keep abreast of the latest developments not only in their field of specialisation but also in areas of educational developments and social and cultural issues through continuous inservice orientation. Emphasis on continuing life-long learning has to become an essential concern of teacher education. A nation concerned with erosion of values needs teachers who are professionally committed and prepared to present a value-based model of interaction with their learners. The basic tenets identified in the national basic education scheme - Head, Heart and Hand need now to be linked to another 'H' - highways. Information highways, websites and internet are going to become terms of common usage in teacher education. For sound mind we need strong hand and a vibrant heart. Areas like physical education and vocational education will continue to gain greater emphasis in years to come and will serve as the basis for developing competencies and skills in addition to commitments and values.

A comprehensive theoretical base is essential for a teacher to assume professional role and develop capacity to conceptualise inputs from other disciplines as well and evolve strategies to utilise them. A true professional is capable of perceiving complexities and uncertainties in the society, has a thorough grasp of the subject, possesses skills to make critical diagnosis, takes decisions and has courage and conviction to implement such decisions.

4

Pre-service Teacher Education

Teacher education by its very nature is interdisciplinary. The major areas of inter-disciplinarity implicit in teacher education programmes include philosophy, psychology, sociology, anthropology, economics, history and culture. Recent researches in medical and life sciences are opening new avenues of knowledge which are relevant to education. Besides, teacher education has an essential and inalienable component of practical work including student teaching, internship, field work, working with the community, work education, etc. The country needs teachers with different orientation and specialisations to manage educational programmes. In addition, the teachers are also needed for physical education, music, art, painting, dance, work education and vocational subjects and for the non-formal stream, distance education, adult education, and open learning system. The scope of teacher education curriculum, therefore, gets enlarged.

The curriculum for teacher preparation, in future has to emcompass the broader canvas which is consistently emerging before the teachers and shall continue to change at a much faster pace in times ahead. Teachers shall have to take a global view of the new trends, strategies and practices, and focus on indigenous heritage and thoughts which could fit in the local and national situations. Transplantation of alien educational ideas and practices has not been found rewarding in developing countries. Consequently, the emerging structures and designs of the curriculum shall lay greater emphasis on the ideas, practices and experiences that have emerged in India through the contributions of thinkers like Mahatma Gandhi, Vivekanand, Rabindra Nath Tagore, Zakir Hussain, Sri Aurobindo, Giju Bhai and many others.

The teacher education programmes shall focus on competencies and commitment in much greater magnitude in future. Such a transformation in teacher preparation strategies would emerge only after due familiarity and adequate appreciation of indigenous thoughts developed over decades in India. Gradually an indigenous approach and strategy would emanate and replace the alien practices that have remained in vogue in teacher education over the decades.

Teacher Profile

The profile of a teacher which emanates from the contexts and concerns necessarily implies additional roles besides the conventional ones. The following capabilities and competencies need to be highlighted:

- inculcating the intrinsic and extrinsic values of professional competency, professional commitment and professional ethics
- creating and reconstructing knowledge
- selecting, organising and using learning resources
- effectively transacting curriculum, selecting and organising educational activities and programmes for learners with special needs
- using media and appropriate instructional technologies
- communicating effectively and responding to the challenges of continuity and change
- counselling students for personality development, adjustment and learning attainment
- conducting research, especially action research and initiating innovative practices
- organising student-activities
- inculcating a sense of value judgement, value commitment and value transmission
- understanding the import of inter-relationship between culture and education and 'culture and personality'
- fostering interest in life-long learning
- understanding the aspirations and expectations of the community and establishing mutually supportive linkages between school and community
- acting as a change agent for modernisation and development

The educational programmes for prospective teachers, therefore, need to be so designed as to develop in them the requisite potential and capabilities.

General Objectives

The general objectives of teacher education derived from the contexts, concerns and issues of education, teacher education and the perceived profile of the teacher, could include the following:

- to promote capabilities for inculcating national values and goals as enshrined in the Constitution of India.
- to enable teachers to act as agents of modernisation and social change.
- to sensitize teachers towards the promotion of social cohesion, international understanding and protection of human rights and rights of the child.
- to transform student-teachers into competent and committed professionals willing to perform the identified tasks.
- to develop competencies and skills needed for becoming an effective teacher.
- to sensitize teachers and teacher educators about emerging issues, such as environment, ecology, population, gender equality, legal literacy, etc..
- to empower teachers to cultivate rational thinking and scientific temper among students.
- to develop critical awareness about the social realities.
- to develop managerial and organisational skills.

Characteristics of Curriculum Framework

An overview of the context and concerns as discussed earlier, teacher's profile and general and specific objectives would define the boundaries of a curriculum framework. The perceived characteristics of the envisaged curriculum framework would include the following:

- reflects the Indian heritage, acts as an instrument in the realisation of national goals and fulfills aspirations of people.
- responds to the latest developments in the field of education.
- establishes integration of theory and practice of education.
- provides multiple educational experiences to teachers.
- enables teachers to experiment with new ideas.
- ensures inseparability of pre-service and in-service education of teachers.
- sets achievable goals for various stages of teacher education.
- provides for use of communication technology.

Teacher Education for Early Childhood Stage

The need for early childhood education has long been emphasised on the argument that it would lead to providing healthy and wholesome learning environment. It is also considered as a preparatory stage for the realisation of Universalisation of Elementary Education. In order to provide healthy and enriched childhood to young learners, a new type of teacher specifically sensitized about the perspectives of child development will be required.

The enrichment programmes for early childhood education have been launched under Integrated Child Development Scheme through Anganwadis, Day Care Centres, Balwadies, Pre-primary Schools run by the State Governments, Municipal Corporations, Voluntary Agencies and Private Agencies. All such efforts, though not adequately provided for, are continuing with diverse approaches without making a synergic impact. Concerted efforts are needed for organising early childhood education in a planned manner. It presupposes pooling of resources by the community as well as the concerned agencies.

In order that early childhood education becomes a reality, in terms of its organisation and accessibility, one of the significant inputs in making a success story of it is that of a professionally trained and committed teacher. The professional preparation of teachers for this stage, hitherto unplanned and uncared for, calls for thoughtful planning of training sequences relevant to the developmental needs of early childhood interwoven with commonalities and specificities.

Specific Objectives : The objectives of teacher education specific to early childhood include the following:

- to prepare teachers for facilitating physical, mental, moral, social, aesthetic and linguistic development of children
- to acquaint them with the knowledge of child psychology
- to cultivate social sensitivity, affection for children and respect for their uniqueness
- to acquaint them with techniques of caring for children and enable them to identify their needs
- to provide experiences and organise activities that promote children's self-concept, creativity and inventiveness
- to enable them to select, prepare and use different kinds of resource materials
- to develop a sense of involvement with and appreciation of local resources (human and material) and their utilisation

- to develop an acquaintance with basics of Scientific and Technological Literacy
- to develop a repertoire of children's games, songs and literature
- to empower student-teachers towards creating learning readiness among young learners

Curriculum Framework : The framework given here is suggestive and not a prescriptive one. It has considerable space for flexibility, innovation and use of locally available community resources. The following curriculum framework is suggested for formulating a Plan of Action for developing programmes and activities, devising strategies of negotiating the curricular inputs and methods of obtaining feed-back. These are pre-requisites for improving the interaction processes directed towards the realisation of optimum enrichment of experiences at the early childhood stage.

Inclusion of the following components of theory and practice are suggested:

Theory

- Emerging Indian Society
- Early Childhood Education: Scope, Nature, Status, Problems and Issues.
- Psychology of the Child and Learning during early years (implementing developmentally appropriate curriculum).
- Planning, management and administration of ECCE programmes
- Methods and Materials for facilitating the growth and development of pre-school child through activities for:
- Physical development
- Mental development
- Emotional development
- Aesthetic development
- Language development
- Social development
- Moral development
- Neuro-muscular co-ordination
- Self-expression
- Health and Hygiene
- Habit formation

- Observation
- Sensory-Motor Training

Practical Work

- Drawing and Painting
- Music
- Creative activities
- Story telling
- Dance and Drama
- Games and Physical Activity
- Plays
- Field trips
- Block making and related games
- Activities for children with special needs

Practicum: Teaching, placement and internship

Practical experiences: Observation, planning and implementing programmes related to activities for children

Rationale: The current areas suggested in this framework have been specially designed for understanding early childhood care and education in its realistic perspective. No formal teaching is visualised at early childhood stage. It is not a stage for introducing three R's. In the preparation of teachers for this stage, therefore, the main thrust will be on sensitizing prospective teachers about change and its implications – cultural, social, economic, etc. as also with the change in the learner through motivation and learning. Future need will be to empower the teacher to observe change, interpret it and adopt, adapt, modify, consolidate, accelarate or reject the same. It is not intended here to suggest details of progrmmes and theoretical content. It is, however, expected that the course on Emerging Indian Society' will enable the intending teachers to know about the rights of child, human rights, legal literacy, community dynamics, knowledge of national and local festivals, emerging trends in community life and social living, prominent personalities in various walks of life, familiarity with factors and forces affecting environmental and population equilibirium, knowledge and appreciation of places of historical and cultural significance and landmarks and trends of development.

Another theoretical input which is intended to be given to the prospective teachers is regarding knowledge of nature and scope, status, problems and issues concerning early childhood education in India. These need to be understood in terms of Indian reality and perspective, foundations of child behaviour etc. In addition, it may include, among others, progress of early childhood education, its historical development, problems, need for looking at it from the point of view of diversity, flexibility, local relevance and specificities, and the agencies involved in the process of promoting early childhood education.

Basic to designing programmes and activities for children at this stage is a thorough understanding of various aspects of growth and development of the child which the prospective teachers will be required to internalise. Since, it is being recommended for intending teachers of pre-schoolers, it will be necessary to know about the fundamentals of early childhood care and education. Most of the training programmes of teachers for this stage will have major concentration on organisation and activities as mentioned above. In addition, the teachers will be required to have a practical training at early childhood education centres and the like. At this stage, greater emphasis will be given on propagation of early childhood care.

Transacting Curriculum

Theory

India is a conglomeration of diversities with a variety of manifestations and yet bound by a thread of commonality. Teacher is expected to recognise commonalities and specificities in order to shape the personality of children for living together in a perpetually changing complex society. The suggested theoretical components included in the framework are essentially, meant for broadening the intellectual horizons of intending teachers who will become conversant with the culture and traditions of the country with due appreciation of the diversities. The seeds of democratic living are sown from the beginning of childhood and education needs to be regarded as a vehicle for maintaining equilibirium in the growth of individuals from childhood to adulthood.

It would be worth experimenting with modular approach of teaching combined with interventions of realistic nature by way of field trips, visit to museums, zoo, educational excursions, visit to mountains, forests, intermediary interventions with real life situations and through audio-video devices, wherever possible. Teaching in teacher training institutions be directed towards empowering prospective teachers to enable to use their experiences in actual work places for enhancing growth and development of young children.

There is to be a planned amalgam of theory and practice in a way that these two constitute a continuum of experiences. The teaching of theoretical components, in addition to what has been elaborated above, will combine various methods and approaches like lecturing, tutorials, seminars, term-papers, discussion groups, gaming, role planning, etc.

Pedagogy

The teachers at this stage are being initiated into and introduced to the art of teaching. Teaching to them is romance with innovativeness and inventiveness. It is love for children. It is caring for children. It is seeking for optimum enrichment of experiences of children. It is providing happiness to children. It is making their stay joyful in schools. The early childhood education includes transacting developmentally appropriate curriculum which includes within its fold concept development, convergent and divergent thinking, creative activities, language acquisition, etc. It is an arduous task of equipping prospective teachers with competencies and skills needed for making the learning experiences of a child joyful and memorable. It must be admitted that the training of pre-school teachers is complex and full of challenges.

The pedagogical aspects of training will be planned around activities and programmes for children, attending to their needs, identifying interests of learners by gender and their background, identifying children with special needs and devising strategies for their optimum growth and development, organising games, recreational activities, plays, etc.

Practicum

Theory and practicum have to be linked and integrated in the training process. Much of what goes by way of practicals is intrinsically related with pedagogy and much of the essence of pedagogy lies in the practical work. The practical work may include comprehensive case studies of children including children with special needs, gifted children, children coming from different socio-economic and cultural backgrounds, etc. Development and use of schedules, assessment checklists and other evaluation tools and techniques will form an important aspect of practicum. The maximum utilisation of environmental and community resources can be done only when the teacher is thoroughly conversant with environmental resources. Community survey, therefore, is one of the several activities of practical work which requires systematic exploration.

The practical work of the prospective teachers will centre around evolving and devising programmes and activities for physical, psychomotor, cognitive, emotional and other aspects of development. Health and hygiene, habit formation, are certain other areas which require practical work. In addition, art, drawing and painting, using clay/plasticin, music, dance, recreation, story telling, games, and physical activity are a variety of examples of other practical experiences which a student teacher will be required to undertake for creative expression of children.

Evaluation

Evaluation for the theoretical component may include assessment of sessional work, term papers, participation in seminars, discussion groups, etc. besides semester examinations, which can be oral, written, practical and objective type. The written tests have to be reliable, valid and representative of the totality of experiences. Different tools and techniques of evaluation can be used for assessing the pupils' growth. Visits to and partcipation in activities of Anganwadis, Balwadis, Day Care Centres will make a part of training towards understanding the dynamics of working with children and educating them. The evaluation of this component is will be in the form of a cumulative record of the performance of the intending teachers. External evaluation of practical activities will defeat the purpose as the practical work is, by and large, activity-based. It is essentially sessional work, day-to-day internal assessment, feed back and monitoring. A record of some of the activities is all that may be suggested for purposes of evaluation in this regard.

Elementary Teacher Education Curriculum Framework

The constitutional provision of providing free and compulsory education to all children upto 14 years of age includes both the lower primary and upper primary classes, that is from class I to class VIII. There seems to be a compelling need for having multiple models for preparing teachers - for primary and upper primary classes. Incidentally, in a number of Elementary Teacher Education Institutions (ETEIs) in the country, the nomenclature of the training programme from pre-service training of primary school teachers has been changed to pre-service training of elementary school teachers. But in actuality, the transformation in programmes has yet to take place effectively.

There are three distinct possibilities of designing courses in teacher education for elementary stage:

- Teacher education programme exclusively for primary school stage (Classes I to V).
- Teacher education programme for elementary school stage (Classes I to VIII).
- Teacher education programme exclusively for upper primary school stage (Classes VI to VIII).

In view of the requirements of Universal Primary Education and Universal Elementary Education, only the first two alternatives are being recommended. However, the third suggested above, could be attempted by offering credit oriented modular courses after successful completion of primary teacher education programmes. It is significant to note that we have nearly 5.98 lakh primary schools which are mostly in rural areas as compared to upper primary schools numbering about 1.76 lakhs only*.

Teacher Education for Primary Stage

Specific Objectives: The formulation of curriculum framework for this stage (classes I to V) has been guided by general and specific objectives of teacher education and perceived characteristics of curriculum development. The specific objectives of primary teacher education may include the following:

- to develop understanding of the psychological and sociological foundations relevant to the primary stage.
- to enable teachers to manage appropriate resources for organising learning experiences of children.
- to acquaint them with methods and techniques of caring for children with special needs.
- to enable them to acquire necessary skills so as to develop curiosity, imagination and creativity.
- to develop in them the capacity to understand and analyse the social and emotional problems.
- to develop communication skills
- to enable them to establish mutually supportive linkages with the community focussing on the objective of UPE/UEE.
- to enable them to understand implications of research for teaching-learning and undertake action research and use innovative practices.
- to enable them to organise games, sports, physical activities and other co-curriculur activities.

Keeping in view the teacher profile particularly the facilitative and resource management aspects, general and specific objectives of teacher education, the following framework which is flexible with ample scope for adaptation and for making it relevant to local enviornment is being suggested :

Curriculum Framework

Theory

- Emerging Indian Society
- Primary Education in India : status, problems and issues
- Psychology of Teaching and Learning with special reference to children of age group 6-11 years
- Assessment, Evaluation and remedial teaching
- Health and Physical Education
- School Management
- Education of Children with Special Needs
- Guidance and Counselling
- Content Areas for Primary Schools
- Action Research

Practice Teaching

- Pedagogical Analysis of Primary School Subjects
- Practice Teaching in Schools
- Observation of Model Lessons

Practical Work

- School Experience inclusive of Internship
- Work Education
- School-Community Interaction
- Action Research Studies (planning and execution)
- Organisation of relevant Educational Activities

Rationale: The teacher needs to be empowered through training inputs to gain greater insights into the complexities of the society and the historical perspective of the developmental process. The paper on Emerging Indian Society is being introduced at this stage with a purpose of making the teacher aware of the contextual realities in which he or she has to work. The paper would take into account rights of children, human rights education, values and their broad features, perspectives of educational, social, economic and political development in the country, significant landmarks in the process of development in various fields including science and technology, etc. Theoretical component is essential for understanding the learner, community and the society, the internal and external forces impinging upon the school and the internal and external variables operating upon the learner. The inclusion of Courses on Psychology of Teaching and Learning, Health and Physical Education, Education of Children with Special Needs has been made for accommodating this point of view in the Framework.

In the proposed training programmes, the prospective teachers would be imparted training in a manner that theory and practice are organically integrated. Correlation within the curricular areas of learning and external environment is established. Psychology of Teaching and Learning, School Organisation and Pedagogical Analysis of primary school subjects will provide a sound base for the adoption of integrated approach to teaching and learning and for establishing meaningful and interactive bonds between theory and practice.

The intent of including Action Research and Education of Children with Special Needs is guided by the fact that every student-teacher is expected to know the elements of action research, surveys, community services etc and is capable of educating children with special needs. Additional areas may be included for making the course content relevant and region specific.

Transacting Curriculum

Theory: Transactional strategies invariably need to emphasise interactive, partcipative and activity-oriented approach. The transaction of curriculum will have place to place and intra-and inter-content variations. The theoretical component of the curriculum can be transacted by lecture-discussion, self-study approach, seminars, media supported teaching wherever possible, tutorials and through practical activities. It is expected that the intending teachers during the course of training acquire mastery of competencies and skills that are basic to making an effective, reflective and committed teacher.

Pedagogy: Practice teaching remains to be a weak link of curriculum transaction. This point of view has been substantiated and re-inforced by field surveys conducted by NCTE at different places throughout the country. In this framework, pedagogical analysis of school teaching subjects has been thought of as an essential component of practice teaching. By way of pedagogical analysis a student teacher becomes conversant with the objectives of teaching a unit, the entry behaviour of pupils, classroom management and evaluation strategies. With this background of having looked into the pedagogical aspects of school teaching subjects, the student teacher is likely to become more effective and confident in his/her interventions in the classroom.

As a necessary part of the training of primary school teachers, knowledge of content is given due importance during the course of training. Mastery of subject matter, the insight gained through pedagogical analysis and the foundation courses when thoughtfully integrated and used for classroom instruction will lead to improving the quality of education.

Practicum: Practical work is an essential component for internalising the theoretical concepts. Thus it will have to be planned on each aspect of theoretical inputs. In addition, practical activities centring around different school experiences, work education, school community interaction, action research projects and other educational activities directed towards development of personality of students will also be undertaken by intending teachers. It needs continuous planning, analysing, monitoring and evaluation throughout the duration of the course which will necessitate the involvement of teacher educators more vigorously than what it is presently.

Evaluation: It is expedient to employ the formative evaluation for obtaining continuous feedback, motivating students and guiding their efforts. There is an increasing felt need to replace external examinations by internal continuous and comprehensive examination system. External system of evaluation, until such times it is replaced, may be perceived as a corrective, moderating and balancing factor. It, therefore, needs to be carefully planned and testing tools made valid and reliable.

In different situations evaluation of theoretical component may be based on essay questions, short answer type questions, objective type questions, objective-based questions, oral examinations, participation in discussion groups etc. Evaluation of practice teaching can be done internally, externally or through judicious combination of both. Gradual transition to continuous and comprehensive internal evaluation of practice teaching and assigning grades instead of marks would be a professionally sound step. Evaluation of practical work would also be done internally.

Teacher Education for Elementary Stage

Justification: The justification for suggesting a separate model of teacher education curriculum for the elementary stage in addition to the one suggested for primary stage is given below;

- There is a constitutional commitment for providing compulsory education upto 14 years of age.
- The gradual transition of the teaching and learning processes from concrete operational stage of development to abstract reasoning process and change over of teaching-learning strategies from one stage to another needs to be ingrained in the minds of teachers for ensuring a continuum of learning experiences from class I to class VIII and matching the learning experiences with the maturity of learners.

  The present status does not reflect the gradual transition implicit in the development of thought processes from one stage to another.

The formulation of the curriculum framework for the elementary stage will also be guided by general and specific objectives of teacher education and characteristics of curriculum development.

Specific Objectives: The specific objectives relevant to the stage may include the following :

- to develop understanding of the psychological and sociological principles relevant to elementary stage of education.
- to enable teachers to select, prepare and use appropriate resources for organising learning experiences.
- to acquaint them with methods and materials of teaching children with special needs
- to develop among them the capacity to solve the social and emotional problems of children.
- to enable them acquire necessary skills so as to develop curiosity, imagination and self-confidence among children.
- to develop communication skills
- to enable them to mobilise and utilise community resources as educational inputs.
- to enable them to organise supplementry educational activities
- to undertake action research projects
- to enable them to establish mutually supportive linkages with the community

- to enable them to organise games, sports, physical activities and other co-curricular activities.

Curriculum Framework

Theory

- Emerging Indian Society
- Elementary Education in India -status, problems and issues
- Psychology of Teaching and Learning with special reference to learners of age group 6-14 years
- Health and Physical Education
- School Management
- Education of Children with Special Needs
- Assessment, Evaluation and Remediation
- Guidance and Counselling
- Action Research

Practice Teaching

- Pedagogical Analysis of elementary school teaching subjects
- Practice Teaching in Schools
- Observation of Model Lessons

Practical Work

- School Experience inclusive of internship
- Work Education
- School-Community interaction
- Organisation of educational activities
- Organisation of games and sports and physical education activities.
- Action Research-proposals and studies.

It is expected that detailed curriculum plan would adequately provide for aesthetics, culture, arts, music, dance, drama, value inculcation, etc.

Rationale: The course on Emerging Indian Society will enable the prospective teachers to understand the demands that society expects education to fulfil. Similarly, proposed course on 'Elementary Education in India - status, problems and issues' will promote the capacity to examine if these expectations can really be met. The course on Psychology of Teaching and Learning will teach them how to formulate their teaching strategies to promote learning among children. Health and Physical Education will enable them to plan exercises for development of sound physiques of formative evaluation. They will be able to deal with children with special needs and adopting problem solving approach, a capacity built by Action Research. The course on counselling and guidance will enable them to help children when they are confronted with problem of any kind.

The pedagogical analysis will provide the prospective teachers an understanding of the complexity involved in the teaching of the subjects at the elementary level. This will enable them to plan their educational strategies. A critical observation of model lessons and practice teaching in the actual class room situation will make them effective and competent teachers.

Internship in a school will offer the prospective teachers the varied experiences needed for working in a school. They will internalise educational value of the work and experience the dignity of manual work. The school community interaction would not only promote the interactive support between both but also enable them to evolve suitable pedagogy for children. The organization of education activities will develop the capacity for planning and undertaking such activities as are essential for the development of personalty of the student. The theoretical and practical courses suggested in this frame are capable of preparing a competent elementary school teacher.

Transactional Strategies: The prospective teachers are to be prepared as to enable them to perform successfully in the pre-instructional, instructional and post-instructional phases of teaching. For this, several well-designed approaches like lecture discussion cooperative study, self-study and project methods etc. may be adopted. Depending on the nature of the subject, the teachers may combine different strategies and instructional aids, utilize media supported teaching, organise field trips and practicals and demonstration techniques. In this process due attention be given to children with special needs. The curriculum transaction will have to be adjusted with the needs of students and locally available resources.

During the process of teaching and learning, the existing transactional strategies marginally promote the capacity for independent study, self-discovery and self-study and rarely seek prospective teachers' participation and remain one way traffic with the result that the subject matter communicated is partially assimilated and not fully utilized. Teacher education has to inculcate professional commitment, develop competencies and make teacher reflective to deal with specific situations.

Practice teaching, the weakest link of teacher education, possesses the potentiality of converting itself into a strong component if properly organized. The process of curriculum transaction needs improvement and enrichment. Pedagogical analysis of teaching subjects is sure to refine teaching and learning as it will transform the teachers' performance and develop competencies not covered by the method-cum-content approach. With the background of pedagogical analysis and model and demonstration lessons given by the teacher educator, the class room performance is sure to improve if it is supervised in detail by the subject specialist. Work education is an important component of practical work and its potentiality has to be utilized by teacher education for developing certain qualities of character. Community surveys helps to formulate a proper social perspective. The mutually supported school and community interaction helps the teachers to evolve suitable teaching strategies.

The teachers will be required to organise educational activities in school. They have to learn to plan and organize such activities as are essential to provide opportunities for self-expression and lead to development of personality of students. They have to be trained for utilizing supplementary materials essential for accelerating and promoting learning among students.

The teachers will be required to facilitate physical, social, emotional and aesthetic development of students. Their creative and constructive potentialities have to be fostered. Practical activities suggested in the document will help to achieve these ends. It is, therefore, necessary to organize these activities on continuing basis. The influence of teachers' personality and behaviour has lasting impact on students. In the selection and adoption of transactional strategies the teacher has to ensure that teaching becomes participatory, cooperative, activity-centred and joyful.

Evaluation: The success or failure of the curriculum transaction is ascertained by evaluation done by means of valid and reliable tools. At this stage, evaluation has to be continuous, formative and comprehensive to bring improvement in teaching learning process. Systematic evaluation will enable a teacher to select proper teaching strategies and effect suitable changes in the curriculum process.

The evaluation of the pupil teachers at the elementary stage will not differ much from the primary stage and the same principles and similar practices which have been adopted at the primary level may be utilized at this stage.

Teacher Education for Secondary Stage

For teaching at secondary stage, the qualification most sought after is one year B.Ed. which is in fact B.Ed. for secondary stage. However, at present, there are several variations for first degree level qualification which are also available. These include B.Ed. (Elementary); B.Ed. (Special Education); which too are programmes of one year duration; B.Ed. through correspondence or distance education mode which is now of two years duration. There are certain other variations in the form of vacation courses or part-time courses which were available before NCTE norms came into force. In addition, there are four-year integrated courses for elementary stage and also for secondary stage. Teacher education programme at this stage, like at all other stages, will include the theory, practice teaching in schools, and practical work in the light of contexts, concerns, profile of teachers and general and specific objectives.

***Specific Objectives*:** The specific objectives at this stage may include the following:

- to enable the prospective teachers to understand the nature, purpose and philosophy of secondary education.
- to develop among teachers an understanding of the psychology of their pupils.
- to enable them to understand the process of socialisation.
- to equip them acquire competencies relevent to stage specific pedagogy, curriculum development, its transaction and evaluation.
- to enable them to make pedagogical analysis of the subjects they are to teach at the secondary stage.
- to develop skills for guidance and counselling.
- to enable them to foster creative thinking among pupils for reconstruction of knowledge.
- to acquaint them with factors and forces affecting educational system and class room situation.
- to acquaint them with educational needs of special groups of pupils.
- to enable them to utilise community resources as educational inputs.

- to develop communication skills and use the modern information technology.
- to develop aesthetic sensibilities.
- to acquaint them with research in education including action research

Curriculum Framework

Theory

- Emerging Indian Society
- Secondary Education in India -status, problems and issues
- Psychology of Teaching and Learning
- Guidance and Counselling
- Assessment, Evaluation and Remediation
- Curriculum Design and Development
- School Management
- Comparative Education
- Action Research

Optional Courses -any two of the following :

- Pre-school Education
- Elementary Education
- Educational Technology
- Vocational Education
- Adult Education
- Non formal Education
- Distance Education
- Environmental Education
- Computer Education
- Education of Children with Special Needs
- Health and Physical Education
- History and Problems of Education
- Population Education

Practice Teaching

- Pedagogical analysis of two school teaching subjects
- Practice teaching in schools
- Observation of Model Lessons

Practical Work

- Internship and School Experiences
- Field Work with community based programmes
- Creativity and Personality Development Programmes
- Work Education
- Sessional/practical work
- Physical Education Activities, games and sports and other school activities
- Aesthetic Development Programmes and Activities.
- Action Research studies

Rationale: A teacher helps in improving the quality of human life in the context of multiple internal and external forces impinging on man and the society. The course on 'Emerging Indian Society', would develop an insight into the nature of Indian society, its variety and complexities and making teacher education programme relevant to the community. Ingenuity of teachers lies in first understanding national ethos and then planning for teaching within this framework as a professional. A professionally trained teacher is expected to identify the strengths and weaknesses of secondary education in India and after having gained insights into the status, problems and issues concerning education at this stage, develop a mental make-up of evaluating the system and utilising the same for promoting excellence in education.

A teacher in the classroom has to make adjustments in teaching strategy according to the nature and scope of the curriculum and evaluate the success of teaching in terms of students' growth. The foundations of curriculum, pedagogy, evaluation and remediation need to be laid down firmly during the course of professional preparation of teachers. What kind of pedagogical strategy will give optimum results in specific units of curriculum and in what ways the outcomes need to be evaluated will be the main thrust.

Distinct departure from the existing programme is noticeable in including a course on psychology of teaching and learning. The teaching of educational psychology to the B.Ed. trainees was done extensively even earlier but without establishing linkages with actual teaching and learning. The attempt to put teaching and learning together does not in any way undermine the importance of educational psychology. Now the basic thrust will be on teaching - learning processes, group dynamics, learners' background, the internal and external forces of the institution and the community. Psychology of teaching and learning would require adjustments at different levels of schooling and for different grade levels. Foundation courses lend support to refining the education processes implicit in teaching and learning. Comparative perspective of educational systems in developing and developed countries would enable teachers to acquire a global vision of contemporary context and gain greater insight into ways of improving the quality of education.

The understanding of some specific areas of education in detail and in depth is needed for becoming an effective teacher. Guided by this consideration and having been supported through field interactions with different target groups, courses on pre-school education and elementary school education have been included as optionals. Teachers will also be required to get indepth understanding of areas like non-formal alternatives to school education. Similarly avenues for indepth studies in emerging areas of concern like vocational education, environmental education, population education etc. Have also been suggested.

The message of educational technology has to reach the classrooms in the form of its application. Prospective teacher has to be so equipped in the course of training as to enable him to think of using appropriate educational technology for improving the quality of instruction and for obtaining optimum results in terms of the students' growth.

Physical education has been considered as an integral part of education. In each system of schooling tremendous amount of emphasis is laid upon building up the cognitive base of students and the affective and psychomotor dimensions of human personality, do not receive adequate attention. A teacher fashioned in the culture of physical education would be conscious of catering to the physical dimension of human personality with concern. The inclusion of this course, however, may not be taken as an alternative to preparing teachers for teaching Physical Education.

Transacting Curriculum: The impact of teacher training programmes has not been perceptible over the years in terms of transacting curriculum in schools. Lecture method, mostly taken recourse to by teacher educators, is generally not supplemented by using instructional materials. Interactive teaching, co-operative teaching-learning, self-discovery approaches seldom find place in the day-to-day teaching practices. What is of importance and calls for top priority in the training programme, is to lay appropriately proportioned emphasis on 'why to teach', 'how to teach' and 'what to teach' aspects of teaching. It has to be reflected in the teaching-learning situations planned by teacher educators.

Theory: Education as a field of specialised studies is inter-disciplinary in its nature. Since different branches of learning are involved in understanding the presage, process and product variables of education, it is essential that formulation of teacher education programmes adopts a holistic approach in order to promote proper understanding, insight and thinking on matters pertaining to this field. The complimentary character of theory and practice needs to be emphasised at every step. The prospective teachers are encouraged to organise, express and communicate their ideas clearly in the class. It has to be accepted as a communicative process of an intensive teacher-learner dialogue and renewal of a two-way process as opposed to 'the banking concept' of teaching. The emphasis must be laid on cultivation, formation and development of power of mind in contrast to the prevalent tendency of aiming at the success in examination alone. Student teachers, it is hoped, in classroom transactions, will employ the use of divergent thinking and problem solving strategy.

The teacher educators will be required to have clarity of thought in respect of components of a course, objectives of teaching, and their relevance to educational and social goals. One of the approaches may be the modular approach. Each module, though a complete teaching unit, remains a part of the total syllabus with built-in linkages and feedback mechanisms. Learning through this approach can be reinforced by library work, seminar readings, tutorials and small group discussions. Self-study and self-motivated learning become an integral part of the curriculum transaction. The outcomes would result in better understanding of concepts better leading to mastery learning.

The interdisciplinary approach in teaching has to be accepted and implemented for developing comprehensive understanding and vision of educational studies. Learning outcomes have to be assessed continuously, which is the basic tenet of the modular approach. This would help in modifying, adjusting and improving transaction strategies for better acquisition of knowledge. Universities have options to evolve their own examination system. Too much reliance on external examinations, however, would inhibit the progress of moving in the direction of quality education.

Student Teaching and Practical Activities: There is no denying the fact that practice of education is as important as its theory. Each good theory leads to a good practice and vice-versa. To strike a balance between theory and the practice of education, therefore, is a matter of judicious planning and scheduling in order to give proper direction to teacher education.

Changes in the pattern and practices of student teaching have been only peripheral. The content-cum-method approach, wherever attempted, remained limited to the introduction of an additional component of content without fully achieving the objective of integration. The problem-solving approach, discovery method, competency based teaching learning and the indigenous contributions, like those of Gandhi, Tagore, Aurobindo, Zakir Hussain and several others have the potential for bringing in innovative ideas in teacher education. The application of educational technology, informatics, telematics, cybernetics etc. Have yet to make a discernible headway. The learning resources wherever available in the training institutions and the community as also in the schools have not been optimally utilised.

Prerequisite to preparing a prospective teacher can be thought of in terms of providing certain inputs such as, induction programme, an exposure of school experiences with special focus on the educational environment of the school, socio-economic and cultural background of the community constituting the catchment area, observation of classroom teaching and other related activities etc. Induction programme might include acquainting the intending teachers with the school settings, the school programmes - curricular and co-curricular. In addition, they will be prepared for actual classroom teaching and the roles they are expected to assume during the course of practice teaching/internship by way of focussed discussions, demonstration lessons, preparation of lesson plans in a way as to encompass teaching for cognitive, affective and psychomotor development.

Practice teaching is essentially a joint responsibility of teacher training institution and the school involving teacher educators, prospective teachers and school teachers. Teacher educators will help in facilitating and guiding the activities as implied by the pre-instructional, instructional and post-instructional phases through which a student teacher has to progress. The role of a school teacher in this joint effort lies in extending cooperation to the teacher educator and the intending teacher. Various aspects as referred to above will have to be suitably adapted to varying structures and designs at different stages of teacher education.

Practical work other than classroom instruction can be viewed in terms of school and community experiences and activities related to personality and leadership development.

Efforts need to be directed towards developing in a teacher trainee certain competencies and skills which would be helpful in the shaping of a teacher for effective role play. It is essentially directed towards capacity building which may embrace, among other competencies, managerial skills , organisational efficiency, leadership skills, democratic attitudes, innovative and creative abilities etc.

The teachers' role, which they will be required to play in the school situation other than classroom teaching, may extend to a variety of activities, such as, maintenance of school records and registers, management of laboratories and library, preparation, repair and selection of instructional aids and equipments, selection and preparation of textual materials, preparation of tests and assignments, admission and selection of students, maintenance of progress reports of students, preparation of school budget and development plans, beautification of school and classroom management etc. The institutional activities within the school environs may include dramatic clubs, stage activities, literary activities, inter-house activities and sports and games, organisation of educational tours, etc.

Community Experiences: Interaction between the institution and community is gaining importance in the modern context. One can think of several activities promoting school-community relationship, such as, celebration of birthdays of children, celebration of parents day, activating parent- teacher association for the welfare of the schools, organisation of school and community games, sports and other functions, utilization of community resources for education, understanding the background of children, celebration of national days in collaboration with the community, environmental education , adult literacy, plantation and social forestry.

Likewise, community involvement and school development activities may lead to community awareness generating competency through community - institution interaction activities; mobilizing community resources for organising literacy programmes, environmental education, work education programme, health awareness programmes, etc. It is expected that organisation of such activities would lead to developing self confidence and initiative among student teachers and also develop among them positive attitude towards plurality of cultures.

Practical Work: The modalities to be employed for organising activities other than teaching for all round capacity building and empowerment of a teacher-trainee will involve joint supervision by the teacher educator and a school teacher.

The transaction modes, for example, for motivating adults for making them literate can be through mass participation, folk songs, street plays etc. The identification of various sports and a variety of activities for cleanliness in the community, collecting success stories and disseminating them in the community, preparing simple write-ups of all the activities undertaken; utilizing community resources for the developmental needs of library building, students scholarships, awards, student aid funds, celebration of festivals etc; student-parent-community contact programmes and organisation of welfare shows for better institution- community participation are certain other strategies of transaction of practical work.

It is expected that a student-teacher undertakes several practical activities which facilitate instruction as also those that relate to management. Relevant to teaching and learning, the intending teacher develops competencies, like identification of support material, skills in preparation of indigenous and low-cost materials, judicious choice and utilisation of material for enhancing the learning and use of community resources for education. The likely activities may include preparation of an inventory of community resources, instructional material, development of software and use of hardware . The teacher-trainee also gets acquainted with the techniques of diagnosis, remediation, guidance and counselling, classroom interaction inclusive of understanding of context variables implicit in the process of teaching and learning, knowledge of educational rules and regulations/laws, in addition to maintenance of cumulative and comprehensive evaluation records, maintenance of school records and is conscious of professional accountability and ethics. It is hoped that most of the activities will be undertaken by the teacher trainee during the internship period of a reasonable duration. Some of these activities will have to be integrated with practice teaching. For meaningful organisation of practical work pre-internship stage may be utilised for demonstration lessons, lectures, simulation, role- playing, micro-teaching etc.

The transactional mode of community related practical work may include interaction between school teacher and intending teacher and members of the community representing parents, panchayats, senior citizens, voluntary organisations, etc. Student -teachers may undertake a case study of a school (generally a practising school) for identifying its strengths and weaknesses, needs and problems, specific learning problems, such as, drop-outs, drug abuse, behavioural problems, learning difficulties etc. Street plays can be organised by the student teachers to sensitize the community in the ways in which community resources could be utilised and also motivate the community members for greater participation in the school welfare activities.

Work Education: To come to its present form, work education has undertaken a long journey. From Marx's 'combination of productive labour and learning' to Abbot Wood's 'vocationalisation', it came to Gandhi's 'handicraft as the medium of education' and again took the form of Kothari's 'work experience' which Ishwar Bhai Patel thought to be devoid of 'social value' and coined the term 'Socially Useful Productive Work' (SUPW). Its central purpose is to shift the centrality of education from excessive verbalism to practicality. It has raised certain academic questions apart from the availability of teachers and other resources. These questions may be summarised as follows :

- how to integrate it with other curricular and co-curricular activities?
- how to inculcate dignity of labour and morality of workmanship among students and teachers ?
- how to utilise the community resources available for work education in community and breaking the status-quo for promoting economic and social mobility?
- how to combine community and school-based work education programmes?
- how to make synthesis between its educational, economic and social values?
- how to enable teachers to understand the relationship between human personality and a particular type of work?
- what is its impact on culture and values?

Work education is a powerful medium for personality development. There can be a variety of activities which are necessarily school based and which may be included under work education like maintenance of the school plant including its playgrounds, cleanliness, repair of furniture and production of material to be used as instructional aids. It will be a great educational experience if community visit, field work, nature study, school co-operatives saving bank, games and sports and other co-curricular activities are carefully organised as part of the programmes leading to development of qualities needed for the success of work education.

Value Education: The rapid erosion of values in the society is causing concern, necessitating imparting of value education. It is generally agreed that cognition is basic to volition which by implication would mean that prospective teachers are expected to understand critical issues regarding values— concept, types, and problems involved in imbibing the values. It is also expected of them to be well-versed with the values enshrined in our Constitution and the values that have the cultural contexts and can be derived from our heritage.

In the process of capacity building of intending teachers, what is of importance is to ensure that they become capable of understanding the import of value education, interpreting values in the contemporary contexts and evolving strategies of imbibing these by their students.

Increased Duration of B.Ed. Programme: An overview of the preceding details would bring in focus the duration required to transact the curriculum and ensure achievement of objectives of teacher preparation at this stage. Through the national consultations initiated by the NCTE, a strong consensus emerged in favour of enhancing the duration of B.Ed. Programme from one year to two years.

The new curriculum frame not only transforms the nature and content of the traditional foundation courses but also includes several additional components. Emerging Indian Society will deal with factors and forces operating in the Indian society leading to the emergence of a new social order. The psychology of teaching and learning has been given a new thrust. It will also include findings of researches in life sciences, medicine, neurology, genetics and communication technology having their relevance for teaching and learning. A new course on Secondary Education has been included to provide deeper understanding of issues related to secondary education. Likewise, Guidance and Counselling has been incorporated to make teachers more functional in their jobs.

The course on Curriculum Design and Development will promote the capacity of curriculum development evaluation and transaction. A component of Assessment, Evaluation and Remediation has been added. The school management has been incorporated as a compulsory course because all the teachers must possess its knowledge and acquire its techniques. A new component of action research has been included to develop the problem solving approach. Comparative education has been added to broaden outlook of student teachers and to develop their insight into educational problems and issues. A number of optional subjects out of which the students will select only two has been suggested in the frame. These optionals are intended to develop certain additional competencies among the prospective teachers. The whole spectrum of theoretical courses has therefore not only been enriched but also given a professional shape and outlook which cannot be achieved within the short period of one year.

The practice teaching is now not merely confined to the teaching of certain subjects. Pedagogical analysis of the subjects offered for practice teaching has been made compulsory. The prospective teacher will analyse the subject before going to class and evolve a need-based pedagogy and transactional strategy. The teacher educators will now deliver model lessons of different types in actual classroom situation and the prospective teachers will not only learn the techniques but make its critical appraisal and evaluation to be subsequently discussed with the teachers. Teacher educators supervising the classroom performance, pupil teachers will discuss their observations with them for providing proper feedback to improve their performance. The practice teaching will, thus, require thorough preparation, detailed supervision and adequate time. Its gain would be acquisition of higher level of teaching competencies.

The practical work has been made comprehensive and meaningful. Internship programme shall be enriched to provide all the experience that a teacher needs. After completion of the period of internship the prospective teacher will acquire necessary experiences for working in school and the training received would be complete as against the partial one at present. The implementation of internship in this format will also need increased duration.

The field work, community interaction, school community relationship and similar programme will enable the pupil teacher to develop a need based pedagogy. The organisation of physical education and the educational activities, work education, sessional and practical work related to practice teaching and optional, the formulation of programmes for the development of personality, creativity and aesthetic sensibility and action research will lead to the promotion of skills and competencies needed for a teacher. The practical activities mentioned above will enhance the competence of the teachers. The duration of the B.Ed. pogramme will therefore have to be increased.

Besides these, a perceptible change in the pedagogy of teacher education itself has been suggested. Its centrality has shifted from the training colleges to schools and its transactional strategies have been transformed. The teacher educators have to make pedagogical analysis of the subjects to be taught and achieve integration between the theory and practice and also the methodology of teaching. They are expected to evolve a culture-specific and need-based pedagogy and develop the potentiality needed for independent learning and self study for which a number of suggestions have been made. The lessons will have to be supervised intensively and formative approach has to be adopted. The teacher educator has now to devote more time in the preparation and planning of his own activities for the professional uplift of the prospective teachers by developing certain additional competencies. All these demand more rigour and need more time.

Professionalism involves its own compulsion and pressure. It needs a change in attitudes and value systems of the teachers. They have to earn social sanction from the community by improving the quality of their work. The scope of teacher education has been enlarged. Teachers have to perform many additional roles in society.

Apart from teaching, they have to act as the agent of change and modernisation, cultural reconstruction and social development to earn recognition as a professional from the society by acquiring new competencies and commitment. They have to become effective and result oriented to enhance their knowledge and develop skills for its communication. These are not possible to be achieved within the short span of one year. Hence the need to increase the duration of the present B.Ed. programme from one year to two years. Existing programmes of two years duration leading to Bachelor's degree in education like B.P.Ed. may continue to be of the same duration.

Two years B.Ed. programme will provide a strong base for pursuing M.Ed. course duration for which may continue to be the same as at present.

Teacher Education for Senior Secondary Stage

Teacher education programmes have to respond to three major determinants: the stage-specific developmental characteristics of the students, the courses of study they pursue and the academic qualifications the prospective teachers possess. At the Senior Secondary stage all the three become distinctly different from that of the secondary schools which offer a common curriculum upto class ten. The main features of the three determinants are given below:

The Characteristics of Students at + 2 Stage : The development of students at this stage, the later part of adolescence, is characterized by

- maturity of body and brain
- development of abstract thinking and logic; goal fixation and symbolization
- self-consciousness, self-identity and self-assertion
- sex-consciousness and sex interest
- personal preferences and choices and ideal formation and differentiation
- peer group influences, strong likes and dislikes, reactions and adventurism
- changes in reference group, imitation of adult behaviour and roles and a tendency of defiance
- moral reasoning and challenging attitude towards the established ideas, practices and authority
- self-esteem and ego-involvement
- attachment to friends
- self-defence and self-exhibition
- argumentation and rebelliousness
- fixation of ideas, development of aptitudes and demarcation of academic or vocational preferences

In short, they acquire many characteristics of youth and adults. Their educational potentialities, inclination and preferences become evident.

Course of Study: For the students of +2 stage, two types of courses - academic and vocational - have been designed. The characteristics of courses responding to the above are mentioned below :

Academic Stream

- differentiated, demarcated and specific contents
- subject and discipline orientation preparatory to specialization
- enriched and comprehensive curriculum with goal specificity
- regrouping of subjects into compulsory and optionals
- emphasis on abstract and creative thinking and higher mental faculties to deal with complex ideas and complicated concepts.
- directed and focussed towards higher studies

Vocational Stream

The main characteristics of vocational courses are in their being

- job oriented,
- skill based,

- useful,
- practical,
- manipulative,
- rich in economic values,
- employment or self-employment oriented,
- terminal in nature, and
- suitable for middle level workers in economy.

Teacher Characteristics: In order to deal with the above, the teachers of academic stream require the following :

- enriched and higher academic qualifications and standards
- additional teaching competencies
- different curriculum transactional strategies and modalities
- competency to promote desire for pursuing higher studies and develop academic interests and pursuit of independent study

To deal with vocational subjects different kinds of teachers are required. They must possess

- expertise in a vocational subject;
- capacity to inculcate workmanship and dignity of labour;
- ability to transfer skills from one trade/vocation to another;
- competencies to explain scientific principles involved in a trade or vocation;
- capability to impart knowledge and skills for achieving success in a trade or vocation;
- desire to produce an educated citizen, not only a narrow specialist or trade's man;
- ability to inspire students for the constant upgrading of their skills; and
- an understanding of the interrelationship between culture and a vocation.

Rationale for Separate Teacher Education Programmes for the +2 Stage : At present there exists a common programme for the education of teachers for the secondary and senior secondary schools. It is undifferentiated and generalized. But the courses at the senior secondary stage have been enriched. Their nature and goals are dufferent. They have been divided into two broad streams. The characteristics of students have also changed. Under these circumstances certain additional competencies are needed for teachers teaching at this stage. Hence the separate programmes for the academic and vocational streams of teachers.

Teacher Education for Senior Secondary Stage - Academic Stream

Objectives : The objectives of teacher education for academic stream may include the following:

- to develop among teachers an understanding of the nature, purpose and philosophy of the academic stream
- to develop necessary competencies and skills for curriculum development, transaction and evaluation
- to communicate difficult concepts and complex ideas
- to inspire students for higher and independent study and promote library and laboratory skills and habits
- to develop abstract, creative and critical thinking among students
- to enable them to reconstruct knowledge and experience
- to enable them to develop and use different kinds of tests
- to foster academic interests and values.

Curriculum Framework - Academic Stream

Theory:

- Emerging Indian Society
- Senior Secondary Education - Nature, Purpose, Status, Problems, Issues etc.
- Psychology of Teaching and Learning
- Curriculum, Pedagogy and Evaluation
- Research Methodology
- Methods of Teaching of one subject at the +2 stage

Optional: One from the following :

i) Educational Evaluation
ii) Educational Technology
iii) Population Education
iv) Environmental Education
v) History and Problems of Education
vi) Comparative Education
vi) Educational Management, Planning and Finance
vii) Innovations in Education

viii) Physical Education

ix) Computer Education

Practice Teaching

- Pedagogical Analysis of one subject at this stage
- Practice teaching

Practical Work

- Internship and School experiences
- Project work in the method and content
- Sessional and practical work in the area
- Action Research
- Field work
- Organization of student and physical education activities
- Personality and leadership development programmes
- School and community relationship programmes
- School development plans/projects
- Library and Laboratory work
- Preparation and use of tests
- Preparation and use of teaching aids/instructional technology

Rationale: An understanding of emerging Indian society and factors and forces operating behind it are essential for developing educational insight among teachers. The knowledge of various components of senior secondary education in the academic stream will enable them to understand its nature, purpose, philosophy and problems. They will be aware of the curriculum, pedagogy and evaluation techniques relevant to this stage and acquire the knowledge of psychology of teaching, learning and transacting the curriculum and the action research to solve day-to-day problems. Teachers will acquire knowledge of the methods of teaching in depth and develop related competencies by means of the specialized programmes. Practical work, the pedagogical analysis of the subject and practice teaching in the class under the supervision of the expert will inculcate among them needed competencies. The related practical activities like action research, field work, project work and sessional and practical work will develop problem- solving approach. The preparation and use of instructional technology will make them more effective in the classroom. The preparation and administration of teacher-made objective tests will transform their approach to evaluation. They will be able to guide the students how to use library and laboratory for independent studies. The theoretical and the practical components mentioned in this curriculum frame will, thus make them competent and reflective teachers.

Transacting Curriculum

Theory: For the purpose of transaction a course may be divided into units and then modular approach may be followed. Pupil teachers may be encouraged to pursue independent and group studies. Seminars and workshops may be arranged. Lectures should only be indicative. The teacher may start the lecture analytically and through interactive interventions arrive at synthesis at the end. The skills of listening, drawing conclusion, conceptualisation, and identifying the central theme and its relevance to life be established. After each lesson, reference materials may be suggested. The main thrust of transactional modality will be on the development of abstract, critical and creative thinking alongwith inculcation of habit of precision and comparison and use of appropriate words and concepts.

Practice Teaching and Practical Work: Pedagogical analysis should precede the actual teaching. The notes of lesson may be only indicative. Its centrality should be focussed on the realisation of objectives. Supervision shall be the joint responsibility of the school and training colleges. At least three fourth of the lessons will be supervised by the expert in detail. Its nature should be formative. The projects shall be completed under the guidance of an expert and sessional/practical work shall be properly planned. The organisation of the student and physical education activities and services will be supervised by teacher educators.

Evaluation: Multiple approach will be adopted for the purpose of evaluating achievement for the theoretical content. It will be continuous as well as annual, internal as well as external. Teacher-made objective type of tests, diagnostic and prognastic tests, etc. shall be used for the purpose. The essay-type question will also be used for identifying abilities not detected by other tests. Continuous progress record of the students maintained by the teacher will be considered at the time of evaluation of the practice of teaching. The different kinds of practical work, project report, sessional work, tests and records of various activities shall be evaluated by experts in the area internally and continuously for giving proper feedback. The evaluation strategy at this stage shall aim at identifying the students' potentialities teaching at the senior secondary stage.

Implementation Strategy: A separate B.Ed. programme as envisaged in the framework may be organised by colleges of education and university departments of education.

The teachers who have undergone a B.Ed. course for secondary stage and Master's degree in any of the academic subjects may subsequently undergo a bridge course or earn additional credits needed for developing competencies relevant to this stage under a specially designed programme of suitable duration.

Teacher Education for Senior Secondary Stage - Vocational Stream

The focus of vocational courses is on self-employment or employment which demand different capabilities, competencies and practical and academic skills from the teachers.

The teachers of vocational subjects should not only possess high competency in a trade or vocation but also be able to enthuse their students to undertake it as a career and develop qualities essential for achieving success in this area. The preparation of teachers for teaching vocational subjects, therefore, becomes an important function of teacher education programme at this stage.

Objectives

- to make the teachers understand and appreciate the philosophy, purpose and need of vocational education and its relevance in Indian context.
- to enable them to impart knowledge and develop necessary competencies
- to enable them to develop an understanding of the scientific principles involved in a trade or vocation.
- to develop among them the necessary skills and values for success in a vocation.
- to enable them to foster among their students the desire to achieve high productive skills and competencies.
- to empower them to induce their students for self-employment.
- to develop insight among the students to transfer their vocational skills from one area to another.
- to make them able to develop the spirit of self-reliance and self-confidence among the students.
- to enable them to organise on-the-job training and apprenticeship programmes for students.

Curriculum Framework

Theory:

- Emerging Indian Society
- Vocational Education : principles, purposes, needs, status, problems and issues
- Psychology of Teaching, Learning and Developing Vocational Competencies
- Entrepreneurship
- Organizational Behaviour
- Management
- Project Formulation
- Marketing and Advertising
- Computer Education

Practice Teaching:

- imparting theoretical knowledge about a trade or vocation
- developing skills and competencies in a trade or vocation
- teaching workshop practices

Practical Work:

- Organising
- apprenticeship
- on-the-job training
- workshop practices
- Formulating and Implementing Projects
- vocational projects
- projects in imparting vocational education
- Advertising
- Marketing
- Elementary Financial Management
- Working with Computers

Rationale: The suggested curriculum with all its theoretical and practical components will develop among the teachers of vocational subjects knowledge, skills and competencies needed for a teacher of this stream. The teacher will not remain a narrow technician but possess a broader educational outlook. The success of vocational education depends on obtaining practical skills and competencies on which enough emphasis has been laid. The apprenticeship programme, on-the-job training and workshop practices have been given due importance. Teachers will be able to teach elementary financial management, advertising, conducting market survey and project formulation for starting a vocation. They will also acquire knowledge about management, entrepreneurship and organizational behaviour with reference to a vocation. All these will make them competent teachers of vocational subjects.

Transacting Curriculum: Curriculum transaction will highlight the applicational aspect of theory to actual practice. Demonstration shall be one of its techniques. Practice of teaching shall be arranged in actual work situation by means of apprenticeship. Laboratory and workshop will be fully utilised. Projects will contain all the details. The evaluation of theoretical component will be done as in the academic stream. But the practice of teaching and practical activities will be performance -oriented. Both process and the product will be evaluated. The workshop practices and work done during apprenticeship will be evaluated and the quality of the product will be judged jointly by the teacher educator and technical expert.

This programme is for the education of teachers who have already acquired degree or diploma in a vocation or trade. In case of teachers who have no such previous training an alternative programme of increased duration may be designed. An alternative and more effective programme of teacher preparation for vocational education may be a 4 or 5 year integrated programme.

Tasks Ahead

In the preceding sections it has been attempted to modify the curriculum framework in keeping with the emerging challenges and demands for better schooling and quality education. Teacher education in India, with a view to making it relevant to the school system as well as training needs for preparing teachers at different levels will have to be further restructured, reorganised, and revamped. Multiple models of teacher education may have to be evolved by the universities and other agencies including National Council for Teacher Education. The innovative models to be undertaken have to be relevant from the point of view of the teacher educator as well as those who will assume the role of a professional, requiring interdisplinarity, broader vision and goal consciousness and commitment. These would lead to the improvement in the standards of teacher education and develop professional competencies. Another significant feature of such models would be their feasible and cost effective. The detailed course outlines will be developed by the universities through their various academic bodies. It, however, pre-supposes that the duration is suitably adjusted with the entry qualifications. Mis-matches between the needs of teacher education institutions and the professional preparation of teacher educators working in such institutions will have to be bridged.

There are several workable propositions for evolving a variety of models like school based model, community based model, discipline-oriented models, integrated models, comprehensive models etc. Needless to say, it would be necessary to initiate integrated and comprehensive programmes of teacher preparation in both academic and vocational streams. The stage-specific and need-specific models will have to be evolved. These innovative models should be promoted and financially supported.

Table:*Suggested Eligibility Qualifications And Duration For Various Teacher Education Programmes*

	Pre-Primary	*Primary*	*Elementary*	*Secondary*	*Senior Secondary*	*M.Ed. (General)*	*M.Ed. (Teacher Education)*
	General Courses						
Eligibility	10+2	10+2	10+2	Graduate	Post-Graduate	Graduate with first degree in education	Post Graduate with first degree in education
Duration	2Yrs.	2Yrs.	2 Yrs.	2 Yrs.	2 Yrs.	1Yr.	1 Yr.
	Integrated Courses						
Eligibility	10	10	10	10+2		-	-
Duration	4 Yrs.	4 Yrs.	4 Yrs.	4 / 5 Yrs.		-	-

The above table gives the eligibility qualifications and duration suggested for various teacher education programmes. The course structure for these programmes has been given separately under the three broad sections of theory, practice teaching and practical work. Weightage for various components may be arranged so as to give total weightage of 40% to theory, 20% to pedagogical analysis of school subjects, 20% to practice teaching and 20% to other practical work. Weightage for various components may be same for time allocation as well as for the scheme of examination. This distribution however, would not be applicable to pre-primary teacher education programmes for which theory and practice would have 30% and 70% weightages respectively. There has been a strong demand from a large section of teacher educators and educationists to increase the duration of

B.Ed. course from one year to two years. However, change-over from one year to two years duration may require two-three years preparatory time. It is, therefore, recommended that the two year B.Ed. courses may be instituted after careful planning, development of detailed curriculum, suitable augmentation of infrastructure and necessary orientation of teacher educators, during the next two/three years. During the interregnum, the general teacher education programmes, as suggested in this section, may be offered. However, if some institutions have the necessary infrastructure, staff and other resources and are willing to start these two year programmes early, they need to be encouraged and assisted.

In-service Teacher Education

In-service teacher education within the overall framework of teacher development, has a crucial role to play. It is no cliché but a reality that those who teach should never cease to learn. The National Policy on Education, 1986 stipulates that teacher education is a continuous process and its pre-service and in-service components are inseparable. The initiatives taken in setting up District Institutes of Education and Training (DIETs), Colleges of Teacher Education (CTEs), and Institutions of Advanced Study in Education (IASEs) are some of the major developments in this regard.

Professional development of teachers begins with pre-service and gets renewed through in-service programmes. It, however, does not mean that there is a simple linearity between the two. There are elements of 'change' and 'continuity' in teacher education system which necessitate renewal and upgradation of skills and competencies. The in-service programmes are also organised to sustain the 'survival competencies' which the teachers acquired years ago, during pre-service education.

Rationale

In the professional updating of teachers, changes in the societal goals, educational structure, curriculum framework, transactional strategies, evaluation techniques and management processes play a significant role. New advances emerging on the educational horizon have to be addressed to and teachers made aware of the same as well. Teacher development is a complex process. Teachers update themselves by putting in various efforts of self-learning, peer learning and interactions with the community. Other alternatives to professional development are participation in recurrent programmes, extension activities and continuing education programmes.

In-service teacher education programmes are essential in view of obsolescence as well as explosion of knowledge and are necessitated on account of changes in educational and social realities. Whenever teachers are required to execute new and different roles or get promoted to a position that requires new set of competencies, participation in appropriately designed in-service programmes is called for. Advances in the fields of curriculum, evaluation, audio-visual aids, telecommunication, etc. demand updating and orientation of teachers. Innovations both at macro and micro levels, would fail if teachers are not equipped and properly oriented to implement. In the Indian context, the developments, such as the 10+2+3 pattern, the making of science compulsory upto class X, new practices in evaluation like internal assessment, question banks, continuous and comprehensive evaluation, scaling and grading, introduction of new areas like environmental education, population education, computer education, AIDS education, gender sensitivity, etc. Demand in-service training of teachers.

In-service training programmes are offered in various ways. Resource institutions at the national level offer orientation programmes of varying duration for different target groups. Besides this modality there are others like attachments, visits, national exchange programmes and international study visits; which form a significant component of in-service programmes. Pre-service and initial teacher education is reinforced by self-initiated learning, in-service teacher education programmes and recurrent and continuing education. Self-initiated learning involves study on one's own for professional development. Recurrent and continuing programmes are organised through seminars, workshops, orientation courses etc. As per the professional requirements.

In the changing context of globalisation, liberalisation and advances in tele-communication, teachers and teacher educators need to become conversant with international trends, internationalism, multi-culturalism, multi-racialism and other pluralities. Both pre-service and in-service teacher education programmes should be receptive to new thinking and new changes. However, reforms and innovations in education can reach schools in large magnitude and expeditiously through in-service education programmes.

Functions

In-service teacher education broadly perform the following functions:

- updates teachers in issues concerning content, methodology and evaluation,

- upgrades serving teachers in tasks with which they are currently occupied,
- initiates and orients teachers to new roles and technologies,
- provides opportunities for unqualified or underqualified on-the-job teachers to update and upgrade their knowledge.

While content, design and duration of each programme would be determined by one or more functions identified above, long range efficacy of any programme would also be judged by its impact on the following :

- personality of the trainees ;
- motivation and commitment in matters relating to professional and self growth ;
- awareness of social realities; and
- communication and evaluative skills;

Objectives

In-service teacher education has to be organised for achieving the following broad objectives :

- to upgrade the qualifications of under-qualified and/or untrained on-the-job teachers.
- to upgrade the professional competence of serving teachers.
- to prepare teachers for new roles.
- to provide knowledge and skills relating to emerging curricular changes -content, process and evaluation.
- to make teachers aware of critical areas and issues, like, competency-based learning, multigrade, multi-level and multi-channel teaching, teaching students of disadvantaged groups, meeting educational needs of children with learning problems, developing enquiry skills, use of mass media in education, community participation and educational development of dyslexic children.
- to overcome gaps and deficiencies of pre-service education.

In-service programmes need to be built around 'transformational objectives', i.e. increasing motivational level, enriching self-concept, building climate of enquiry and making teachers reflective practitioners. The thrust of transformational objectives is to develop such qualities in teachers as would enable them to become receptive, perceptive, reflective, innovative and dynamic.

Strategies

Strategies adopted in in-service teacher education programmes would vary programme-wise and theme-wise. One has to judiciously select an appropriate training strategy or a mix of training strategies keeping in view the theme, programme duration, background of participants, availability of resource persons, support material and technologies of training at hand. Training strategies would range from lecture-cum-discussion to project work, library work, group interaction, field visits.

There may be many models of in-service training. Some of these are given below:

Face to face Institutional Model: In this model, the training institution offers in-service training programme on its premises using direct face to face training approach. It is most effective when the number of participants is around 30 to 40. Besides lecture-cum-discussion mode many other transactional strategies are also used namely project method, case method, library work, peer learning sessions, buzz sessions, and small group techniques. The merit of this approach is that there is a direct and sustained interaction between participants and resource persons. The limitation of this approach is that it cannot be used when the institution wants to train a very large number of participants within a short time.

Cascade Model: In this model number of persons to be trained is very large and training design is built on two or three tier systems. In the first level the key resource persons are given training. They train resource persons who in turn train teachers. The advantage of this model is that a large number of teachers can be trained within a short duration of time. However, it has its limitations. Knowledge and information passed on at the first tier of key resource persons and then at the second tier of resource persons get somewhat diluted resulting into transmission loss of training effectiveness.

Media Based Distance Education Model: With the advent of satellite technology and computers many training programmes are imparted using electronic media. Audio-conferencing and tele-conferencing are already being used. In these the electronic media play the key role and print material play a supportive role. The advantage of this model is that training objectives can be achieved within limited time period. The constraint of this approach is the limited availability of the technology itself, and its high initial investment.

Besides the above three models, some other important considerations contribute to effectiveness of an in-service training programme.

i) *Locale :* Training institutions at the national, state and district level organise training programmes generally at their respective institutions. These institution based trainings have their own strengths in terms of availability of resources. Their limitations are that they dislodge participants from their work place. This approach is often known as off-site approach. On the other hand using on-site approach many institutions organise training programmes at the school site itself. Thus participants are not dislodged from their work place. Extension programmes and on-site programmes take training to the doorsteps of schools/ institutions.

ii) *Target Groups :* At present in-service programmes are organised largely for teachers. A few programmes are also organised for headmasters, principals and other supervisory staff. This net has to be widened and many more categories of personnel brought into the fold. In-service teacher education programmes ought to be offered to all teachers working at pre-primary, primary, elementary, secondary and senior secondary levels. These could cater to teachers working in formal schools, non-formal centres, open and distance teaching institutions and institutions of physical education, adult education, special education, etc.

Teacher educators, in general, have limited exposure to in-service education. There is a need to train teacher educators at all levels. In fact, an apex institution needs to be set up for training of teacher educators. Alternatively some selected institutions may develop special expertise in training of teacher educators. Such institutions would have to develop relevant support material and undertake critical research studies relevant to in-service programmes of teacher educators.

Besides teachers, supervisors and administrators, there are other categories like Zila Pramukh, Pradhan, Sarpanch etc. connected with Panchayat Raj System who have the responsibility to look after primary level education. Depending upon the resources available staff of the support system, including librarians, hostel wardens, etc. should also be exposed to various programmes to enhance their professional competence.

iii) *Transactional Strategies :* An effective in-service education and training programme would use various transactional strategies like case study method, brain storming sessions, panel discussions, seminars, symposia, small group techniques, project work, library work and lecture-cum-discussion sessions.

The organisers and the resource persons can make an in-service teacher education programme more effective and interesting if the age, experience and background of participants are appropriately used at the planning phase. Since in-service participants bring a lot of experience and way of looking at educational events, they can significantly contribute to the design and development of programmes.

iv) *Content :* Content of in-service programmes would depend upon objectives of each programme which could be grouped under the following major categories :

- school subjects.
- pedagogy and methodology.
- emerging issues.
- teacher's new role.

The focus of in-service programmes is on developing competencies and commitments. The overall aim of in-service programmes is to enable teachers to improve their classroom activities, out-of-the-classroom activities, school activities and community activities.

v) *Evaluation and follow-up :* Evaluation is a weak link in many in-service training programmes. In most of the cases in-service programmes are evaluated, if at all, on an *ad hoc* basis. Each in-service teacher education programme should have monitoring as an integral component so that effectiveness of a programme can be properly assessed and apraised. Programme evaluation should assess whether the required inputs were provided to the programme on time, the logistics properly looked after and coordinated, the reading materials provided to participants etc. Another aspect of programme evaluation should be to assess the gains of each participant. The other subtle aspect is the impact evaluation to assess the impact of the programme at the grassroot level and in the field situation.

Success of an in-service teacher education programme may be assessed by collecting perceptions of trainees and of resource persons. A comprehensive view on quality assurance could be obtained by taking note of the following:

- how has the programme been implemented?
- what is the context? Is the programme relevant to the existing education context?
- has the programme been planned properly in terms of objectives, duration, and resources?
- does the programme satisfy the need of all or most of the participants?
- is the programme cost-effective?

Pointers for Future

- Education and training programmes become more productive and effective when programme planning is participative and transactional strategies are interactive. The need of all in-service teacher education programmes must emerge from the grassroots. For example, under the centrally sponsored teacher education programme, District Institutes of Education and Training are expected to organise programmes for teachers in such a way that every elementary teacher gets a chance to participate in the programme of his or her choice at least once every five years. In this venture state level coordinating agency like SCERT can play a faciliative and co-ordinating role to ensure that need based in service programmes are launched.
- In some states due to certain reasons and other considerations, untrained and under-qualified teachers get recruited. These untrained and underqualified teachers need training and content upgradation. The backlog of untrained and underqualified teachers has to be cleared at the earliest.
- Whenever teachers are promoted from elementary level to secondary level or from secondary level to senior secondary level, intensive in-service training programmes should be designed and offered to them. Whenever a teacher takes up new educational assignments (headmastership or principalship), he/she would require task oriented in-service training.
- There is a need to make a shift in organising programmes from training institutions to schools and school clusters. Concerted efforts may be made in this direction.
- Development of support material is very important for in-service education. Unless quality support materials are developed, face-to-face training alone may not be enough. Good quality support material in the form of print, video cassette

and computer programmes have to be designed, developed and disseminated.

- Some in-service programmes be made credit oriented. On successful completion of specified programmes, participants may be considered for professional mobility.
- Participation in in-service programmes within a stipulated period should be made obligatory and appropriate incentives thought of.
- Organising in-service training porgramme using mobile training teams may also be thought of.

Teacher Preparation For Alternative Systems / Approaches in Education

Global upsurge for universal education, explosion of knowledge, expectation and aspirations for better quality of life have led to the exploration of alternatives to formal system which suffers from inherent inadequacies of rigidity and structural deficiencies. These alternatives include non-formal education, adult education, distance education, etc. While a good deal of work has been undertaken to spread and improve education through various alternatives, a major problem has been lack of trained functionaries. However, these functionaries cannot be prepared on the formal models of teacher preparation. Since they are required to perform functions of different nature, their training has essentially to be job-specific. Developing skills, competencies and commitments in the personnel involved in alternative strategies demand preparation and use of teaching and learning materials to be specifically designed for the programmes.

Non-formal Education

Non-formal education consists of an organised sytematic and planned educational activity, essentially characterised by inbuilt flexibility and carried on outside the framework of the formal system. It provides learning experiences to children in the age group of 6-14 years who are not able to avail of the facilities of formal schooling. Children from the non-formal system are eligible to appear in the examinations leading to certification to join the formal stream.

In certain respects formal and non-formal education are similar as both are organised to augment, promote and facilitate learning. They differ in their institutional management and the organisation of the course content. The training of the functionaries at different levels including instructors, supervisors, material writers, project officers and managers is significant. The objectives of the training of the functionaries may be the following :-

- to familiarise the functionaries with the latest developments in knowledge and technology specific to their job performance.
- to develop among them critical awareness about India's social reality.
- to acquaint them with special requirements of the groups they have to deal with.
- to provide them knowledge and skills as may help in the socio-cultural development of the clientele.
- to enable them to draw support from a wide variety of sources.
- to develop among them positive attitudes towards the under-privileged sections of society.
- to promote among them the desire to actively participate in the developmental activities.

Course Content

The curriculum for the functionaries of the non-formal education would be need-based and job-specific, depending on the nature of the task they have to perform. However, there are certain essentials which need to be considered. These include :

- a sound background in India's composite culture, its unity and diversity
- science as an element of thought, its role in history and its impact on society.
- Indian national movement and Constitution of India
- economic planning in India and its impact on economy and society.
- national development problems and issues.
- educational development and systems of contemporary Indian education
- environmental and population related issues.
- basics of human psychology and behaviour.
- communication skills, use of media and educational technology.
- production of instructional materials
- Identification of learners' needs and community interaction.
- practical / field work

Transactional Modalities

- organisation of induction and recurrent orientation programme of suitable duration.
- organisation of refresher courses and orientation programmes in the method and content.
- utilisation of community resources -human and material
- summer schools and short term training programmes.
- seminars, symposia and workshops
- interaction with local experts and skilled persons.
- use of supplementary educational devices, media and educational technology.
- evaluation.

Methods and Approaches

- Non-formal education may be included as an optional/ compulsory course in all teacher education programmes and also in courses like MA (Education), MA (Community Development), MA (Social Work), MA (Rural Economics), etc.
- Resource Persons may include Principals and school teachers, teacher educators, experts from different academic disciplines and administration and social activitists.
- Participation of Non-Governmental Organisations and voluntary agencies may be encouraged in implementation of the programme.

Adult Education

To achieve its present status, adult education has undertaken a long journey. Literacy campaigns during the thirties led to strengthening of social education. In sixties, it took the shape of functional literacy programme which was further reinforced to include functional literacy, numeracy and technocracy. It is now seen as an integral part of life-long learning. It duplicates certain functions of non-formal and continuing education. Adult education is expected to provide the skills needed to survive in the modern world for leading an effective and 'good life'. It includes adults of all ages. National literacy programmes focus specifically on those in the age group of 15-35 years in Indian context. It aims at developing the capacity of 'learning to learn' with or without the help of adult educator. Adult education concerns those who are not full time learners and have not been exposed to formal education. The knowledge gained and skills developed from it are utilised in a variety of situations. Thus, it has become need-based.

Objectives of Training of Adult Education Functionaries

The objectives of the training of the functionaries may include the following :

- to enable them to develop social awareness.
- to develop skills related to functional literacy programmes.
- to liberate adults from the bondage of prejudice, bias, ignorance, superstition etc.
- to prepare them for the participation in developmental activities.
- to develop among the learner the desire and potentialities of 'learning to learn'.
- to enhance their economic efficiency.
- to inspire the adult learner with the sense of patriotism, global consciousness and the will to live together.
- to promote among them a sense of national and social cohesion.
- to enable them to combine personal dignity with civic responsibility.
- to understand the learners and their needs.
- to develop awareness of human rights and legal literacy.
- to enable them to understand environmental and population concerns.
- to develop humanistic, moral and ethical values.

Training Programme and Content

The programme should be participatory, flexible, relevant, diversified and need-based. It might include, among other things, the following :

- Psychological and Sociological Principles of Adult Learning
- Problems and Issues of Adult Education.
- Indian Heritage
- Freedom Movement, Indian Constitution, administrative system of India including Panchayat Raj.
- Contemporary India and the World.
- Scientific and Technological Literacy.
- Planning and Developmental Activities.

- Economic and Social Problems.
- Problems of women, minorities and the under-privileged sections of the society.
- Acquaintance with approaches and methods of teaching adults.
- Right to information, social activism and legal literacy.

Transactional Modalities

For the functionaries in this field it is essential to promote their capacity of 'learning to learn'. Lectures should, therefore, be reduced to the minimum and emphasis should be laid upon self-learning through techniques, like :

- workshops, seminars, debates and discussions
- tours and excursions
- library work, laboratory work and actual experience of work situations
- basics of language learning
- organisation of refresher courses and orientation programmes.
- short term training programmes.
- extension lectures
- use of supplementary educational devices, media and educational technology.
- evaluation

Methods and Approaches

- adult education may be included as an optional/compulsory course in all teacher education programmes and also in courses like MA (Education), MA (Community Development), MA (Social Work), MA (Rural Economics), etc.
- Resource Persons may include principals and school teachers, teacher educators, experts from different academic disciplines and administration and social activitists.
- Participation of Non-governmental Organisations and voluntary agencies may be encouraged in implementation of the programme.

Distance Education

Distance education is emerging as an alternative to the formal education system. The emphasis on education for all, explosion of population alongwith the desire for education, limitation of the formal system in providing greater accessibility and the rising expectations from education are some of the factors for its increasing demand. The new communication technology has brought it within the reach of all. Originally designed to provide alternative educational avenues to the poor and the working people for higher education, it has now developed as a parallel system in India from the primary to tertiary levels and covers not only liberal but scientific and professional studies as well.

Distance education implies the provision of educational opportunity at the place of learner from a distance by means of multiple media such as self-learning materials, audio-visual gadgets and short-term personal contact programmes. Information technology and cybernetics are simultaneously being utilised for upgrading the knowledge and skills.

In order that learning through distance education mode becomes effective, the following categories of functionaries need special inputs of training for persons involved in:

- development and production of reading materials including assignments.
- organisation and conduct of personal contact programmes.
- production of radio, television and computer programmes.
- use of teaching aids and technological gadgets and tele-conferencing.
- academic counselling and resource persons manning regional / study centres.

Objectives

Objectives of the training programme for distance teacher educators are as follows:

- to enable the distance educators to understand the nature and purpose of distance education.
- to develop among them the technique to prepare self-learning and self-instructional materials.
- to facilitate learning at one's own pace.
- to promote the habit of self-appraisal.
- to organise personal contact programmes.
- to identify and utilise learning resources.
- to enable them to establish a healthy linkage with the formal system and make distance education an effective means for the national and social development.

- to train them to make use of various interactive techniques.
- to enable them to prepare, utilise and evaluate the assignments.

Courses, Modalities and Strategies

These will be need-based and have to be evolved depending upon the specific requirements of the target groups, nature and extent of resources and professional support available and the potentialities of the identified approach courses on distance education may be included at graduate and post-graduate levels. Considerable experience has been gained in the area by organisations like National Open School (NOS), Indira Gandhi National Open University (IGNOU), and others. Expertise exists to plan and design effective programmes in these sectors.

Preparation of Teachers For Students With Special Needs

Democracy intrinsically implies provision of equality of educational opportunity to all according to the learner's age, ability, and aptitude. It envisages equality not only in terms of access, but also in achievement and the life chances. Every child in the classroom is unique and therefore, deserves individual attention. There are also children having mild or moderate disabilities who can be served by the general classroom teachers only if they are properly sensitised to the needs of such children. Similarly, gifted and talented children also need to be identified and provided necessary educational inputs. In addition, there may be children lagging behind due to specific learning difficulties which may have remained unidentified.

Objectives

Teachers with different skill levels are needed for special education programmes. Most of the general classroom teachers require sensitisation programmes whereas some teachers require specialised training to deal with severely disabled children.

The general training objectives in the area of special education are listed below :

- to create an awareness among all student teachers about education of children with special needs.
- to equip student teachers with skills to manage mild and moderately disabled children in general classrooms.
- to prepare resource teachers to serve specific categories of disabilities.

- to prepare multi-category resource teachers to serve more than one category of disability.

The general training objectives mentioned above will lead to the course objectives. These will vary between the levels of training like sensitisation, single category specialisation, multi-category specialisation. The course objectives may include the follwowing :

- to understand the nature and causes of disability
- to acquire knowledge about the physiological and psycho-social implications of disability
- to understand the educational implications of various disabilities
- to develop positive attitudes towards students with disabilities
- to acquire skills to identify and assess levels of disabilities and provide appropriate educational services
- to apply the knowledge and skills acquired in the rehabilitation of students with disabilities
- to acquire competencies and skills to prepare and use relevant teaching-learning aids, technology and support materials.
- to develop skills in management of children with multiple disabilities
- to familiarise with education policies and programmes of the State and Central Governments regarding disabled children
- to understand practicalities of integrated education of disabled children
- to acquire techniques in educational assessment, evaluation and placement of disabled children
- to develop skills in encouraging family and community participation in rehabilitation of disabled.

Curriculum Framework

For All Teachers: The curricular input of special education in general teacher preparation programme right from the pre-primary to secondary levels may be as follows :

Theory

- Development of special education in the emerging Indian society
- Handicapping conditions
- Trends and issues in special education
- Psycho-social aspects of disability

- Curriculum development and its adaptation to different disability areas
- Instructional and evaluation strategies
- Management of children with disability.

Practicum

- Practice Teaching in a mainstream class
- Visits to special education institutions
- Identification of disabled children using functional assessment procedures
- Preparation of teaching-learning materials
- Case Study and Project Work

For Special Teachers (Pre-service)

For each category of impairment and disability special courses shall have to be designed to prepare specialised teachers. Products of such courses would qualify to work as resource teachers in general schools and general classroom teachers in special schools.

Areas:

- Visual Disability
- Hearing Disability
- Mental Retardation
- Learning Disabilities
- Dyslexia
- Locomotor and Neuromuscular Disabilities

The Curricular Input for special teachers of disabled children may be as follows :

Theory:

- Nature and characteristics of specific disability
- Social aspects of disability
- Medical aspects of disability
- Psychological aspects of disability
- Curriculum construction and adaptation
- Plus-Curricular areas
- Methodology of Teaching
- Management of disabled children

- Special areas of concern : Student Activities and Physical Education
- Rehabilitation process
- Therapies

Practicum :

- Observation of disabled children
- Practice Teaching with appropriate adaptations for children with special needs
- Use of aids and appliances relevant to the area of specialisation
- Preparation of instructional materials
- Case study and project work
- Use of functional assessment procedures and identification of disabled children
- Visit to special education institutions and rehabilitation programmes
- Vocational modifications; removal of architectural barriers in access to playgrounds, dining hall, toilets, etc.

In-service: In-service programme is needed for all serving teachers to renew and upgrade their skills in dealing with children with special needs. In-service programme becomes imperative for the special education teachers to update themselves with the latest innovations and techniques of teaching in the field of special education. These would also apply to preparation of multi-category special teachers.

Teachers for the Gifted

In every society or school one can find children who are much above the average and possess certain special abilities. They are referred to as the gifted or talented children. It has been observed that generally teachers are not properly trained to nurture the talent of such children. Every society needs the gifted and the talented for its progress. It is, therefore, necessary that proper provisions are made for their education.

In India certain schools have been started for the education of the gifted and the talented children. In these schools as well as in the general schools the teachers are appointed from the general pool of trained teachers whose training, by and large, is not oriented towards meeting the educational requirements of such children. Since giftedness and talent, like disability, have different shades and colours, the preparation of teachers should also be multi-dimensional.

Teacher Education for the Gifted in Common School System

Objectives:

- to develop among the prospective teachers the capacity to identify the special talent and the potentiality of the gifted and talented.
- to enable them to understand the psycho-social aspect of children.
- to develop among them the capacity to identify learners' needs and make suitable educational provisions.
- to empower them to evolve suitable curriculum, appropriate methods of instruction and evaluation and to promote self-learning.
- to enable them to promote proper socialisation among students.

To achieve the above objectives the following may by included in the general teacher education programmes.

- Giftedness -Meaning and Concept,
- Identification of the Gifted and the Talented,
- Methods of Nurturing the Talents of the Gifted,
- Continuous Monitoring ,
- Case Study and Project Work.

Teacher Education for the Gifted in Specialised Institutions/Classes

Objectives:

- to develop among the prospective teachers the capacity to identify the special talent and the potentiality of the gifted and creative children.
- to enable them to understand the psycho-social aspects.
- to develop among them the capacity to identify their needs and make suitable educational provisions.
- to empower them to evolve suitable curriculum, appropriate methods of instruction and evaluation and to promote self-learning.
- to enable them to improve power of abstract thinking, critical faculty, originality and creativity among their students.
- to build the capacity among the prospective teachers to foster the problem-solving attitude among the students.
- to enable them to promote proper socialisation among the students.

Curriculum Framework: To sensitise teachers in catering to the requirements of talented and gifted children, relevant components from the following curriculum frame have to be incorporated in the curriculum already identified for each stage. The suggested curriculum structure is only indicative.

Theory:

- Education of the Gifted and Talented Children-Status, Issues and Problems
- Psychology of Teaching and Learning of the Gifted and the Talented (This course would be talent specific)

Optionals:

- Psychology of thinking
- Psychology of creativity

Practical:

- Pedagogical analysis of one or two school teaching subjects
- School and Community Experience
- Work Education

Activities: Specialised activities may be undertaken for the development of the following :

- Creativity
- Abstract thinking
- Reasoning, analysis, synthesis and evaluation
- Judgement
- Self-learning and self-evaluation
- Socialisation
- Intellectual independence

Training Strategies:

- Special inputs on gifted and talented in elementary level teacher training (certificate/diploma)
- Optional paper in B.Ed. on gifted and talented
- B.Ed. (gifted and talented) in specially identified institutions
- In-service education programmes.

Education of Teachers For Physical Education

Physical education is an integral part of the education system. It aims at building a sound body, a sharp mind and wholesome personality. It is essential for the cultivation of vitality, courage, self-confidence, cooperativeness, leadership, obedience, discipline and positive attitude towards life and the world. The great educational thinkers like Plato, Rousseau, Gandhi, Aurobindo and Russell have laid great emphasis on it. Physical education stresses :

- development of sociability, obedience and discipline, acceptance of authority, positive attitude, equanimity, rapport with others and group consciousness.
- development of emotional stability, control over one's own feelings and temptations.
- development of mental health, ability to take immediate decision and prompt action.
- cultivation of the power of concentration.
- inculcation of democrative values.
- development of neuro-muscular skills
- formation of character and development of willpower.

Development of physical fitness and health of students is not the responsibility of the teachers of physical education alone. In fact, every teacher has a role to play in this direction, especially at the elementary stage and must have substantial exposure to physical education and health education. The teachers other than physical education teachers also need to take interest in games and sports and physical activities.

Every prospective teacher irrespective of the level needs to be made conversant with the basics of physical education. In addition, every trainee is required to participate in at least one major group game and two items of sports. It needs to be provided for in the curriculum with a view to enabling them to generate a climate for promotion of physical activities.

Curriculum for Physical Education should be viewed from the following two angles:

a) Physical education as an integral part of teacher education programmes at all levels.
b) Physical education specifically for preparing teachers of physical education.

Physical Education as an Integral Part of Teacher Education

Objectives : The objectives of physical education as an integral part of teacher education may be as follows :

- to enable teachers to be conversant with the basics of physical education
- to enable them to understand the relationship between general education and physical education
- to enable them to organise games and sports and physical activities

The expected outcome of such an approach will lead to universalisation of physical education activities in schools.

Strategies

- Inclusion of physical education component in teacher education at all levels.
- Compulsory participation in at least one major group game and two items of sports.

Teachers of Physical Education at the Elementary Stage

These courses leading to a certificate or diploma are being suggested for the teachers of physical education at the elementary stage. The programme aims at realising the following objectives :

Objectives:

- to enable prospective teachers to understand the nature and purpose of physical education at elementary stage
- to develop among the students awareness of basic principles of health, hygiene and nutrition
- to enable them to develop good health and sound physique of students
- to foster interest in physical exercises, games and sports
- to inculcate the spirit of healthy competition and leadership
- to develop team spirit and fellow feeling
- to promote among them the competencies for organizing different kinds of activities in physical education
- to enable them to develop among students the physical and mental alertness
- to enable them to develop emotional stability and self-control

Curriculum Framework

Theory:

- Emerging Indian Society
- Physical Education : principles, purpose, status, problems and issues

- Psychology and Sociology of Physical Education
- Methods and Techniques of Physical Education
- Basics of Anatomy, Physiology and Kinesiology
- Health and Safety Education
- Management and Organization of Physical Education
- Yoga - basics of theory and practices

Practice Teaching and Practicals

- Demonstration
- Coaching
- Organization of games and sports
- Organization of indigenous and local games and sports
- Organization of community games and sports
- Lessons in Yogic exercises
- First aid, care of minor injuries, bandage and massage
- Upkeep and use of materials and equipment
- Marching
- Swimming
- Gymnastics
- Relaxation exercises

Teachers of Physical Education at the Secondary Stage (B.P.Ed.)

B.P.Ed. programme is intended to prepare the teachers of physical education for the secondary schools . The programme aims at realising the following objectives :

Objectives:

- to enable teachers to understand the nature, purpose and philosophy of physical education at the secondary stage
- to prepare teachers of physical education with broader educational perspective
- to develop potentialities for planning and organising physical education programmes and activities
- to develop capacity to organize leisure and recreational activities
- to empower them to inspire their students to actively participate in physical and yogic exercises, games and sports
- to enable teachers to develop personality, character, will-power, democratic values and positive attitude towards life among their students

- to make teachers capable of imparting basic knowledge about health, hygiene and nutrition
- to develop skills and competencies to organise school and community games and sports
- to cultivate the spirit of sportsmanship, mental and physical alertness, scientific temper and optimism
- to promote mental health, power of self-decision and self-control, correct judgement and action, emotional stability and equanimity, respect for others and acceptance of authority and rules
- to promote appreciation and interest for indigenous games, sports and yogic exercises.
- to create awareness about health and hygiene in the community.

Curriculum Framework

Theory

- Emerging Indian Society
- Foundations of Physical Education
- Management of Physical Education, Games and Sports
- Kinesiology and Physiology of Exercises
- Anatomy, Physiology and Health Education
- Psychology and Physical Education
- Guidance and Counselling in Physical Education
- Evaluation in Physical Education
- Adapted Physical Education

Specialization

- Sports Medicine
- Rules of Games and Sports
- Science of Training and Coaching
- Yogic Education and Indigenous Games
- Education of Athletes

Practicals and Practice Teaching

- Demonstration
- Practice of Coaching
- Organization of Games, Sports and Recreational Activities
- Organisation of Meets/Camping

- Participation and Training in major games and sports
- Participation and training in major indigenous games and sports and yogic exercises
- Track and Field Events
- Gymnastics and Tumbling
- Marching and Calisthenics
- Defensive Martial Arts
- Aquatics
- First aid, bandage and massages
- Care and Management of minor injuries
- Conditioning Exercises
- Relaxation Exercises

Masters Course in Physical Education (M.P.Ed.):- The Masters programme is intended to prepare teacher educators for physical education. Its objectives may be the following :

Objectives:

- to enable prospective teacher educators to understand the nature, purpose and philosophy of physical education
- to develop competencies necessary for physical training and coaching
- to develop knowledge, skills and competencies necessary for imparting physical education
- to enrich knowledge of personal and community health
- to promote the capacity to organise games, sports and recreational activities
- to provide knowledge of sports medicine and physiotherapy
- to develop competence to undertake research in physical education, games and sports
- to enable them to prepare good athletes
- to inculcate the spirit of sportsmanship
- to foster interest in physical education and appreciate its role in school and society
- to prepare for evolving stage-specific curriculum, pedagogy and evaluation techniques in physical education
- to develop an understanding and appreciation of indigenous approach to physical education, exercises, games and sports

Curriculum Framework

Theory:

- Emerging Indian Society
- Physical Education in Historical, Philosophical and Social Perspectives
- Psychology and Physical Education
- Physiology of Exercises
- Curriculum Development in Physical Education
- Evaluation in Physical Education
- Mechanical and Scientific Principles of Coaching
- Research Methods in Physical Education

Specialization:

- Management of Physical Education, Games and Sports
- Sports Medicine
- Physiotherapy
- Principles and Practice of yogic exercises and Indigenous games and sports
- Training Methods : Exercises, Games and Sports
- Rules and regulations of games and sports

Dissertation/project work

Practical Work

- Demonstration
- Advanced Coaching
- Organization of games and sports meets, camps and recreational activities
- Tests -Development, administration and scoring
- Sports Skills tests
- Major Fitness tests
- Strength tests
- General Motor Ability tests
- Psychomotor tests
- Cardiovascular tests
- National Physical Fitness tests
- Physiotherapy

- Dislocation Reduction
- Yogic therapy
- Hydrotherapy
- Electrotherapy
- Relaxation
- Massage
- Bandaging
- First Aid and Care for Minor Injuries
- Reconditioning

Transaction and Evaluation: Detailed curriculum planning will accord due considertion to region or area specific practices and approaches to transactional strategies. Explanation, demonstration, participation, performance and evaluation would be major components of transcational strategies. Corrective measures and remediation inputs would flow from evaluation leading to attainment of levels of performance. Group evaluation and community appreciation would provide much needed motivation to both the teachers and trainees.

5

Education of Teacher Educators

The role of teacher educator is of prime importance for effective implementation of teacher education curriculum. Education and training of teacher educators is a pre-requisite for effective changes in the training and orientation of teachers. India has a large system of teacher education. There are more than 2000 elementary teacher education institutions, Colleges of Education and University Departments of Education. Nearly 30,000 teacher educators are engaged in the preparation of school teachers. In addition, there are teacher educators working in pre-primary training schools as well as institutions concerned with the preparation of teachers for the education of children with special needs and alternative education such as non-formal education, distance education etc.

It is well recognised that the overall quality in education mainly depends on the quality of teachers and a sound programme of professional preparation of teachers is essential for imparting quality education. However,Teacher educators' own education leaves much to be desired. Teaching is an art which can be inculcated through a series of well designed activities in respect of education and training of teachers and is equally valid for professional preparation of teacher educators.

The teacher educators would not only be training pre-service and in-service trainees but would also be associating themselves with several other activities. New strategies and techniques of material development, the changing approach to evaluation, intensive interactions with the community, creating an activity-based environment in the training institutions, acquiring skills for resource mobilisation and several other such competencies at mastery level would be essential for professionals to function as teacher educators.

Changes in the school curricula would be faster in the near future. Corresponding changes in training programmes and strategies shall have to be perceived and given a shape by the teacher educators.

In the context of universalisation of elementary education, teacher educators will be expected to display a deeper understanding of the issues pertaining to access, participation and attainment in their specific regions or areas. They need adequate professional competence to conduct such surveys and studies would reveal the region specific and area specific issues and problems which would help the functionaries of the education department and the community. They will prepare the trainees in responding to these issues during the training period and also in schools subsequently. The professional quality of teacher educator will determine the quality of the training of teachers, both pre-service as well as in-service. The professional level at which teachers are prepared would, in turn, determine the quality of school education. Again, teacher educators have to be fully familiar with the school realities, social environment and community expectations to realistically perform the challenging tasks before them. On the professional side, teacher educators need to be actively associated with policy formulations, implementation strategies and monitoring of programmes.

Existing System

At present, the only programme which is often treated as preparing teacher educators is that of M.Ed. Scrutiny of the curriculum of most of the M.Ed. programmes would reveal that these have not been specifically designed to prepare teacher educators. There are some M.Ed. programmes where provisions do not exist for writing a dissertation. The products of these programmes would certainly not be in a position to conduct research, initiate innovation on their own and induct teacher trainees in these areas which are essential functions of teacher educators.

Prior to the establishment of the NCTE as a statutory body, NCERT acted as its secretariat and organised several professional development programmes for teacher educators in areas like micro-teaching and simulation, student teaching and evaluation, preparing research proposals, improvement of teacher education curricula and so on. The University Grants Commission (UGC) has been organising national and regional level workshops for improvement of the teacher education programmes. Through various schemes it offers financial support for seminars, workshops and research projects for teacher educators for such themes as higher education, educational technology, non-formal education, population education, environmental education, research methodology, etc. The National Institute of Educational Planning and Administration (NIEPA) organises programmes for Principals of Colleges of Education, Heads of University Departments of Education and other administrators concerned with teacher education. The SCERTs and State Boards of Teacher Education organise continuing education programmes for teacher educators on teaching methodologies for new subject areas and on innovations in education.

Some University Departments of Education organise seminars, workshops, and orientation programmes for teacher educators on teaching, development of instructional skills, interaction analysis, teaching behaviour, educational technology, guidance and counselling and research methodology. Certain Colleges of Education and University Departments of Education have been upgraded as Colleges of Teacher Education (CTEs) and Institutions of Advanced Study in Education (IASEs) for taking up innovations in teacher education. NCTE after its establishment in 1995 as a statutory body, has initiated several programmes aimed at enhancing professional competence of teacher educators. These include seminars and workshops in the area of human rights and national values, indigenous thoughts in education, indigenous approach to teacher preparation, institutional networking and capacity enhancement and production of good quality enrichment materials for teacher educators. These institutions have considerable experiences in organising training and development activities. Based upon the experience gained they will have to evolve programmes of sequential nature with in-built mechanism for assessment and impact evaluation.

In the absence of an appropriate policy of recruitment, specially at the pre-primary, primary and elementary stages of teacher preparation, the manpower in the institutions of teacher education does not necessarily possess the professionally required qualifications for the preliminary stages. At the pre-primary stage one comes across teacher educators who have passed high school or higher secondary examination and possess a certificate in teacher training, not necessarily meant for the pre-primary stage; graduates or those with higher qualification with absolutely no training background or with the background not appropriate for that stage or level. As regards the primary and elementary stages, the teacher educators, generally, possess graduate or higher qualification with teacher training mostly at the B.Ed. level. There are serious lacunae in the recruitment policies in as much as the professional qualifications prescribed are not stage-specific and mostly not suited to the education of teachers for the stage or level concerned. This situation calls for fresh thinking regarding recruitment policies for teacher educators and well-planned programmes of education for teacher educators.

Rationale and Objectives

Education and training of teacher educators has to focus its attention on the new role of teacher educators on the problems which reflect the emerging global trends in education and the overall needs and aspirations of the people in India. It has also to deal with specific problems confronting teacher education institutions and to make teacher education more responsible and responsive. It also has to encourage teacher educators' continuing professional growth. In addition, there are certain practical problems as well. For instance , what would be the basic qualifications of teacher educators at various stages of teacher preparation? What would be the requirements in respect of the core education courses and for the organisation of procedures and practices in the institutions. Answers to several of such issues have to be sought in the very rationale of providing professional education.

The rationale behind the education and professional training of teacher educators lies in providing qualitative instruction through well-designed programmes of professional education. The following questions are relevant for designing a programme for education of teacher educators :

- What exactly should the education of teacher educators aim at?
- What are the significant issues and problems concerning the education of teacher educators?
- What are the possible models of both pre-service as well as inservice education of teacher educators?
- What patterns, contents and techniques are envisaged?
- What are the possible agencies and organisations which could be profitably employed in providing continuing abd recurrent inservice education to teacher educators?

Based upon the issues raised above, the following objectives can be comprehensively identified for the programmes of preparation of teacher educators :

- to develop competencies and skills needed for preparation of teachers and teacher educators
- to enable them to organise competency-based and commitment oriented professional programmes
- to enable them to develop pedagogy relevant to the education of teacher educators
- to acquire an understanding of the needs and problems of teacher educators and teacher education institutions
- to develop skills related to management of teacher education institutions
- to develop competencies of curriculum development and preparation of learning and evaluation materials
- to enable teacher educators to acquire capabilities to organise in-service continuing education programmes
- to enable them to organise need-based and commitment oriented on the job training
- to develop competencies for evaluating educational programmes and teaching learning materials
- to develop the capacity of examination, analysis, interpretation, elaboration and communication of educational ideas
- to relate education and the national needs and develop critical awareness about Indian realities
- to enable them to understand the relationship between Indian ethos, modern technology and education
- to promote the global perspective of educational development with special reference to the developing countries.
- to enable them to undertake meaningful educational research.
- to develop the capacities to reinterpret Indian heritage, culture and values to meet the requirements of the present-day Indian society.
- to develop the capabilities for self-directed and life-long learning.
- to enable them to appreciate and adopt emerging communication technology and innovative practices in Indian context.

Evolving Models of Pre-Service Education of Teacher Educators

The present system of pre-service education of teacher educators is characterised by lack of perspective in terms both of contents as well as qualifications. For instance, while it is well accepted that the B.Ed. qualification entitles a person to teach at secondary stage , it is doubtful if the M.Ed. programme adequately prepares a person to become teacher of secondary school teachers.

The existing M.Ed. programme has little provision of training in and working out teaching and evaluation strategies suited to the needs of teacher trainees. And yet one finds M.Ed. degree holders entrusted with the responsibility of teacher preparation not only at secondary stage but also at the pre-primary, primary and elementary stages of teacher preparation.

Likewise, while the B.Ed. qualification legitimately entitles a person to teach at the secondary stage, it cannot, at the same time, be accepted as a good enough qualification for being a teacher educator at the primary stage. The existing B.Ed. programme is designed mainly to teach high school students and not for preparing primary school teacher educators. Thus, it is imperative that the professional qualification of teacher educators is made stage-specific suited to the needs of teacher trainees of different categories.

It is time for seriously considering designing of definite programmes to prepare teacher educators rather than depend on the conventional B.Ed. or/and M.Ed. course. Education of teacher educators has necessarily to correspond to teacher preparation programmes.

It is nonetheless necessary to consider alternatives and institute programmes like M.Ed. (Teacher Education) catering to the needs of stage-specific and category-specific preparation of teacher educators alongside general M.Ed. programmes. M.Ed. (Teacher Education) could be conducted for the following specific categories and areas:

- M.Ed. (Pre-primary)
- M.Ed. (Elementary)
- M.Ed. (Secondary & Sr. Secondary)
- M.Ed. (Special Education)
- M.Ed. (Distance Education)
- M.Ed. (Physical Education)

Existing M.Ed. courses in Indian Universities are by and large academic in nature and not adequately professional in content. In as much as the Master's level courses in Education need to be formulated for making it a professional course, some additional areas of study will have to be introduced with changed orientation.

Curriculum Framework

The course structure in respect of the above alternative M.Ed programmes has to correspond to the course structure of teacher education at various stages and categories.

For instance, the M.Ed (Elementary) programme may comprise the following courses.

- Contemporary Indian Society
- Philosophy of Education
- Educational Sociology, Social and Cultural Anthropology
- Child Psychology including the researches in life and medical sciences having bearing on elementary education and psychology of teaching and learning with reference to child
- Curriculum Development, Transaction and Evaluation
- Comparative Education with reference to developed and developing countries.
- Pedagogical Analysis of School Subjects
- Research Methodology
- Dissertation
- Field Work, Practical and Internship

Coverage, Emphasis and Focus in the Above Courses will be on Elementary Education Sector.

Optional Courses:

- Management, Finance and Planning of Education
- History and Problems of Education
- Educational Technology
- Education of Children with Special Needs
- Alternative Education
- Guidance and Counselling
- Pre-School Education
- Secondary Education

These are some of the areas. More of these could be added. Further, several courses within each area could be devised.

The Course Structure in M.Ed (Pre-Primary) M.Ed (Secondary) etc. be suitably adjusted accordingly with reference to the stage or category concerned.

Strengthening the Programmes

An altogether fresh look is necessary for first developing need-based programmes for the preparation of teacher educators and then working out well planned strategies for implementing these programmes. Needless to say that the preparation of teacher educators would concern itself with the relevant theoretical courses as well as the consonant practicum. At the theoretical level, the choice of pedagogical inputs has to be guided by various contexts and their educational and professional concerns. In addition to theory courses, specialisation courses with reference to teacher education have to be included. The theoretical courses will have a bearing on the practice of teacher education. It will be necessary to develop competencies and skills in prospective teacher educators relating to their work situations. What goes on in teacher training institutions by way of educational programmes and activities has to be reflected in the education and training of teacher educators. It essentially implies that the preparation of teacher educators has to be made an integral part of the system of teacher education.

It will be pertinent to evolve a pedagogy relevant to the stage or category specific programmes. It will lay due emphasis on societal goals, values specially those enshrined in the Indian Constitution, higher order learning processes, curriculum development and theory and practice of educational research including action research. Competence to carry out research and innovations needs to be acquired by all. Training in curriculum development and preparation of learning materials is inalienable aspect of entire process of teacher education. Similarly, development of evaluation materials would result into more effective utilisation of evaluation in teacher education institutions.

The practical work has among other things necessarily to include internship programme by way of attachment to the stage-specific and category-specific teacher education institutions. This will give the prospective teacher educators an adequate knowledge of the total functioning of teacher education institution, the improvements needed and also provide insights into the problems and issues concerning maintenance of institutional plant, classroom management, organisational climate of the institution etc. As for practice teaching, the main thrust has to be on a variety of techniques such as team teaching, micro-teaching, panel discussion, seminar, demonstration, etc. as integral part of classroom-teaching-learning-evaluation procedures. Practical work other than internship and practice teaching has to develop competencies and skills in organising activities concerning work education and working with community as per the practical work requirements in the teacher education institutions.

Thrusts in In-service and Continuing Education

The present provision for continuing education of teacher educators is inadequate in respect of both quality and content. Planning in respect of in-service education of teacher educators needs to be evolved for different stages and levels. The major thrusts in respect of programmes for teacher educators among others, may be as follows:

- Designing short-term programmes for those who are already placed in these institutions.
- Specific short-term induction programmes for those who do not have the experience for the stage they are supposed to be working at.
- Identification of certain university departments of education and Institutions of Advanced Study in Education as institutions which may work mainly for teacher educators. They may focus on induction training, recurrent training, orientation programmes, research studies and surveys, curriculum development, preparation of training materials, evaluation strategies and techniques, use of educational technology, media and others.
- Establishment of institutions for preparation of teacher educators for special education at different stages. These may be open to primary and secondary trained graduates willing to become teacher educators. Such programmes need to be designed with particular focus on the practicum that would familiarize the trainees with school situations in totality.
- Networking of various institutions and organisations for designing and carrying out collaborative programmes by pooling and sharing of resources.

The fact that our education system has inadequate facilities for preparation and orientation of teacher educators has been a major factor for not taking due care of the education and training of teacher educators in several respects. With the policy focus changing to quality and relevance of education, it is necessary that only those, who are professionally competent, committed and willing, are charged with the responsibility of preparing teachers for the nation. Teachers for various stages, levels and categories are prepared professionally by teacher educators. The quality and character of teachers therefore, would largely depend on the professional education of teacher educators.

Towards this, It is necessary, therefore, that their education should be given a new orientation and improved qualitatively and adjusted properly with the demands of the new curriculum.

Managing the System

This Curriculum Framework is characterised, by among other things, ample measure of flexibility and responsiveness to the needs of teacher education system in the country. Teacher education institutions and organisations at various levels will initiate the process of development of curriculum after indepth perusal of this document. The exercise has to be need-based and in tune with demands and directions of the National Policy on Education. The extent of success in implementation would largely depend on the support and assistance provided by the management system.

Imposition of a rigid and uniform management system ignoring the regional variations and cultural diversity of Indian society may not be conducive to achieving the targets of teacher education. Consultative in policy planning and decentralised implementation are bound to be more acceptable and productive. Institutional autonomy for the experimentation of innovative ideas and practices needs to be assured.

This, however, would be possible only if autonomy and corresponding accountability are blended together. Accountability within the system is to be transparently reflected and judged to the extent to which it responds to the regional expectations and requirements. The system need not merely be concerned with the needs of the present but also be dynamic and forward looking.

Objectives

- to contribute effectively in development and promotion of professional efficiency among the teachers and teacher educators.
- to promote the sense of commitment and belongingness.
- to assure optimal utilisation of resources.
- to increase their general awareness about education and society.
- to enhance institutional linkages with other institutions and the society.
- to make the system functional at the optimum level.
- to correlate teacher education and manpower needs.

- to achieve a mutually supportive collaboration with different agencies engaged in human resource development and welfare activities.
- to help and participate in enhancing overall institutional efficacy.

Curriculum Planning: While developing the curriculum of teacher education, disciplinary and professional components need to be interwoven to improve the quality. An attempt of this kind will give it a more meaningful direction. The research findings in the areas of life sciences, anthropology, etc., when included in the curriculum of teacher education, will increase its relevance and make it more functional. The use of indigenous educational thought will enhance its relevance to Indian situation. Various types of dichotomies and misconceptions need to be carefully identified and subsequently weeded out from the content of studies.

The increased duration of the programme of teacher education may be properly utilised for the professional development of teachers. It would also require inclusion of additional inputs of theoretical, pedagogical and practical components and proper allocation of time and resources for improving the quality of teacher education.

Implementation Strategies: Any sudden and abrupt departure from the prevailing practices would only destabilise the existing programme and may prove to be counter-productive. The teachers must be fully exposed to philosophy and purpose of this curriculum framework. A time bound programme for its implementation should be prepared, its priorities be fixed and strategies evolved after careful planning. The gaps of the existing system be identified and removed.

In this document certain alternative models of teacher education have been proposed. It will depend on the concerned organisation/ institutions to select one or the other for implementation after due consideration of its possible professional gains and availability of resources and expertise.

A favourable climate at the national level needs to be created for implementation of the recommendations. Seminars and meetings of teachers, teacher educators, administrative functionaries at the state level will have to be arranged. The regional language versions of this document will be widely circulated. The NGOs working in the field of education and other welfare activities may be involved. The meetings of Education Secretaries, DPIs, Principals of DIETs, Principals of CTEs/IASEs, Directors of SCERTs, Chairmen of Faculties of Education,

Heads of Departments of Education and conveners of the Boards of studies may be arranged. Short term training programme in the form of seminars, workshops, summer schools and orientation courses may be organised. These exercises of awareness generation will prepare institutions, universities, state Govts. bodies and others to evolve specific plans of implementation in their own areas. The NCTE should take the responsibility of assisting in preparation of relevant materials. The professional association of teachers and teacher educators will have to come forward and play a constructive role for upgrading the quality of teacher education. For putting the suggestions into actual practice supplementary materials will be required in the form of teachers' guides, handbooks etc.

Role of the State: Within the educational system, there is a need of creating a separate cadre of teacher educators with an inbuilt provision for upward mobility. Such an arrangement is bound to be more professional. With improved professional competencies they would perform better as supervisors, administrators and policy planners.

Improvement in the standard of teacher education may require additional inputs in terms of money, material and manpower. Arrangements for these will have to be made and the priorities of implementation will have to be fixed. The changes which require no financial involvement should be implemented first. The optimum use of money, men and material be made by curtailing non-academic expenditure. Whenever required, adequate inputs for the professional development of teachers be made available The expenditure on education, particularly on teacher education, is an investment in nation's future.

Institutions willing to launch innovative pre-service, in-service teacher training programmes specially of long duration, should be given financial assistance over a period of time. This special assistance should come from centrally sponsored schemes.

NCTE has been mandated to ensure planned and co-ordinated development of teacher education. Since the task is massive, there is a need to revive the concept of establishment of State Boards of Teacher Education (SBTE). These Boards in close collaboration with SCERTs and NCTE may draw state level long term plans to ensure that:

- Pre-service and in-service becomes mandatory mutually re-enforcing.
- Comprehensive plans are developed for teachers at all levels so that each teacher gets an opportunity to participate in in-

service programmes and undertakes continuing education programmes.

- Multi-channel learning, distance education techniques and communication technologies should be fully utilised.
- Quality study materials be developed and made available to all teacher resource centres.

Curriculum development is a continuous process and demands system approach. Merely by periodic summative evaluations, implementation of curriculum can not be assured. It needs a system view to look at all components simultaneously like curriculum structure, curriculum content, teacher training, support materials and evaluation strategies. Monitoring and feedback should become important segments of the developmental process. Each university or state board needs to evolve micro-level monitoring systems. At some stage meta-level monitoring systems be designed to ensure that quality teacher education is imparted to every serving and prospective teachers and teacher educators.

Need for Vocationalisation of Education in India

Vocational Education and Training (VET) is an important element of the nation's education initiative. In order for Vocational Education to play its part effectively in the changing national context and for India to enjoy the fruits of the demographic dividend, there is an urgent need to redefine the critical elements of imparting vocational education and training to make them flexible, contemporary, relevant, inclusive and creative. The Government is well aware of the important role of Vocational education and has already taken a number of important initiatives in this area.

The objective of this note is to assess and describe the need for introducing Vocational education at higher and tertiary levels and for establishing a Vocational University. The note also summarizes the present Indian and International Vocational Education scenario and its problems. The note also puts up recommendation for policies with the need for implementation at State and National Level and suggests possible models to introduce Vocational Education at the higher / tertiary levels.

Current Scenario of Vocational Education and Training in India

The structure of current education system can be described as below:-

In India, skill acquisition takes place through two basic structural streams – a small formal one and a large informal one.

Status of Vocational Training received: The World Bank report of 2006, shows that among persons of age 15-29 only about 2 per cent reported to have received formal vocational training and another 8 per cent reported to have received non formal vocational training. The proportion of persons (15-29 years) who received formal vocational training was the highest among the unemployed. The proportion was around 3 per cent for the employed, 11 percent for the unemployed and 2 per cent for persons not in the labour force. The activity of persons receiving vocational education is as shown below-:

Comparison with other Countries: There is little capacity in vocational education in India and even that is under-utilized. World Bank Report suggests that the enrolment figure is less than three per cent of the students attending Grades 11-12. This implies that between 350,000 to 400,000 students are enrolled in vocational education, which works out to less than three per cent of the 14 million students or more in Grades 11 and 12, implying that less than one per cent of students who had entered Grade 1 over the last decade or so would have eventually participated in vocational education. In comparison the status in various other countries is as shown below-:

Problem Areas in Present Vocational Education and Training System

Through, the study of the prevalent Vocational Education System in India the following problem areas have been identified -:

1. There is a high drop out rate at Secondary level. There are 220 million children who go to school in India. Of these only around 12% students reach university. A large part of the 18-24 years age group in India has never been able to reach college. Comparing India to countries with similar income levels – India does not under perform in primary education but has a comparative deficit in secondary education.
2. Vocational Education is presently offered at Grade 11, 12th – however students reaching this Grade aspire for higher education. Since the present system does not allow vertical mobility, skills obtained are lost. Enrollment in 11th & 12th Grade of vocational education is only 3% of students at upper secondary level. About 6800 schools enroll 400,000 students in vocational education schemes utilizing only 40% of the available student capacity in these schools.

3. International experience suggests that what employers mostly want are young workers with strong basic academic skills and not just vocational skills. The present system does not emphasize general academic skills. The relative wages of workers with secondary education are increasing.
4. Private & Industry Participation is lacking. There are no incentives for private players to enter the field of vocational education.
5. Present regulations are very rigid. In-Service Training is required but not prevalent today. There is no opportunity for continuous skill up-gradation.
6. There is a lack of experienced and qualified teachers to train students on vocational skills. In foreign countries Bachelors of Vocational Education (BVE) is often a mandatory qualification for teachers. However, in India no specific qualifications are being imparted for Vocational Education teachers.
7. Vocationalization at all levels has not been successful. Poor quality of training is not in line with industry needs.
8. There is no definite path for vocational students to move from one level / sector to another level / sector. Mobility is not defined and hence students do not have a clear path in vocational education.
9. No clear policy or system of vocational education leading to certification / degrees presently available for the unorganized / informal sector. No Credit System has been formulated for the same.

   Over 90% of employment in India is in the Informal sector. JSS offers 255 types of vocational courses to 1.5 million people, Community Polytechnics train about 450,000 people within communities annually and NIOS offers 85 courses through 700 providers. None of these programmes have been rigorously evaluated, till date.
10. Expansion of vocational sector is happening without consideration for present problems.

Trends related to Labour Market

An analysis of the labour market has brought the following issues to the fore-:

1. Labour market requirement for skilled workers without general education skills is declining.

2. Labour force participation is declining while student participation is increasing. Thus more students are joining higher secondary education and looking for vertical mobility.

Government Initiatives

National Vocational Qualification Framework: To stimulate and support reforms in skills development and to facilitate nationally standardized and acceptable, international comparability of qualifications, a "National Vocational Qualifications Framework" is being established by the Central Government.

Central Advisory Board of Education (CABE) has resolved to set up an inter-ministerial group which would also include representatives of State Governments to develop guidelines for such a National Framework.

The unified system of national qualification will cover schools, vocational education and training institutions and higher education sector. NVQF will be based on nationally recognized occupational standards which details listing of all major activities that a worker must perform in the occupation or competency standards – a detailed listing of the knowledge, skills and attitude that a worker should possess to perform a task written by the particular employment-led sector skills council.

The National Skill Development Policy 2009 has proposed the following features for the framework:-

a) Competency based qualifications and certification on the basis of nationally agreed standards and criteria;
b) Certification for learning achievement and qualification;
c) A range of national qualification levels – based on criteria with respect to responsibility, complexity of activities, and transferability of competencies;
d) The avoidance of duplication and overlapping of qualifications while assuring the inclusion of all training needs;
e) Modular character where achievement can be made in small steps and accumulated for gaining recognizable qualification;
f) Quality Assurance regime that would promote the portability of skills and labour market mobility;
g) Lifelong learning through an improved skill recognition system; recognition of prior learning whether in formal, non-formal or informal arrangements;

h) Open and flexible system which will permit competent individuals to accumulate their knowledge and skill through testing & certification into higher diploma and degree;

i) Different learning pathways – academic and vocational – that integrate formal and non-formal learning, notably learning in the workplace, and that offer vertical mobility from vocational to academic learning;

j) Guidance for individuals in their choice of training and career planning;

k) Comparability of general educational and vocational qualifications at appropriate levels;

l) Nationally agreed framework of affiliation and accreditation of institutions;

m) Multiple certification agencies/institutions will be encouraged within NVQF.

Analysis of National Vocational Education Framework in Other Countries

Australia: Australia, a country that has had an NQF for many years, has re-introduced vocational courses into schools (entitled 'VET in Schools') but the courses have been developed as 'foundation' vocational skills already defined and standardized by the Australian National Training Authority, the single tripartite body responsible for training standards.

Level-I Certificates from the VET system are regarded as educationally equivalent to Senior Certificates from secondary schools, and Diplomas and Advanced Diplomas may be issued by the VET system or by higher education institutes. Depending on the courses of study, credits may be allowed to be accumulated as participants choose to move between the three sectors. Some VET certificates may now be issued with little or no formal training, for example, to enterprise workers who have obtained their skills over a number of years on the job.

United Kingdom

The National Qualifications Framework (NQF) in UK is a credit transfer system developed for qualifications in England, Wales, Namibia and Northern Ireland. The Framework has nine levels covering all levels of learning in secondary education, further education, vocational, and higher education. Different qualifications are divided into different levels, according to three important frameworks namely, the National Qualification Framework (NQF), the Qualification and Credit Framework (QCF) and last, but not least, the Framework for Higher Education qualifications.

Proposed Education Model for India

Based on the comparison of various education models across the world, the following education model is recommended for us-:

National Board for Vocational Education

1. A national level Board for vocational education should be established, called as National Board for Vocational Education.

For Example, In Australia, there is a similar authority established by the state and federal government called Australian National Training Authority (structure may vary) which plays a major role in :

a) developing a national TVET system and national strategies with respect to vocational education
b) ensuring close interaction between industries and TVET providers
c) developing effective training market for public and private needs
d) enhancing efficiency and productivity of TVET providers National Vocational Education Policy

2. A National Vocational Policy should be formulated. The policy should establish equivalence for degrees, diplomas and certifications in the vocational education sector for lateral and vertical mobility across various learning sectors that is, secondary, vocational and higher education.

National Vocational Education Assessment and Accreditation Council

3. National Vocational Assessment & Accreditation Council should be established to formulate a regulatory and quality/standards framework.

Introduction of SSC (Vocational)

4. SSC (vocational) or its equivalent 10th grade certification in vocational stream should be created on similar lines as HSC (Vocational) at both national and state level. Vocational Stream should be introduced at 8th Grade through Bivalent Schools which may provide both conventional and vocational stream of education at secondary level. Presently, in India only sporadic

courses as electives are being offered to students under bifocal scheme. However, a separate vocational stream offered by means of bivalent schools does not exist. Statistics reveal that employers prefer students with some general education skills in addition to vocational skills. Thus, in all schemes related to SSC (Vocational) general education courses should be emphasized. Eg. Problem Solving, English, Soft Skills, Business Management etc

For Eg, In China, there are three levels of vocational education: junior secondary, senior secondary and tertiary. Junior vocational education refers to the vocational and technical education after primary school education and is a part of the 9-year compulsory education i.e from age group of 13-15 years.

Credit Banking and Accumulation

In ITI's and ITC's or other vocational education providers, a credit banking system can be established to accumulate required credits in order to grant SSC certificate. This will be especially useful for non-formal and unorganized sectors who do not have any prior formal education. These students in non formal sector may be allowed to take courses worth requisite credit points to obtain SSC Vocational.

In Philippines, the Non-Formal Education - Accreditation and Equivalency (NFE A&E) System enables Filipinos who are unable to avail education through the formal school system or who have dropped out of formal school, obtain elementary and secondary education. NFE A&E test is a standardized paper- and pencil-based test featuring multiple-choice questions based on the expected learning outcomes articulated in the five learning strands of the NFE A&E Curriculum framework which enables students to obtain secondary level certification.

Lateral/Vertical Mobility

5. To ensure vertical mobility, ITIs, MSBVs, Community Colleges and other State Vocational Education Institutions may be granted recognition and accreditation from the respective State Board for Vocational Education to award SSC (Vocational) certification. Vocational Education Providers, Community Colleges, JSS, CP's, Vocational Junior Colleges may also be allowed to award Diplomas and Associate Degrees in addition to HSC (Vocational) certification. Students from Vocational Institutions can be given opportunity for lateral mobility into

conventional stream by providing bridge (preparatory) courses. The proposed mobility structure is as indicated below-:

Industrial Participation

7. Private Participation from Industry and other players must be encouraged and is critical for the success of the vocational education growth in India. Industry participation must be at all levels especially in Governance, Curriculum Design, Placements and Funding, Monitoring Outcome. Industry participation is also required for creating production oriented Research and Innovation Labs. A PPP Model can be also created where GOI and Industry can come together to invest in infrastructure and train students in latest skills

For Example, Penang Skills Development Centre is a joint company training centre. The Government invests in the centre and uses it to carry out public training programmes. The State provided the infrastructure and the industry partners donate equipment, labs, training modules and trainers. Industry thus has access to shared training facilities for in-service employees training. The Government uses the centre as a training institute.

In India, National Skill Development Corporation India (NSDC) is a one of its kind, Public Private Partnership in India. It aims to promote skill development by catalyzing creation of large, quality, for-profit vocational institutions. Three business models established till date are as under-:

B-Able - Tie ups with corporate like L&T and Tata dealers have been established. Six centres providing classroom training and guaranteed 4 week apprenticeship with a prospective employers have been established.

Gram Tarang - Targeting tribal/naxal affected areas. 4 training centres created to train people in Auto CAD, advanced welding on advance machinery funded by NSDC.

8. Teachers training is an important aspect for ensuring quality education in vocational stream. Vocational Educational Qualifications should be insisted (eg. BVE). Higher salaries must be offered to attract skilled teachers. Additional income incentive can also be given through in-service training programmes which can be conducted by teachers for industry employees. Continuous skill development and up-gradation of teachers can be done through Teachers Training Programmes conducted by Teacher Training Centres

Salient Features of a Vocational University

1. A Society registered under the Societies Registration Act, 1860 (Central Act No. 21 of 1860); or Any Public Trust registered under the State Public Trusts Act, or the Indian Trusts Act, 1882 (Central Act No. 2 of 1882) or under the relevant laws in any other State or Union Territory or a Company registered under Sec 25 Companies Act 1956. The University may be established by State Government or by Private players (self-financed)
2. Land, construction and infrastructure requirement may focus on the need for creation of production oriented labs, training centres, innovation/testing labs, latest industry specific equipment etc.
3. Authorities of the University shall have active Industry participation. The administers of the University must have industrial experience.
4. Vocational University will offer all kinds of degree and diploma programmes in vocational higher education sector (Bachelor, Masters, Doctoral) – New Degrees should be created eg. Bachelors in Vocational Studies

For example, In Germany, some of the examples of vocational degrees offered by Vocational Universities are as under-:

(a) Bachelor in Automotive engineering, Clothing design by Berlin School of Applied Sciences (HTW),

(b) Bachelor of Jewellery and Objects of Daily Life by Pforzheim University of Applied Sciences.

(c) Bachelor of Motor Vehicle Industry, Bachelor of Printing and Media by Munich University of Applied Sciences

(d) Bachelor of Arts in Facilities Air Conditioning by Biberach University of Applied Sciences.

5. Vocational University will emphasize on a different teaching – learning pedagogy with a special focus on skill based and hands-on learning and training. Vocational University may offer vocational programmes through online, distance and life-long learning mode.
6. Vocational University Curriculum will emphasize life coping skills and general educational skills such as Liberal arts subjects, English competency, entrepreneur skills, problem solving, team work, leadership, management courses etc.

7. Vocational Education Junior Colleges offering HSC (Vocational), Agencies / Community Colleges offering Associate Degrees or Diplomas may be given affiliation to the Vocational University to provide entry into the Bachelors Programmes.
8. The University shall have a well defined Credit Banking and Transfer System. The Credit System will allow multi-entry and multi-exit to students. The Credit System will also enable students to pursue opportunity for life-long learning and skill development.

For example, in Scotland, the Scottish Credit and Qualification Framework (SCQF) is a credit framework that promotes mobility and credit transfer within and between sectors of learning. Similarly, in UK, the National Vocational Qualification Framework simplifies credit transfer between different awarding bodies, especially for vocational qualifications.

9. Industry participation shall be sought on the Board of Management. Industry representatives will be involved in governance and curriculum design. Production oriented Research and Innovation Labs will be setup in collaboration with Industry to promote regional economic growth. Industry collaboration shall be sought for funding, placements and apprenticeship for students. Department of In-Service Training shall be setup to encourage industry to send employees for regular skill development and up-gradation (this will also gain additional income for teachers).
10. Teachers training will be given special emphasis by the University. The Vocational University will setup a separate department for Teachers Training and Development in order to build teaching resources and research component. Continuous teacher training programmes shall be emphasized by the University Management. A separate degree called Bachelor in Vocational Education (B.V.Ed) or B.Ed with specialization in vocational education is proposed to be introduced. This would be a mandatory requirement for hiring teachers for vocational education and training.

For Example, In United States, Bachelor of Vocational Education degrees are offered for teachers teaching vocational courses. In Sri Lanka, Research Cell of University of Vocational Technology has carried out research study on "Contribution of Instructional Resource Development programmes in improving Teaching & Learning environment of TVET Centres"

Conclusion: The industrial and labour market trends clearly indicate the necessity of strengthening of vocational education in India. The introduction of vocational education at secondary level through bivalent schools and SSC (vocational) will enable us to broaden the vocational education base at secondary level of education. A clear pathway for vocational students to enter higher education streams is the way to move forward. Through this concept note we have made an endeavour to provide some of the possible solutions to address these issues. Framing of vocational qualification framework, introduction of vocational degrees and setting up of a Vocational University with polytechnics, community colleges, CPs and other VEPs as affiliated colleges are some of the recommendations which require further deliberation at National and State level.

Importance of Vocational Education in India

One of the weaknesses of Indian education system is that it does not gives due importance to vocational education. As a result there is a mismatch between the skilled manpower required and skilled manpower available. Every year, various colleges churn out millions of graduates who do not have the specific skill sets required by the market. This has resulted in a situation where on the one hand there are scores of unemployed graduates and on the other hand there is a huge shortage of skilled workers such as plumbers, electricians, etc.

To rectify this situation vocational training programmes need to be promoted in a big way. This may include secretarial practices, computer operator and programme assistant, library assistant, architectural draughtsman ship, desktop publishing, electrical technician, electronics mechanic, refrigeration and air conditioning, plumbing, tailoring and dress making, hair and skin care, fruit and vegetable preservation programmes, etc.

In fact, education is useless if it does not make people fit for a livelihood. While educational institutes have increased by leaps and bounds since Independence, many products of these institutes are found to be not even capable of earning a livelihood. This is the result of bad and haphazard planning on the part of the educationists. Educational institutions have failed to lay any stress on the quality of the education that they impart, or the subjects they teach. These institutes still follow the subjects of study introduced in our curriculum by the British rulers which have lost their significance for us today being free Indians. Hence, there is a bankruptcy of achievement by our educated children.

Besides a lop-sided curriculum, our primary education has been neglected which has led to a vacuum in the basic literacy standards. As a result colleges turn out plain and simple graduates and postgraduates who are absolutely unemployable when they come out of their colleges. Hence, instead of increasing the numbers of colleges for general studies, it would be better to introduce more of vocational centres and institutes for the large number of children coming out of schools.

At present, vocational educational in India aims to develop skilled manpower through diversified courses to meet the requirements of mainly the unorganized sector and to instill self-employment skills in people through a large number of self employment oriented courses. Vocational education is being imparted through Industrial Training Institutes (ITIs) and polytechnics. However, this has to start at school level itself. When children leave school, they should posses some skill which can be further developed and they can get a job based on that skill. Students can be taught skills like painting, drawing, and clay modelling etc., as a part of the syllabus.

They could have it as an extra-curricular activity which they would enjoy and at the same time get groomed for the skill. These children, as they enter college they can start learning repair and mechanical jobs etc. This process would enable the students to develop some skills and also show their aptitudes. For these children college would be their vocational centre. These centres could, at a higher level also give degrees or diplomas in the skills of the study.

The entire educational system has to be built in a manner that will guarantee to the children a basic livelihood, once they come out after completing their education. Once the students get vocational education, their main aim of getting employment will be fulfilled and many a problems would be solved. It will be good for the country also, for the masses of the young will be in a position to join the mainstream of nation building as soon as they come out of their education outfit.

Today, the economy's the world over are changing into knowledge based economies. This changing face of technology the world over requires an individual to be specialized in a particular skill. Only a person who is expert in a particular field can get a good job. Vocational education training institutes impart specialized and practical knowledge to a person and help them become independent at a particular age. Vocational education training can be provided for a number of courses like health, technical, art, administration and other courses. These subjects can be further classified into specialized courses. For example, health can be divided into massage therapy, dieticians, and nutritionist. Any person can select any course of his choice and inclinations.

Vocational education training should be such that even working people can join the course, and even select the timings as per their convenience and nature of job. The vocational institutes should also allow the students to study online and attend either evening or morning classes. Moreover, financial aid should also be provided to students who are economically weak.

The faculty of these Vocational education training institutes should be highly experienced and be able to impart practical knowledge to their students. As a result the students should be able to have a real life and practical industry experience. The students may also be provided with internships and stipend for motivation to perform better and excel in their jobs. Doing their job under the supervision of an expert would be a great learning experience for them as it would help them perform better in their job. For working professionals it would be a way to hone their skills while making money.

As a precautionary measure, appropriate and necessary rules should be framed by the central and state Governments. Vocational training institutes should be required to follow the rules or else their recognition should be cancelled. Similarly, it should be necessary that a student fulfils the eligibility criteria of the training institute. The procedure of getting admission into any vocational institute should be very simple and easy.

Care should be taken to regularly update the course structure of the training institutes because the technology and the fundamentals of economy are changing very rapidly. In the present scenario, providing practical knowledge based on the old concepts do not make sense.

Scope of Vocational or Technical Education in India

Technology is touching every aspect of life and society. So, there is a dire need of backing up conventional study and teaching with technical education, as it will not only help in the development of the country, but also the person possessing those skills. A technically sound person is never short of jobs. Thus, technical education as per the needs of the present market will assist in uplifting society. Technical education is a part of education that is directly related to the gaining of information and skills needed in manufacturing and service industries.

In India, overall education can be divided into social, spiritual and vocational. Concerns related to society are covered under social education, personality development is the part of spiritual education and vocational education consists of technical education that further deals with branches like agriculture, medicine, engineering and commerce. Technical education is a skill-based education that primarily keeps the job prospects in mind. It provides training to the individual in a specific field

For acquiring technical education, there are two structural streams in India – formal and informal. Polytechnics, Industrial Training Institutes (ITIs), Industrial Training Centres (ITCs), Centrally Sponsored Scheme of Vocationalisation of Secondary Education by the Ministry of Human Resource Development are few of the formal sources of technical education in India. Whereas self-learning and small private institutes providing short term technical course are covered under informal ones.

In the past few decades, India has seen a mushrooming of many small to medium technology-based enterprises because of the easy availability of labour. Though students are opting these formal technical institutes for training but interest of students in these institutes is quite less in India. Also the rate of enrollment in these vocational institutes is very low, as there is a high drop rate at secondary level in India. Vocational training is given in class 11 and 12, but students who reach at this level focus on higher education rather than technical training. Moreover, employers look for candidates with strong academic record rather than just having a vocational training. Training institutes too lack trained staff and teachers. Most of the teachers who impart basic technical training are not well qualified. Also, we do not have quality institutions in India for technical education. Then the lack of interest and interaction from industry is another big challenge for the growth of technical education in India. Also, less emphasis is given on skill up-gradation during employment in India.

To overcome these hurdles, old curriculum must be updated with a new and advanced one. Also, new institutes must be set in to provide advance information regarding this field. Classes should be more interesting and interactive with full industry participation. Students must be made aware of their growth path in the selected stream. It is not that our education system is full of flaws. We have a rich educational heritage and a very strong primary education system. Subject knowledge is extensively given in India, and Indians have vast theoretical knowledge as well. As compared to developed countries,

India has a good number of higher educational institutions. But on the other hand, lack of an updated curriculum and specialized technical education are the flaws in our education system. Teachers do not play any role in addition to teaching. Once these hurdles are crossed, growth in technical education can be seen in India.

Historical Background of Technical Education in India

With British rule came the establishment of technical centres in India as they needed skilled labour for constructing roads, buildings and for other such works. Also, there was a requirement of skilled artisans and craftsmen to help the British army. Though superintending engineers, foremen and artificers were hired from Britain, skilled craftsmen were hired locally for all other low grade jobs. To improve their efficiency, they were given basic lessons in writing, reading, geometry and mechanics.

Also with the industrial revolution, the importance of technical education was felt because it brought the need of operating machines and completing the task skillfully within a short span of time. So, the perspective towards education started to change. Education in India that earlier used to focus more on personality development than skill was now focusing on the latter.

Though technical schools were present in Calcutta and Bombay even during 1825, an industrial school was established at Guindy, Madaras in 1842. To train civil engineers, the first engineering college was established in 1847 in Uttar Pradesh. In November 1856, the Calcutta College of Civil Engineering was established in Bengal. After a year, its name was changed to the Bengal Engineering College. With time and need, more and more such colleges came into existence in India. Great need of all kinds of engineers was felt after independence, so a number of engineering colleges were established keeping this in mind.

Government Initiatives

The Central Government has established the National Vocational Qualification Framework for motivating skill development. The basis of the National Vocational Qualification Framework are the nationally recognized occupational standards. For the proper functioning of the Framework, the National Skill Development Policy 2009 has proposed many features such as certification of learning, national qualification levels, quality assurance, lifelong learning, open and flexible system, framework of affiliations and accreditation, multiple certification agencies, etc.

New industrial and labour trends in India have clearly specified the need of vocational and technical education. But the base of technical education must be made strong at secondary level of education and a clear-cut path for the students to move ahead in this field must be made. More vocational and technical degrees of high quality along with vocational universities must be established.

Importance of Vocational Training in Indian Educational Scenario

In India, every year thousands of graduates are produced and most of them do not have the specific skills required by the market. If this trend continues for a long time, our economic growth would soon be hampered. To prevent this situation, it is very important for us to change our mindset first. In India, people are obsessed with just achieving a graduation degree without thinking about the nation's long-term growth and development. This has led to a situation where, on the one hand, there are a number of unemployed graduates and on the other hand, there is a huge shortage of skilled workers in the market.

In the previous times, vocational courses were thought to be meant for the people who were lacking aptitude to study in a college and thus, needed skills in a particular field, to gain employment. This scenario, however, does not exist anymore in today's world. In the recent years, people have realized the importance of Vocational Education and Training (VET) and are opting for such courses to enrich their skills related to a particular sphere to face career challenges easily.

Vocational Education and Training is an important aspect of the nation's educational system. It offers specialized and practical knowledge to an individual in a particular field by having an in-depth study of the specific subject. It also helps one in preparing to get the desired job for a successful career. Vocational education basically comprises of practical courses through which one attains skills and experience directly linked to a career in future. Vocational training offers the student a fast-track education which gives way to job opportunities and growth in the existing workplace. Thus the student gets a job faster and becomes capable of becoming a responsible citizen of the society instead of an unproductive burden.

The aim of vocational education is to equip students with all the practical knowledge and social skills necessary for them to take on a productive role in the economy, by training for a specific career or business. It is also an essential tool to educate the employees for better performance and to earn profitable outcomes.

Who Can Opt for Vocational Courses?

There is no age boundary in acquiring this type of knowledge. In India, vocational training is open to students, who leave school after 10th or 12th standards. After completing the school, choosing a career-specific training would be a better idea than just simply going for a regular four-year degree programme.

Vocational Training V/S College Degree

VET is very different from the traditional way of learning as it does not follow the simple teaching format. In traditional courses, wide array of courses are taught and most of which are not directly related to the goal of the individual.

Students are realizing that their regular college education does not equip them with the adequate communication and practical knowledge which is essential to perform well in their professions. The current education system focuses more on providing theoretical knowledge, which is not enough for the young student to start his/ her career and succeed in it. Even after a three year graduation, the youth often has to spend considerable amount of time in hunting for jobs, which becomes very frustrating. Just earning degrees does not make one educated. Rather, the person must have an in-depth knowledge of the concerned subject which is easily possible through vocational education.

The Basics of Vocational Education Training

- Vocational training in India is provided on a full time as well as part time basis.
- India is a pioneer in vocational training in Film & Television, and Information Technology.
- Often the curriculum for the courses is prepared after taking suggestions from the local employers.
- These type of courses are mostly certified or diploma courses.
- Vocational education training institutes impart graduation and post graduation courses to students.
- The best part of these institutes is that even working people can join the course, and even select the timings as per their convenience and nature of job.

- Financial aid is also often provided to students who are economically weak.
- According to the NSDC (National Skills Development Commission) report India will need 83 million skilled workers across different industry verticals by 2015. Unfortunately with our current training capacity India will produce only 3 million!!
- In India, vocational education is imparted through Industrial Training Institutes (ITIs) and polytechnics.
- The skill shortage in the Indian economy today is largely due to neglect of vocational education

Methods of Teaching in Vocational Courses

Along with classroom instructions, practical knowledge is also imparted through field work. This prepares the student for the job at hand and thus, he is able to give full justice to his profession, due to his vast knowledge. Vocational schools give plenty of hands-on training, so that the individual already gets some experience of his/her future profession. The students have a real life and practical industry experience. They are also often provided with internships along with stipend for their internships. This gives them the motivation to perform better and excel in their jobs.

Benefits of Vocational Training

- Enhances skills and knowledge – vocational education provides job specific skills and contributes to career success. It imparts specialized knowledge, which is the need of the hour today!
- Promotes entrepreneurship – In certain cases, the completion of this sort of course provides the learner with a license to allow them to start working immediately. The individual is also equipped enough to start his own business.
- Offers a wide range of options – It prepares the youth for a vocation of their own choice and interest by providing a diverse range of subjects.
- Builds up a formidable work force of international quality, which would be in demand not only in India but also in all other countries. In India, only IT training is world class. In the manufacturing and service sector, there is worldwide shortage.
- Demand for skilled men – A recent study by global HR consultancy Manpower Inc says that 41 per cent of employers worldwide are having difficulty filling positions due to lack of suitable talent in their markets. We need millions of trained

people in agriculture, floriculture, horticulture, sericulture, fishery, healthcare, tourism and in other manufacturing sectors.

- Easy employment – It is often seen that employers prefer to hire a student who has done a vocational course rather than a college pass out, as by doing a vocational course, a student is trained specifically for a particular job. Thus, the student gets a job faster, is able to support & provide for his family and self, becoming a responsible citizen of the society instead of an unproductive burden.
- A way to earn early – With the changing face of technology, the world requires an individual to be specialized in a particular skill. Only a person who is expert in a particular field can get a good job. Vocational education training helps them to become independent at a particular age. After completing a vocational course, the student already possesses the right temperament, skills, qualities and education for the job.
- Helps to develop the economy – Vocational Training provides an instrument for the promotion of worker employability through the enhancement of human capital and for productivity improvement and competitiveness at the level of the firm or nation. Manpower shortages can cripple economic growth. It can escalate wage rates, thereby reducing the competitiveness of the country.
- Reduces unemployment by supplying world-class skilled people. Vocational courses increase the number of small businesses, which further increase employment, thus reducing the stress on the government to provide jobs for the unemployed.
- Serves as an alternative to those who cannot afford to take a three-year break to pursue a college degree. The time duration for a vocational course is less and the skills which are imparted to the students are highly adequate.
- Lesser education costs – It is the most effective way to gain the right career resources in exchange of minimum amount which costs much less than the regular forms of learning in colleges. Many vocational courses provide placement to the students. This makes it quite useful for those who do not have the means to shell out money for a college degree.
- Flexible form of learning – They are often provided by various community colleges with proper learning infrastructure. Some organizations also use online education system to help students

learn at their own convenience. It is suitable for working people also as they can select the timings as per their convenience and nature of job. The vocational institutes allow the students to study online and attend either evening or morning classes.

- Financial aids are also readily available from various public and private sectors for these types of courses. Government funding is also offered to students of vocational training in certain countries
- Contributes to national development – Enhancing the employability of a student is extremely important since it will not only help in youth empowerment, but also contributes to national development.
- More practical-oriented – Vocational courses offer the students not just classroom learning but also hands-on practical training in various aspects like customer relationship, people management, personality development etc. are in top demand now.
- Offers a wide range of job opportunities – Retail, Hospitality & BFSI are the fastest growing sectors and would need 20 million skilled candidates by 2015. Specialized sectors like Auto and Hair & Beauty are projected to need 5 million resources while the Construction sector alone will require over 15 million skilled workers.
- Helps in promoting education – There is a high dropout rate at Secondary level. Comparing India to countries with similar income levels – India does not under perform in primary education but has a comparative deficit in secondary education. This can be prevented by introducing flexible and cheaper ways of vocational training.
- The faculty is highly experienced – A separate degree called Bachelor in Vocational Education (B.V.Ed) or B.Ed with specialization in vocational education is proposed to be introduced.

Vocational Training and Courses

Due to rapid development in science, technology and business practices, one has many options to choose from, such as:

- Art and design: Computer animation, computer aided design, video game design and web design

- Automotive Courses: Aviation technology, diesel mechanic and marine mechanic
- Business: Administrative assistance, accounting, bookkeeping and E-business
- Healthcare: Massage therapy, dietitian and nutritionist

Role of the Government

According to a National Sample Survey Organization (NSSO) report two types of vocational trainings are available in India:

a) Formal - Formal vocational training follows a structured training programme and leads to certificates, diplomas or degrees, recognized by State/Central Government, Public Sector and other reputed concerns.

b) Non-formal – Non-formal vocational training helps in acquiring some marketable expertise, which enables a person to carry out her/his ancestral trade or occupation.

The Government is well aware of the important role of Vocational education and has already taken a number of important initiatives in this area. Government funding is also offered to students of vocational training in certain countries.

Choosing a Suitable Vocational Training Institution

One can choose from both online and campus options for vocational training. Before opting for a vocational course, a student should ensure that the institute in which he/she is applying is a reputed one, both in terms of the quality of the education provided and placements in the past. For this purpose, the person can research on the internet and also talk to friends who have done such courses. The institute should have accreditation that is recognized by the industry. This will ensure that the course is reliable. Only when these things are settled, a student should invest his time and money in a particular course. It would also be more beneficial if the institute is a government recognized one.

Conclusion

Vocational Training and Education (VET) is a sure way to add a new dimension to the career for a successful future. These courses enhance the employability of a student and are vital as they not only help in youth empowerment, but also contribute to national development. Today, it has become important for employees in every sector

Vocational courses must be seen as a necessary addition to the regular school or graduate education, since the college education will only provide knowledge enhancement while the vocational courses gives training to get a job and start a successful career. Vocational courses can also be incorporated in regular college environment, wherein the students will have easier access to the skills, training and can complete the course easily along with his graduation. Vocational education is also as good as college education!

Vocational training can be considered as a launch pad for a career that can lead to participants becoming masters in their field. Vocational training is a must and should be compulsory as it provides the learner with practical knowledge of the theoretical concepts learned in school. Vocational training should be considered as a stepping stone to success. This type of knowledge is surely going to be an enabler to help India shine in the future years.

6

Importance of Vocational Training in Generating Employment

Despite the fact that the Indian economy has witnessed a considerable growth in the last two decades, this growth rate has not been uniform. Underemployment, low educational levels, a high rate of dropouts and lack of proper vocational training which can provide better employment opportunities, are still prevalent. The shortage of skilled workforce is evident from the discrepancies of demand and supply in the market.

According to the reports of a Boston Consulting Group, India will have a surplus of 56 million working people while the global shortage of skilled working people will be 47 million by 2020. With a 'demographic dividend' of more than 50% of the population within the age bracket of 25, the 11th Five Year Plan identified the potential of India emerging as an important global entity in skill development. Currently only 10% of the youth population has proper vocational training. Realizing the importance of proper vocational training and skill development programmes, the 11th Five Year Plan established the PM's National Council for Skill Development (for framing policies), the National Skill Development Coordination Board (for coordinating the various skill development programmes), and finally the National Skill Development Agency (NSDA – a catalyst to enhance the skill development programmes).

Later the PM's Council and the Coordination Board had been absorbed in NSDA, which is now empowered to serve as the flagship for countrywide skill development programmes undertaken by the Government. The 12th Five Year Plan outlines strategies for further improving the vocational training programmes at both the Centre and State levels.

Important Vocational Training

Some Important Vocational Training Programmes Undertaken by the Government

Craftsmen Training Scheme (Cts): Under the Ministry of Labour and Employment, the CTS aim at providing vocational training to the school leavers and educated youths (so that they can meet the industrial requirements). There are separate reservations for the SC/STs, physically handicapped and women.

Modular Employable Skill (Mes) Based Training Programmes: Under the Ministry of Labour and Employment, MES has been designed specifically through consultation with the Industries and backed by the opinions of the experts in the field of vocational training. MES aims at providing a 'minimum skill set' that is just sufficient to gain entry in the employment sector. MES is an extremely flexible programme with the objective of providing vocational training to the school leavers, ITI graduates etc., to increase their chances of employment through optimal utilization of the existing infrastructures of the Government, private sector and the industries.

National Rural Livelihoods Mission (Nrlm)/Aajeevika: The objective of this scheme is to harness the capabilities of the rural poor population by supplementing them with knowledge, skill sets, tools and finance so that they can have proper livelihood options. The primary target of this scheme is to deliver market driven skill training to the rural BPL youths in the age bracket of 18 to 35 years and provide placement in suitable sectors.

National Urban Livelihood Mission (Nulm): An integral part of the SWARNA JAYANTI SHAHARI ROZGAR YOJANA (SISRY) under the Ministry of Housing and Urban Poverty Alleviation, NULM's objective is to provide the urban poor with proper vocational training so that they can undertake self-employment and increase their chances of employment in different sectors. The primary target of this project is the urban poor population below poverty line with special reservations for the SC/ST and women. A special 3% reservation is also there for the physically challenged.

Support To Training and Employment Programme (Step): Under the Ministry of Women and Child Development, STEP aims at upgrading skills of women converting them into viable assets for employment. This programme also provides placements for women and access to credit facilities. Other than that this programme has a complete package of support services, awareness generation, gender sensitization, educational programmes, nutrition and nutrition oriented awareness programme, legal literacy including day care facilities for dependent children.

Parvaaz: It provides comprehensive vocational training and education programme for the rural below poverty line (BPL) areas. Operating under the Ministry of Rural Development, the primary objective is to include the BPL youths, minority youths especially school dropouts/left outs in the mainstream by providing them with a platform through extensive vocational training and educational programmes and employment opportunities.

Rural Self Employment Training Institutes (Rseti): The main objective of the RSETIs is to provide the rural BPL youths with free and unique, intensive, short term, residential, self employment training programmes, which includes free food and accommodation so that they can undertake micro enterprises and wage-based employment.

Polytechnics: Operating under the Ministry of HRD, Polytechnics provide three years diploma courses in conventional disciplines like civil, electrical and mechanical engineering and also on the emerging disciplines like electronics and computer science. The minimum eligibility is secondary level. Employment oriented curriculum is being implemented in the Polytechnics. A new plan of setting up of 300 new polytechnics is currently underway.

Tool Rooms: 10 such MSME tool rooms have been set up with Indo-German and Indo-Danish collaborations. Tool Rooms offer short term courses on manufacturing of quality tools to the school dropouts to assist the MSMEs. Long term courses like 'Post Graduate Diploma on Tool Designing and CAD/CAM' are also available. The Tool Rooms have achieved almost 100% placement with their long term course trainees in different industries.

Udaan: Funded by the Ministry of Home Affairs, UDAAN is specially designed for Jammu and Kashmir, aiming at training 40,000 students in 5 years in various sectors including retail, IT and BPO.

There are other Government endeavours like ROSHNI and vocational training programmes, exclusively designed for the rural youths of the Left Wing Extremism affected areas of India.

Challenges likely to be faced by the vocational training programmes undertaken by the Government as per the 12th Five Year Plan:

- Expansion of the various projects in remote and difficult areas through E-Learning, Internet and simulation packages
- Setting up of vocational training centres in underdeveloped areas
- Designing market oriented projects and extensive promotion of public private partnership
- Introducing AADHAR based tracking of the beneficiaries in pre and post placement programmes
- Revamping the entire Employment Exchange Network to function as an effective human resource development centres
- Increase credibility of the certification procedure and streamlining it to avoid delays in granting certificates
- A strict monitoring of the funds released under various schemes and projects to ensure their proper utilization and avoiding any misappropriation

The target of the 12th Five Year Plan is to create 50 million employment opportunities in the non agricultural sector with an equivalent supply of skilled manpower by the end of the plan. As evident from the above discussions, the ball has been set rolling. The Indian Bank has formulated an educational loan scheme for the underprivileged which is planned to cover tuition fee, exam fee, caution deposits, etc. The loan amount may vary from Rs 20,000 to Rs 1.5 lakh for a course of duration of more than one year. However, a more aggressive persuasion on the part of the Government is essential to generate 50 million work opportunities at the end of the 12th Five Year Plan.

Challenges of Vocational Education in North East India"Role of IGNOU Institute for Vocational Education and Training (IIVET)

The challenges of Vocational education in an Open University like ours are many and impinge upon the very mechanisms and methodologies of a Distance Education and Open University such as IGNOU. These are: technology aided instruction, the use of broadcasts, telecasts and the internet for delivery services. However, in vocational education and, training face to face mode of instruction and especially skill based activities have also to be emphasized.

Vocational education has to be viewed from different multi-layered practices. One is of course the hands on training component. The other is employment generation and sustainability, whether the training programmes or courses can lead to employment/self employment. If so there has to be follow up measures to see what the participants in a vocational training programme have achieved and whether there has been a progress in terms of employability and income generation. Also, whether any industry has employed any participant, especially when there has been in plant or in house training. Another perspective of VET is studying a course on vocational education in a college or a university with the hope that the certificate will lead to an acquisition of jobs. The industry-education alliance which is gradually becoming a force in the country, one reckons that this will play a significant role in the future, what with a Skills Development Council being set-up under the aegis of and with the active support of the CII, will also, I hope, shape future events in this regard.

Skill development is one of the components and outcome of VET but training programmes should also concentrate on unskilled workers thereby giving them an opportunity to learn and earn. The unorganized sector is also a catchment resource in areas such as retailing, marketing and micro businesses.

The history of VET is not very sanguine in India especially as EDPs and allied training programmes have not been followed up. Simply leaving a participant with a certificate to fend for himself/herself has added to the plethora of the unemployed. However, with the Govt. of India's accent on the Public Private Partnership model, one can only hope that such tie-ups will give a prod to the conscience of the industry and corporate houses, especially with Corporate Social Responsibility being such a major issue of debate today internationally, notwithstanding the polemic on ethics and CSR.

In North East India there are hardly any industrial houses worth the name and the local industry in terms of agro based products and raw material remain untapped, the potential being exploited by middlemen. Jute, rubber, bamboo and cane, ginger, turmeric are grown in the different states but how are these to be encapsulated as micro units to generate employment? The other business houses which have come to the region are basically setting up franchisee units in mobile phones, internet connection, computer courses etc. all for marketing strategies and the youth who are employed look unsettled and are trying constantly to search for better opportunities.

Coming again to the context of the Region, indigenous knowledge such as weaving, textile making, music and the arts, performing arts, the oral tradition, medicinal plants can be brought into the gamut of trades. But with the increasing modernization and the technological wave many of such indigenous methods are on the verge of becoming extant. One can only strive for a revival. How many will remember the duitara musical instrument of the Khasis? Technology has no doubt led to the creation of a global community, one world, but it has exacerbated to the tension between the local and the global. Local needs are to be addressed perforce as community needs especially in a country with low literacy rates. Compared to the literacy of the country, the literacy of North East India is fairly better, thanks to the Mizoram boom and this could be a marginal advantage. Yet literacy levels for women are strikingly low in some states and it is here that vocational education training programmes can intervene as basic literacy programmes to earn livelihoods.

Livelihoods have also to do with living in good if not salutary conditions. Floods in Assam every year are cataclysmic but precious little is done to take long standing measures to combat this problem. Flood control management % how to live intelligently with floods, could well serve vocational and training needs of the common populace who finally bear the brunt of such disasters.

VET in the North East Region can be integrated into a whole, a complex process since we have to trace it to components of agriculture and the current despair of the educated unemployed or even the plumber or the technicians eking out a living. This is of course true of the entire country but in a Region where industrial development is in backwaters then education is a strength with the presence of some very good academic institutions in the Region. These institutions should come forward in partnership whether they are general colleges or professional colleges to re-appraise vocational education in the context of the small industries and local habits mentioned above. More than having vocational education courses, short term training programmes will benefit the people keeping in mind the changing order of the 'world' market such as repair of mobiles and computer hardware.

IGNOU's intervention into the area of VET in the form of the establishment of the IGNOU Institute for Vocational Education and Training (IIVET) could well be a benchmark for revival (indigenous knowledge) and survival (linking such knowledge with trades) as well as looking into contemporary realities and needs keeping in mind the training factor. The target group is the youth in particular and the public in general, taking also into cognizance rural women. And of course the oeuvre of distance education technology is always there as a ready support system.

Vocationalisation of Education in India: Current Scenario, Key Challenges and New directions

Gandhi's Philosophy of Education: *"Every handicraft has to be taught not merely mechanically as is done today, but scientifically. This is to say, the child should learn the why and wherefore of every process".*

The greatest challenge in Indian education system today is to provide skill based education to the youth. This is exacerbated by a mismatch in demand and supply for the skilled workforce. The penetration of vocational education and training remains poor not only in rural areas, but also in urban regions where there is a higher installed capacity to impart the same. This post is an attempt to make the readers understand the need of vocational education in India. Also, this is a fumbling first attempt to summarise a few recommendations on the same.

A recent survey (61st round) conducted by the NSSO found that:

1. The percentage of population that completed primary education was 70%, but less than 10% went on to complete a graduation course and above. Almost 97% of individuals in the age bracket of 15–60 years had limited exposure to technical education, which is another indicator of low skills sets among Indians.
2. According to the occupational profile of India's workforce, 90% of the workforce population is employed in skill-based jobs, whereas more than 90% had no exposure to vocational education or training even though more than half of the seats remain unutilised in vocational education.
3. There is a lack of training facilities and skills development in as many as 20 high-growth industries such as logistics, healthcare, construction, hospitality and automobiles.
4. India has roughly close to 5,500 public (ITI) and private (ITC) institutes as against 500,000 similar institutes in China. As against India's 4% formally trained vocational workers, country like Korea had 96% vocationally trained workforce. Even relatively under-developed countries like Botswana had a surprisingly decent score of 22%.

Trends in the Labour Market: Over the past decades, there has been a gradual decline in the labour force market for skilled workers that do not possess higher educational degrees. Today's industrial sector demands workers to possess at least a graduation degree in addition to vocational training. A diploma holder undergoing vocational training desires vertical mobility and hits a glass ceiling after a few years. Thus, while the employers complain that the worker does not stay longer, the employee complains that he does not see growth in the current job. The net result is a decrease in demand for skilled workers with lower degrees.

Current Scenario and key Challenges: Skills in India are largely acquired through two main sources: formal training centres and the informal or hereditary mode of passing on cascading skill sets from one generation to the next. Nowadays vocational courses are becoming quite popular among youth because it is believed that taking these courses would provide more and better employment opportunities than those provided by conventional academic courses. While there remains a requirement for skilled professionals in the industry, the supply for the same is hampered by:

1. High dropout rate at Secondary level: Vocational Education is presently offered at senior secondary level but the students at this level aspire for higher education.
2. At present, the vocational system doesn't put much emphasis on the academic skills hence lower incidences of vertical mobility
3. There is a lack of participation by private players in the field of vocational education.
4. Vocationalisation of education is not in line with industry needs.
5. Lack of opportunities for continuous skill up-gradation.
6. There is no clear provision of certifications and degrees for the unorganised/informal sector.
7. Challenges faced by ITCs and ITIs are poor quality trainers, lack of flexibility and outdated infrastructure

New Directions: Vocationalisation should not be attempted in an unsystematic or haphazard manner. Need of the hour is to understand the trainees' apprehensions and challenges regarding Vocational Education and training (VET). Thus there is a huge opportunity for a vocational training institute that can address these challenges. This will favour the organisations willing to enter the vocational education market as well as the students wanting to take up vocational courses to increase their employability. In summation, it is critical to redefine the essential elements of VET so that it becomes more flexible, inclusive, relevant and contemporary.

New Initiatives to Strengthen Vocational Education in India

The main terminal stages in the general education system are secondary and higher secondary education. This is because the students take important decisions about their career at these points. They have many options like to pursue higher education, join the work force, opt for technical training etc. Vocational education provides training for jobs that are based on traditionally non-academic, manual or practical activities, occupation, or totally related to a specific trade. In this system of education, the trainees get expertise by themselves in a specific group of techniques. So, the vocational education is also referred to as technical education. The practical courses included in the vocational education helps the students to gain experience and skills that are needed for their career in future. As soon as they finished the course, most of the students are offered placements in jobs. It is a fact that most of the employers look for candidates with work related experiences. The training in vocational education help the students to acquire such work related experiences.

Objectives of Vocational Education

The goal of vocational educational in India is to enhance skilled manpower through various courses to meet the requirements of the unorganised sector. It also aims at inculcating self-employment skills in people through several self-employment related courses. Vocational education in India is conveyed through polytechnics and Industrial Training Institutes (ITIs). Some of the vocational courses are Cutting/ Tailoring & Dress Making, Library Assistant, Refrigeration and Air Conditioning, Secretarial Practices, Typewriting, Computer Operator and Programme Assistant, Stenography, Electrical Technician, Plumbing, Fruit and Vegetable Preservation Programs, Architectural Draughtsman ship, Electrical Technician, Desk Top Publishing, Electronics (Radio/TV/Tape Recorder Mechanic), etc. Today, the Indian economy lacks skilled people. This happens mainly due to neglect of vocational education. On the basis of the recent survey, the main reason for unemployment is the shortage of marketable skills.

Advantages of Vocational Education

The advantages in imparting vocational education and training are listed below.

- Build up a work force of international quality.
- Reduce unemployment by providing world-class knowledge to people.

- Prepare the youth for a career of their choice.
- Provide skilled people thereby reducing cost and enhance the productivity of services and manufacturing.
- Supply millions of trained people in floriculture, agriculture, sericulture, fishery, horticulture, tourism, healthcare and in the manufacturing sector.

Importance of Vocational Education

The university degrees were not necessary for most of the occupations. These jobs could be performed by trained higher secondary aspirants. It should be made possible to divert at least half of the students completing their 10th to the vocational stream. Then only the pressure on the universities will get reduced. Besides, this will help the students for profitable employment. Every year in India, more than 6 lakh engineering degree holders and about two million graduates pass out of colleges.

Among these engineering graduates, approximately two-thirds of the total need to be re-skilled. Otherwise they would not get any jobs in the industry. In the mean time, this developed world requires skilled workers and professionals. A survey report says that there will have a shortage of 40 million working people in the developed world. This shortage can disable the economic growth which in turn shoots up the wage rates thereby reducing the competitiveness of these countries.

Role of Public and Private Institutions

Many private institutes offer vocational training accredited to recognised industry bodies by realizing the need for skilled manpower in the country. These institutes also promise better placements for their students. In recent years, the government of India has given a lot of importance on streamlining vocational education. This initiative can fulfil the rising need of the market by aiming on employability skills. Vocational education in India is offered by polytechnics and industrial training institutes. In India, vocational training is widely referred to certificate level crafts training for the students who leave school after 10th or 12th standards. Compared to other states, India has less number of industrial training institutes and polytechnics.

Imparting vocational education at the secondary stage of schooling has achieved only partial success. This is because the students mostly prefer general courses like art and science at +2 level. These students constitute the major part of the qualified unemployed youth in India.

A systematically planned and effectively implemented vocational education system will facilitate the unemployed youth to take up some useful career.

New Strategies Launched by Government

Recently, a new strategic partnership (MoU) has been launched to strengthen instructor training and vocational education curriculum in India. This collaboration focuses at the recognition of India's need in increasing the numbers of skilled and educated young candidates. These candidates are more suitable to compete in a knowledge-based and increasingly globalised economy.

The objective of the MoU is to implement, evaluate, develop, and monitor a technical trade instructor training programme and instructional materials related to them. The team aims to scale-up nationally. The partners of this association are the Jindal Education Initiatives (JE), Montgomery College, and the Wadhwani Foundation.

The Wadhwani Foundation will focus on faculty development, courseware and curriculum development, and facilitating technology platform. With a mutual agreement on cost recovery model, Montgomery College will provide the technical expertise. JE offers fully-equipped trade instructor training facility and recruitment. Jindal Education Initiatives had started many community colleges in various parts of the country.

The OP Jindal Community College (OPJCC) colleges provide many diploma programmes and vocational education certificates. These diplomas and certificates are recognized by the Ministry of Human Resources and Development. The college is registered under the IGNOU Community College Scheme. The OPJCC aims to enroll more than 100,000 vocational education students over the next 5 years.

Jindal Educational Initiatives had launched a partnership with Montgomery College in USA. This partnership demanded workforce enhancement curricula in construction management, automotive technology, and building trades. This acted as an initiative to build significant capacity in the vocational education sector in India. A similar initiative was launched by Wadhwani Foundation in the last year which is called "Wadhwani Skills Colleges."

It focuses at creating capacity for vocational education of three million students linked to industry. The MoU was the latest launch signed at a glittering event in Delhi. We can hope for its success. If so, India will definitely shine in the unorganized sector.

Skills Formation for Economic Development in India: Fostering Institutional Linkages Between Vocational Education and Industry

As national economies are integrated into the global economy, which is increasingly becoming "knowledge-based" (OECD, 1997), and as technological change occurs at unprecedented speeds, it becomes increasingly important for developing countries to develop institutional mechanisms that can foster skills formation at both national and firm levels, to become globally competitive and to promote sustainable economic development. As the knowledge and skills required for today's production activities are becoming more and more tacit, hard to obtain, and costly to transfer between firms, and thus more specific, and often even firm-specific (Najmabadi & Lall, 1995), firms are taking on an increasingly important role. Indeed, they have become de facto institutions for skills development that will improve productivity and competitiveness (Okada, 2004).

These changes pose enormous challenges to institutions of technical and vocational education and training (TVET) in developing countries, in terms of their design, planning, and management, as they affect the adequate supply and deployment of skills needed in the workplace as well as the productivity of the workforce, and thus the growth of economies. Conventional pre-employment school-based TVET may become less relevant and less important, given its difficulty in keeping up with fast-changing skills in demand, caused by:

1) the changing nature of skills,
2) changing production processes, and 3) changing labour markets.

Thus, there is a growing recognition about the need to develop an alternative model of TVET in which the private sector is more deeply involved (Middleton et al., 1993; OECD, 1994; ADB, 2004). Training, whether conducted on-the-job or off-the-job, is an institutionalized form of knowledge and skill transfer. Particularly in the work context, training is a means of acquiring and enhancing firm-level learning: lessons the organization has learned are translated into learning by members of the organization, and knowledge acquired by the firm is shared among them in different parts of the organization. That is, in-firm training promotes the intra-firm transfer of knowledge and skills. Despite the current trend in which production processes converge across different countries, considerable diversity still remains in the various national systems of skills formation, even in the face of globalization (Ashton & Green, 1996).

This study examines the nature of institutional linkages between vocational education and industry in the Indian skills formation system. The Indian case is of particular interest for two reasons. First, India has faced an acute need to upskill its workforce, as India's economic reforms since the mid-1980s, and more notably in the 1990s, have led to dynamic restructuring, a growing exposure to global competition, and an increased inflow of foreign capital. Second, although the Indian TVET has been widely considered to be unsatisfactory, interestingly, it has had a formal apprenticeship training scheme institutionalized by the government in the 1960s, when India was still at a very early stage of its economic development.

This tripartite institutional arrangement involving the government, industry, and TVET institutions, has worked well during India's rapid economic restructuring in more recent years, as it has provided incentives to both firms and workers. The study focuses on the linkages that TVET institutions, such as Industrial Training Institutes (ITI), have forged with firms to accelerate the upgrading of workers' skills. In particular, making special reference to the Indian automobile industry, I examine the changing patterns of interactions between the ITI and the firms, as the industry grew very rapidly in the 1990s; I then consider how such interactions have helped the industry upgrade workers' skills. The automobile industry is one of the Indian industries that has gone through the most rapid transformations in recent years. The existing literature on TVET, particularly in the Asian context, has mainly focused on school-based education and training institutions; as few studies have looked at enterprise-based TVET, we lack sufficient insights into how workers are actually trained inside the firm, and what incentive systems would motivate governments, firms and training institutions to develop the kind of tripartite partnership that will forge the formation of skills that the country and the industries require. This study thus fills this gap by drawing on a detailed firm-level observation of the Indian apprenticeship training scheme.

This micro-level study is based on three rounds of fieldwork that I carried out in India between 1996 and 2004. In this paper I argue that while India's vocational education system has been considered largely unsatisfactory, the institutional linkages that vocational education institutions have forged with firms through state-mandated apprenticeship schemes, have actually played an important role in developing and diffusing the skills that industry requires, thus allowing industry to achieve rapid transformations.

Vocational Education in India: A Big Opportunity

One need not explain the meaning of Demographic Dividend in the present context, as it has been India's trump Card during the recent high growth period. But, the apparent demographic dividend has mostly resulted into a mistake. We need our youth to be productive in a much more effective and extensive way. The 93 % of employment in unorganized sectors is a shame for a country of the size of India. Keeping in mind the nature of work force available in India, we need more jobs which involve semi-skilled and manual labour, or to go a step ahead a more extensive provision for vocational training to better utilise the available labour. This Demographic Dividend might very well have extremely negative effects, if we fail to skill our youth quickly.

India's GDP is split 17%, 28%, and 55% in agriculture, industry and services, respectively. Similarly, the employed workforce splits 52%, 14 and 34% respectively. The disproportionate services GDP is an anomaly in an economically poor country like India. The vast majority of service employment in India is in low-level and low-paying industries. The contribution of higher-level industries to the services GDP is driven by the information technology and software sectors which do not employ large numbers of people.

States like Uttar Pradesh, Rajasthan and Madhya Pradesh contain so much potential than already put in use; these are the states from where the demographic explosion is confirmed. Yet keeping in mind the present scenario they are still likely to contribute insignificantly to the GDP. The laggards will have to be the front runners in every sphere to overcome under performance, but the challenges are insurmountable.

Indian spends $600 billion yearly on education. With this India's education sector is bigger than that of the US. India is the 9th highest in the world in this context. India's yearly growth in overall education expenditure at 15% is also one of the fastest in the global system.

The estimated Compound Annual Growth Rate (CAGR) of private revenue in Indian education is roughly 19% from 2011 to 2015, one of the highest in the world again. On the same lines vocational training is emerging as big opportunities for private players. High growth, scarcity of investable opportunities and the recession-proof nature of the sector are likely to keep valuations high.

From $30 billion in 2012, private education revenue is expected to reach $45 billion by 2015. Some of the estimates are: K-12

(Kindergarten to 12th grade- \$20 billion, technical education- \$12billion, coaching- \$8 billion and pre-school \$3 billion.

The affluent class groups in urban areas spend 10.4% of the total consumer expenditure towards private education. On the other hand rural poor spends just 1.4% of their income on education. With the median income elasticity of demand for education at near 2, a 1% rise in per capita income leads to a 2% jump in spending for education, mostly on private education. This is the key driver of the sector.

Indian education is in a dismal state with only about one out of eight children who start first grade graduating from 12th grade. According to World Bank data, India's literacy rate for ages 15 and above places it in the last quartile of 114 countries.

Inclusive growth can be effective when there is an attempt to uplift more students who are under the Below The Line (BTL) and provide them with vocational training for jobs. Dichotomy between public and private is pivotal to bring both scalability and skill to move things at a faster pace. Speed in execution is mandatory.

State Governments have initiated an array of schemes. One such scheme run by the Andhra Pradesh Government is the Employment Guarantee Marketing Mission Scheme, under which the Government partners with education agencies to train and place students from BTL in a better position. Government further reimburses the entire fee including boarding expenses. The programme prolongs for 400 hours predominantly in retail, sales and marketing customer service. The highlight of the programme has been the placement success which is currently clocking at 70%, companies like Café Coffee day and Macdonald in hospitality sector, Big Bazaar and more in retail, Hindustan Level in FMCG and so on hire extensively. There is a need for many more such Government funded programmes.

58 % of our graduates suffer from some sort of skill deficiency, and require last mile intervention to make them employable. At the same time companies don't want to pay for trained man power as the wages will have to be higher.

"India will account for 20 per cent of the world's global workforce in 2020s. The average age of Indian workforce will be 29 years as compared to 37 for the US and China and 45 years for Europe", Kapil Sibal, minister for human resource development, communications and IT said at the India Economic Summit 2011 in Mumbai.

Never before in the history of any country has human capital development been such a key focus area as 2011 was for India, marking the beginning of better times. The huge demographic dividend India can for sure reap from its large young population, with 250 million to 400 million people joining the employment market between now and 2025 to fuel its growth. This is a staggering number by any standards. However, to become productive these huge numbers have to be suitably trained to avoid large scale unemployment, which needs greater emphasis than rejoicing the fact that we have the largest youngest population in comparison to other countries.

To be more specific, 109 million persons will attain working age during the period of 2007-2012. The net addition to workforce is, therefore, expected to grow to 89 million of which around 13 million are likely to be graduates/post graduates and about 57 million are likely to be school drop outs or illiterates. A significant share of incremental demand is likely to be for skilled labour – graduates and vocationally trained people are expected to account for 23% of incremental demand by 2012. The study further estimates that India is likely to increase deficit of 5.25 million employable graduates and vocationally trained workforce by 2012.

Vocational education could be a great way to counter this challenge. India's current capacity for vocational training is just about 4 to 5 million per year against a requirement of 10 times that. Hence focusing on vocational education is of primary and immediate importance for the country.

7

Learning and Work: New Possibilities

Doug Barkey and Etta Kralove

According to a recent evaluation of the vocational education system in this country, fully one half of all high school students engage in some form of vocational education. Of these students, some are considered vocational concentrators, students whose main area of coursework is in vocational education programmes. Yet 1/4 of these students never enroll in a post-secondary programme and only 18% complete a college degree. A mere 27% work even one day in the job they were prepared for (Silberberg, Warner, Fong, & Goodwin, 2004). In some rural and urban areas in this country, 45% of the students drop-out before completing high school, some suggest the number is actually closer to 60% (Brand, 2003). These students, the least well served by the public schools in this country, face an uncertain future without the skills they need to compete in today's highly volatile and changing job market. What is the responsibility of the vocational education system to meet the needs of these students? And why has it failed to do so? This paper outlines the challenges to vocational education and introduces a new form of vocational education, the learning company, a production learning environment for the 21st century.

A Long History

When John Runkle, President of MIT saw the instruction workshops that Victor Della Vos imported for the Philadelphia Centennial Exposition in 1876, a new vision for vocational education in this country was born. The innovation of these shops was that they provided instruction as an activity separate from production. Prior to the Della Vos innovation, vocational instruction was done in production workshops where students served as apprentices to working craftsmen who taught the trade while doing the work. The rest is, as they say, history. From that time forward, vocational education became disconnected from producing real goods for real people in real work settings and became instead modelled on academic learning in classrooms. Apprenticeships gave way as industry moved forward and the twentieth century was born with a new way to prepare workers for industrial America.

Vocational education proponents spent much of the 20th century building a vocational education system in this country that used instruction workshops to prepare students for work in the real world. Little innovation entered the system, which relied on the largess of congress for funding. As a result, vocational educators had to become champions for their system rather than developers of new ways of conducting the business of vocational education. As a vocal opponents of vocational education, FDR folded the Federal Board of Vocational Education into the Office of Education, limiting the power of the board and clearing the way for new initiatives (Kliebard, 1999).

The workplace of today makes very different demands on workers than did the workplaces our vocational education system was designed to address. Agreement abounds that vocational education as practiced in the twentieth century will fall far short of the needs of the workplace in the 21st century. But what is less certain is what a re-conceptualized vocational education ought to look like and how it ought to be structured to meet the needs of the new economy. In addition, contemporary learning theory suggests that the old behaviourist model for vocational instruction needs to be overthrown. Recent reform initiatives have pointed the system in some new directions.

The New Vocationalism

The current period, called 'new vocationalism,' was given birth by the *Nation at Risk* report (National Commission on Excellence in Education, 1983) and pushed along by the changes in the 1990 Carl D. Perkins Vocational Education and Applied Technology Act, and the 1994 School-to-Work Act. The movement is responsible for providing a vision for re-formulated vocational education programmes. These acts of legislation are attempts to fundamentally alter the vocational education system in this country, freeing it from the sigma of the past and creating a system able to prepare workers for the world of work today. Generally, the new policies call for a three pronged integration:

between academic and vocational education; between secondary and post secondary education programmes and between classroom and work-based learning. In this policy environment, vocational classrooms are seen as only one place where students are prepared for work. Work-based learning programmes place young people in real work places for part of their training programme. In theory, vocational education teachers use these experiences as the basis for teaching academic subjects back in schools.

Many in the movement have argued for a return to Dewey's notion of education through occupations (Grubb, 1997). Dewey conceived of the study of occupations as the centrepiece of education believing it was through participating in the 'work' of life that students could see how intelligence was used. For Dewey, the most important purpose of education was to foster intellectual and moral growth and by engaging in activity, intelligence became manifest and students experienced the use of intelligence to solve problems in the world. Dewey fought against the bifurcation of thought and action and therefore saw learning through occupations as a bridge between these two worlds. Dewey was careful to draw a distinction between his conception of education through occupations and the vocational education system that grew up during his lifetime and was in fact a vocal opponent of the vocational education movement. Dewey feared the growing vocational education system would create a tracked system of education in the country, isolating immigrant and poor students in programmes that provided narrow skills training rather than an education necessary for participation in a democracy:

"This movement [vocational education] would continue the traditional liberal or cultural education for the few economically able to enjoy it, and would give to the masses a narrow technical trade education for specialized callings, carried on under the control of others," (Dewey, 1915)

Those involved in developing and articulating the new vocationalism movement that we are experiencing today like to tie it to Dewey's conception of occupations forming the centrepiece of an educational experience. Dewey conceived of students working at occupations that exist in their communities while at school in order to bring education alive, not to turn students into weavers or farmers. The new vocationalism, on the other hand, has a strong utilitarian focus on the requirements of the new economy. So while Dewey might be pleased to see a new emphasis on the kind of active education that is required by education through the occupations, he would no doubt be certain to warn against a narrowly utilitarian educational focus. Many see in the new vocationalism an avenue for significant high school reform. Advocates highlight project-based instruction as well as structural reforms necessary to facilitate opportunities for work-based learning experiences. Advocates of the new vocationalism know that these changes have the potential to transform high school practice at the same time. They also acknowledge how hard it is to transform the public high school. Before turning to these efforts, it is important to understand the thrust of new vocationalism and it implications.

One chief characteristic of the ideas in new vocationalism is a broadened notion of skills training. New vocationalism advocates building occupational competencies in students that are relatively general and can lead to a number of different career paths as well as post-secondary education since a focus on further education is a crucial component of current thinking about vocational education.

For many, the term, 'vocational education' implies a kind of work life that does not exist today. Most American workers hold at least seven jobs over a lifetime and these jobs are often in very different fields. This 'serial vocations' cycle to work life today requires workers to think of their work as a set of skills rather than an occupational title that defines their job. Some make the argument that common employability skills underlie all jobs and that equipping young people with these skills prepares them for a lifetime of career changes and new jobs. There is a strong consensus about the need for a better trained workforce with a larger complement of skills needed in a knowledge-based society; that education is a life-long process and that degrees and certifications matter (Jacobs & Grubb, 2003). As a result of this consensus, vocational education reform initiatives in the U.S. over the past ten years have included calls to increase an emphasis on standards development and accountability; to build bridges between secondary and post-secondary schools and the workplace; to provide for apprenticeship opportunities and to integrate academic and vocational education (Chappell, 2003).

The fullest articulation of need for building general employability skills and the skills needed for the new world of work can be found in the reports by the Secretary's Commission on Achieving Necessary Skills (SCANS). The commission was appointed by the Secretary of Labour in the late 1980s to determine the skills that young people needed to succeed in high performance workplaces of today. Their 1991 initial report, *What Work Requires of School*, outlines the foundation skills and workplace competencies needed by today's workforce (Secretary's Commission on Achieving Necessary Skills, 1991). The foundational skills include basic literacy and computational skills, and the thinking skills necessary to put knowledge to work as well as personal qualities that make workers dedicated and trustworthy. In addition, SCANS also outlined workplace competencies that include the ability to manage resources, to work amicably and productively with others, to acquire and use information, to master complex systems and to work with a variety of technologies.

The SCANS report suggested a very different notion of vocational education and shifted the focus of much thinking and practice in the field. Enter any One Stop career centre in this country and you are immediately placed at a computer terminal, taking a number of "career aptitude' tests that help you see how the skills you developed in your last job can be used in a job is a very different area. Clients at good One Stop Career Centres are re-trained, in part, to understand themselves not as, for example "paper workers," but as a bundle of transferable skills. The SCANS reports also put a very important idea on the table. Their notion, "learning a living," pointed attention to the fact that life long learning has become a necessity in this age of rapid technological change and job mobility. In this world of skill bundles, employability skills and transferable skill sets, what is an appropriate training for young people and more fundamentally, what should it be called?

The National Centre for Research in Vocational Education issued a major policy statement in 1992 calling for the integration of academic and vocational education. That report discussed the recommendations from educational reformer, Jeannie Oakes, calling for nothing less than new purposes, organization, curricula and language. She recommends that a common vocational curriculum be organized around basic concepts of economics and technology and that it have four major curricular strands. These strands follow the principles from academic disciplines that underline the economic processes and technology and explore how these principles are transformed into work. These principles form the core of learning as students move from classroom to lab to workplace and back to classroom (Plihal, et.al., 1992). This vision of vocational education is much more closely aligned with Dewey's notion of education through occupations than any of the other initiatives like school-to-work and work-based learning which are structurally difficult to connect to academic work.

Career and technical education (CTE) is a term that many in the field suggest should replace the term vocational education. Some have suggested calling the broad field "technology and economic sciences," or "technological and economic literacy," (Oakes, 1986). Regardless of the name, stakeholders in the field of vocational education are, each in their own way, struggling to determine the nature and shape of the endeavour to prepare young people for a rapidly changing world of work.

Legislating Change

The federal legislation that authorizes funding for vocational education, the Perkins Act, requires a national study of vocational education prior to each re-authorization of funds. The recent evaluation, *National Assessment of Vocational Education: A Final Report to Congress* shows that the progress toward these goals has been uneven and that the system as a whole has been plagued by a lack of clarity about purpose and goals (Silberberg, Warner, Fong, & Goodwin, 2004). Citing the historical accumulation of purposes over the last century, the assessment finds that vocational education has moved from the narrow purpose of preparing immigrants and rural workers for life in factories and on farms in the early 20th century to preparing young people for college as well as the work force in the 21st century. The conflicted picture of federal priorities for vocational education that emerged from this report has put educators on the alert that lacking a clear vision for the system as a whole, the system is in danger of losing its historical funding base (Silberberg, Warner, Fong, & Goodwin, 2004). The report recommends clarifying purposes, which in their view means we must choose between a focus on academics with an eye to further education or a focus on workforce development with an acknowledgement that skills like critical thinking and higher levels of literacy are essential for today's worker, but are important as means to an end.

While there may be a lack of clarity about the purposes of vocational education, there is certainly not a lack of policy recommendations on how to fix the system. The most recent is the Bush administration's, *Blueprint for Preparing America's Future,* the Carl D. Perkins Secondary and Technical Education Excellence Act to reauthorize the Carl D. Perkins Vocational and Technical Act of 1998. Briefly, the reauthorization plan links the CTE system to No Child Left Behind principles of higher academic achievement rates and calls for more pathways and smoother transitions into technical education programmes in community college and workforce investment systems and for states to have more freedom in how they spend their Perkins dollars. The plan calls for significantly higher levels of academic achievement, including 4 years of English, 3 years of math and science and 3 years of social studies. While ratcheting up the standards, the plan ratchets down the funding level, with a 25% cut from 2004 to the proposed 2005 funding level.

Another set of recent recommendations from the American Youth Policy Forum calls for a new vision for CTE that includes building theme-based vocational programmes in schools with strong pathways to college and work. In addition, they recommend changing the funding flows, immediately sending the message that vocational education funds are not entitlements, but rather funds to support innovation and change. So, while legislators grapple with periodic re-authorizations of the Perkins Act, educators scramble to implement changes that legislators write into the re-authorization of the Act. The last re-authorization called for the strengthening the academic content in vocational education programmes and called for increased levels of accountability. In addition, initiatives, like the Tech Prep Act and the 1994 School-to-Work Opportunities Act (STWOA) signed into law by President Clinton keep educators in the field aiming at a moving target. Employers want to know why their young workers lack so many of the essential skills they need. With so many heads turned to the issue of vocational education, we would hope that meaningful, lasting change would be the order of the day. But is it?

From Policy to Practice

Discussions and policy recommendations during the new vocationalism period have often focused on providing students the opportunity to learn outside traditional educational institutions, broadly outlined in the STWOA which identifies three major components, each containing specific activities designed to assist students in the transition from school to work. These include a school-based learning component, a work-based learning component, and connecting activities. Paramount to the success of the STWOA is the concept that schools cannot accomplish this task alone. Although the legislation provides federal funds for the states and local jurisdictions to develop STW programmes, a critical component of the school-to-work movement is the successful linkage of schools with communities and business organizations.

Theorists have been exploring the parameters of workplace learning (Marsick & Watkins, 1990), variously called, school-to-work (Steinberg, 1998); work-based learning (Bailey, Hughes, & Moore,

2004), practice-oriented education (Centre for Work and Learning at Northeastern Universtiy), and learning in the workplace (Senge, et. al., 1999). Moving significant portions of vocational education programmes outside the classroom not only broadens our notion of vocational education but demands a much more systematic in our approach to vocational education. Most would agree that learning a job is best done on the job rather in the "instruction shops" invented by Del la Vos in the late 19th century. In their twenty-year study of work-based learning Bailey, Hughes and Moore highlight the possibilities and challenges of the movement. They are particularly interested in the tension that exists between the kind of cognition required in school and that used in a workplace and suggest that this tension can produce important learning gains that either by itself would not support. In addition, they highlight the importance of reflection in the process of work-based learning, without it the experience lacks a strong academic component.

While the benefits of work-based learning can be enormous, the challenges associated with placing young learners in real work environments have been enormous. Building partnerships with workplaces and preparing them to make good use of student's time is an incredibly labour-intense activity for school personnel. Providing structured time for reflection on work-based learning experiences is out of sync with most high school schedules. Perhaps most critical are the findings that mundane tasks that often are the basis of a work-based learning experience can in fact turn students off to learning rather than engage them more fully.

The enormous structural impediments to work-based learning experiences includes some of the most mundane, but hardest to change practices in high schools. For example, to connect student's work in the classroom to work-based learning experiences requires that teachers talk with work-based learning partners. Yet, few teachers have telephones in their classes, so just being able to call teachers has difficult. Time schedules of teachers, state testing mandates all conspire to keep teachers in classrooms and kids at school. In the end, the researchers acknowledge that while work-based learning has tremendous potential for enriching the learning experiences of students, in today's educational climate, our focus should be elsewhere (Bailey, Hughes, & Moore, 2004).

On the other side of the partnership equation are the employers who have to worry about the bottom line and the way mentoring impacts their worker's ability to get the job done. Research on the subject suggests that workers feel rejuventated by working with the students and that the students actually, "help get the work done," (Steinberg, 1998).

One central question about the initial success that is seen in some STW programmes centres on the issues involved in the problems of learning transfer. Some hope that by engaging in work-based learning experiences, student's motivation and academic attainment will be increased. While there may be many benefits to work-based learning experiences, learning transfer does not appear to one of them. In a study of disaffected young people, researchers in the UK found that, "the benefits of work-related learning for young people, where they do exist, ,do not readily transfer to school-based settings and consequently do not necessarily result in improved levels of motivation or attainment at school," (Hall & Raffo, 2004). They found that students would resent teachers who did not 'treat them like adults,' as they were treated in the workplace and at school.

Situated cognition theorists also warn of the difficulty of learning transfer between vastly different settings (Lave & Wenger, 1991). The math learned at work in a kitchen or in a gardening project will only transfer if there is explicit attention to transfer and if what is called for as a demonstration of math competence at schools resembles in some way the math learned on the job (Hall & Raffo, 2004). This is a significant problem and will no doubt become more so as calls for higher academic standards pushes the high school curriculum into narrower and narrower conceptions of knowledge. A lack of recognition of the academic possibilities in vocational education has not been on the public's mind recently. The whole STW movement would have made real headway if it had been able to impact the larger high school environment, rather than merely pushing some problematic students off workplaces.

In some ways, the community service requirement that many high schools now endorse are an off-spring of the work-based learning movement in the early nineties. But while we are seeing more and more community service requirements for high school graduation, these are often nothing more than check-off requirements. The strong recommendations that Bailey, Hughes and Moore have made about the importance of reflection has not seemed to penetrate the community service requirement in schools, which are sadly missing a key factor that can make these experiences educationally rich. In addition, students often are placed in settings that are so far beyond their level of maturity that the workplace experience has the effect of turning students off to a particular workplace. For example, a world renowned genetics research lab in the Northeast takes students from the local high school for a term in internship positions.

These high school students work side-by-side with research associates on real research projects. The experience has left many students unready to think about their future. According to one young lady in the project, "They are all too serious, I don't want to be a scientist if scientists are 'like that'," (Mooser, 1997). Young people are not adults and while they may want to try on adult roles, the support for that experimentation is enormous and must be factored into any work-based learning experience that is meaningful. Ironically, in the end it appears that providing meaningful work-based learning opportunities for our students takes more work on the part of teachers than less.

Some high schools have used the concept of career academies as the basis for whole school restructuring. Typically schools-within-a-school, career academies offer opportunities for students to explore broad occupational areas, like medicine, business or technology. These programmes integrate academic subjects into the career cluster of the academy. Typically, local business or industry leaders are invited to speak in classes, provide internships in their workplaces and mentor young students. The success of these programmes has been well-documented (Steinberg, 1998). The broader focus allows programmes to get beyond narrow skills training, provides the opportunity for more academic material integration and appeals to a broader range of students.

Most educators would agree that tracking has been a significant problem in education generally and that vocational education has be en a hard wired system that perpetuates the unequal educational opportunities offered to students in this country. Career academies hold a promise that tracking can be overcome. A medical cluster, for example, can as easily appeal to a student with aspirations to be a doctor as to a student with more modest aspirations.

The model presents a number of significant challenges. It requires substantial re-structuring of existing high schools, never an easy task. The model has been difficult to implement because of the difficulty of developing a new teaching method to accompany the changed goals and structures of career academies. Teachers are asked to take on new roles as they must learn the industries involved and then develop academic curriculum that builds on the industry.

Learning in a New key: Constructivism

While discussion at the policy level has centred on changes in the vocational education system demanded by the new economy and rapidly changing technology; for educators, questions about pedagogy and learning environment structures are paramount. These questions have to do with how best to link classroom learning with learning in the work place. This question is increasingly important as educators come to understand the implications for vocational education of contemporary learning theory with its focus on contextual or situated learning and constructivism.

This question raises a second set of questions in the field of vocational education having to do with the appropriate conceptual and theoretical underpinnings that should form a reconceptualized approach to vocational education. Most would agree that the field of vocational education has used a behaviourist framework to articulate its approach to pedagogy and practice. While a behaviourist approach might have worked well for preparing workers for factory jobs, jobs in the 21st century will require higher order thinking skills, problem solving and collaborative work skills. Classical behaviourist theory cannot address this latter type of learning (Doolittle & Camp, 1999). We see behaviourism at work in the performance objectives that form the basis of lesson plans in voc/tech classrooms. Behaviourism is operating when criterion-referenced measures are used to gauge task completion and when programmes rely on incumbent worker task lists for the primary curriculum (Fitch & Crunkilton, 1999). Using a behaviourist paradigm, complex work, like welding, has been broken into discrete pieces and students have been taken through these specific skills, one step at a time and are asked to demonstrate their competence of each discrete skill. But educators now ask, is this learning?

Constructivism hit the learning theory scene hard with its inherent critique of behaviourism. In addition, ground-breaking work in the area of situated learning suggests the need to shift the focus in vocational education away from discrete skill sets to an understanding of the way learning occurs in the world naturally. (Lave and Wenger, 1991) Constructivism postulates that learners construct new knowledge using existing mental framework, with new learning building on prior knowledge. The practice emphasizes experience which engages the learner in authentic tasks. The importance of authenticity cannot be overstated according to constructivist educators because for true learning to occur, intrinsic motivation must be present. Constructivists would argue that it is hard, if not impossible, to engage learner's intrinsic motivation with 'classroom' projects whose only evaluation is a teacher's grade. Not unlike the term progressive education that Dewey spent much of his lifetime trying to rescue from mis-use, constructivism suffers from an overuse and a lack of clarity.

Beyond Constructivism: Situated Learning

In addition to the potential contribution that constructivism can make to the pedagogical practices in vocational education classrooms, the insight that learning is context bound and situation dependent has tremendous potential to revolutionize vocational education practice. The idea of situated learning moves beyond constructivism into exciting new territory for vocational educators:

" The activity in which knowledge is developed and deployed. . . is not separable from or ancillary to learning and cognition. Nor is it neutral. Rather, it is an integral part of what is learned. Situations might be said to co-produce knowledge through activity. Learning and cognition, it is now possible to argue, are fundamentally situated," (Brown, Collins, & Duguid, 1989).

Lave and Wenger have worked to bring the idea of situated learning to the forefront of thinking about learning. They argue that learning is a process of participation in communities of practice, in which participation increases by degrees of engagement and complexity. Their notion of legitimate peripheral participation alerts us to the gradual nature with which novices move into higher levels of understanding in their field. Their ethnographic analysis of a communities of practice, everything from Alcoholics Anonymous groups to tailors and mid-wives has spawned a whole generation of research on newcomers entering into existing communities of practices. They use the idea of situated learning to ground their understanding of communities of practice (Lave & Wenger, 1991).

In Japan, practitioners of situated learning have studied the apprenticeship system in place to induct Japanese into systems of art, craft and religion. This work has focused researchers interest in learning in "likely place." By looking at the ways in which learning occurs in these traditional setting, anthropologists have gathered rich insights into the way learning naturally occurs in non-formal educational settings. By watching and documenting situated learning, researchers are able to say that in fact, "knowledge is a property of meaningful activity, not a substance to be injected," (Singleton, eds., 1998).

This theoretical base has been used to structure learning environments that are more effective in increasing student learning. Constructivism has driven the increase in project-based learning in the classroom and the fields of adult education and workplace learning have embraced the idea of communities of practice and have built professional development approaches that rely on the informal communities that exist in workplaces (Bailey, Hughes, & Moore, 2004; Lave & Wenger, 1991).

What is the promise of this work for vocational education? For one, the narrow and utilitarian nature of vocational education is called into question. Vocational education has long relied on outmoded behaviourist practices that destroy the possibility of student's constructing either new knowledge or engaging in meaning-creation, both core to the constructivist notion of learning. If we look at the completion rates and employment figures of vocational education completers, we find, for example, that according to a 1987 report, only 27% of all vocational school graduates were working for even a single day in a job related to their vocational training (National Assessment of Vocational Education, 1994). The 1990 authorization of the Perkins Act responded to these low numbers by calling for a broadened training programme that mandated that students gain experience in all aspects of the industry they were preparing to enter. But merely mandating that students receive a broadened understanding of their fields without changing the content of the daily experience of students in vocational education programmes is doomed to failure. And today, most vocational education programmes look much like their predecessors, students in classrooms, preparing to work in real settings.

So how should career preparation be organized and situated if we are going to build the system on 21st century economic realities and understandings of learning? When the MIT president first saw the Della Voss "instruction shops," the fate of vocational education was sealed. Vocational education stepped out of the world of producing goods and moved into a classroom of producing projects for grades. This shift, while seen as an advance at the time, disconnected students from real work and imposed a system of vocational education into an institutional framework that was perhaps ill-suited for the purpose. Now that the genie is out of the bottle so to speak, is it possible to put vocational learning back in the places where real production happens? The school-to-work movement attempted that, but the enormity of the task of finding business ready to take on an educational mission proved over-powering. What is needed are vocational programmes that are themselves businesses. We would like to present a vision for the future of workforce development and vocational education. Drawing heavily on Training and Development Corporation's 30 years of experience and design work, the model presented here has been tested and refined in urban and rural areas, resulting in the development of the Production Learning Company, which brings together the best of two traditions, vocational education and job training. The model draws heavily on the apprenticeship approach and project-based instructional models and bridges the gap between what mainstream institutions offer and what employers and job seekers need. Perhaps more importantly, the model takes advantage of a reconceptualization of how learning and work gets done, changes the relationship between adults and students, and re-inserts into vocational education the broader purposes of education that Dewey envisioned.

In addition, a production learning company changes the arithmetic of investments in workforce development and represents a new labour market institution that competes favourably with community colleges, career colleges and vocational schools as well as with traditional job training programmes. The production learning company combines the European concept of production learning with constructivist learning methodologies that have emerged from twenty-five years of research in the fields of learning theory and cognitive science.

Overview of Career Development Theories

Career Development is a "continuous lifelong process of developmental experiences that focuses on seeking, obtaining and processing information about self, occupational and educational alternatives, life styles and role options" (Hansen, 1976). Put another way, career development is the process through which people come to understand them as they relate to the world of work and their role in it. This career development process is where an individual fashions a work identity. In America, we are what we do, thus it becomes a person's identity. It is imperative when educating our young people that our school systems assist and consider the significance of this responsibility for our youth and their future. The influences on and outcomes of career development are one aspect of socialization as part of a broader process of human development.

Why Study Theory?

Theories and research describing career behaviour provide the "conceptual glue" for as well as describe where, when and for what purpose career counselling, career education, career guidance and other career interventions should be implemented. The process of career development theory comes from four disciplines:

- Differential Psychology- interested in work and occupations
- Personality- view individuals as an organizer of their own experiences
- Sociology- focus on occupational mobility
- Developmental Psychology- concerned with the "life course"

> *"Theory is a picture, an image, a description, a representation of reality. It is not reality itself. It is a way we can think about some part of reality so that we can comprehend it"* *(Krumboltz)*

Career Development Theories for the past 75 years fall into four categories:

1. Trait Factor - Matching personal traits to occupations-Frank Parson's (1920's)
2. Psychological - Personality types matching work environment-Holland (1980's)
3. Decision - Situational or Sociological- Bandura (Self Efficacy-1970's)
4. Developmental - Self Concept over life span-Super (1950's)

Holland Theory of Vocational Types

This approach gives explicit attention to behavioural style or personality types as the major influence in career choice development. This is described as structurally interactive.

Common Themes:

- Occupation choice is an expression of personality and not random
- Members of an occupational group have similar personalities
- People in each group will respond to situations an problems similarly
- Occupational achievement, stability and satisfaction depends on congruence between one's personality and job environment

Holland Types

Realistic - work with hands, machines, tools, active, practical, adventurous

High Traits - practical, masculine, stable

Low Traits - sensitive, feminine, stable

Occupations - construction, farming, architecture, truck driving, mail carrier

Investigative – thought, analytical approaches, explore, knowledge, ideas, not social

High traits – scholarly, intellectual, critical

Low Traits – powerful, ambitious, adventurous

Occupations – biologist, chemist, dentist, veterinarian, programmer

Artistic – literary, musical, artistic activities, emotional, creative, open

High Traits – expressive, creative, spontaneous

Low Traits – orderly, efficient, conventional, social, masculine

Occupations – artist, musician, poet, interior designer, writer

Social – train, inform, educate, help, supportive, avoid technical skills, empathy, relationships

High Traits – cooperative, friendly, humanistic

Low Traits – ambitious, creative, strong,

Occupations – social work, counselling, police officer, LPN

Enterprising – verbally skilled, persuasive, direct, leader, dominant

High Traits – ambitious, adventurous, energetic

Low Traits – intellectual, creative, feminine

Occupations – lawyer, business executive, politician, TV producer

Conventional – rules and routines, provide order or direct structure, great self control, respect power and status, punctual, orderly

High Traits – stable, efficient, dependable, controlled

Low Traits – intellectual, adventurous, creative

Occupations – bank teller, clerk typist, cashier, data entry

Terms

Differentiation - the amount of spread between one's first and second code letters; denotes how clear one's type is.

Incongruence – lack of fit between one's type and work environment. People leave jobs because of too much incongruence or because of a chance to increase their congruence. Best decision makers are I's; worst are C's.

Consistency – closeness on the hexagon of one's first and second choices. The higher one's consistency, the more integrated one's characteristics (values, interests, traits) and the greater one's vocational maturity, persistence and achievement.

Advantages of Holland Types for Career Counselling

Types are intuitively appealing and easily shared with students. Helps students get oriented to the worlds of work that isn't overwhelming. Provides helpful way of understanding varied work environments.

Disadvantages of Holland Types for School Counselling

Theory doesn't provide insights into how one develops a type or guidance for working with student.

Bandura's Social Cognitive Theory

The concept of self efficacy is the focal point of Albert Bandura's social cognitive theory. By means of the self system, individuals exercise control over their thoughts, feelings, and actions. Among the beliefs with which an individual evaluates the control over his/her actions and environment, self-efficacy beliefs are the most influential predictor of human behaviour. The level and strength of self-efficacy will determine:

- whether coping behaviour will be initiated;
- how much effort will result;
- how long the effort will be sustained in the face of obstacles.

Self-Efficacy - the belief in one's capabilities to organize and execute the courses of action required to produce given attainments- is constructed on the basis of:

Four most influential sources where self-efficacy is derived:

- Personal Performance - Accomplishments-previous successes or failures (most influential)
- Vicarious Experience - Watching others, modelling, mentoring
- Verbal Persuasion - Verbal encouragement or discouragement
- Physiological and Emotional Factors - Perceptions of stress reactions in the body

Self-Efficacy plays the central role in the cognitive regulation of motivation, because people regulate the level and distribution of effort they will expend in accordance with the effects they are expecting from their actions.

It is important to understand the distinction between Self Esteem and Self Efficacy.

- Self esteem relates to a person's sense of self worth.
- Self efficacy relates to a person's perception of their ability to reach a goal.

How Self Efficacy Affects Human Function

Choices Regarding Behaviour-People will be more inclined to take on a task if they believe they can succeed. People generally avoid tasks where their self efficacy is low, but engage when it is high. Self efficacy significantly higher than ability can lead to psychological damage. Significantly low self efficacy leads to an inability to grow and expand skills. Optimum levels of self efficacy are a little above ability, which encourages people to tackle challenging tasks and gain valuable experience.

Motivation- People with higher self efficacy in a task are likely to expend more effort and persist longer than with low efficacy. On the other hand, low self efficacy may provide an incentive to learn more and prepare better than a person with higher self efficacy.

Thought Patterns and Responses- Low self efficacy can lead people to believe tasks are harder than they actually are. This leads to poor planning and stress. A person with higher self efficacy will attribute a failure to external factors, whereas a person with lower self efficacy will attribute it to low ability. (Example: Math Test)

The Destiny Idea- Bandura successfully showed that people with differing self-efficacy perceive the world in fundamentally different ways. People with a high self efficacy are generally of the opinion that they are in control of their own lives: that their own actions and decisions shape their lives. On the other hand, people with low self-efficacy may see their lives as somewhat out of their hands and with fate.

Efficacy vs. Outcome Expectations

Bandura distinguishes between outcome expectancy and and efficacy expectancy.

Outcome expectation refers to the person's estimate that a given behaviour will lead to particular outcomes.

Efficacy expectation is an estimate that one can successfully execute the behaviour required to produce the outcomes sought. Self-beliefs about abilities play a central role in the career decision-making process. People move toward those occupations requiring capabilities they think they either have or can develop. People move away from those occupations requiring capabilities they think they do not possess or they cannot develop.

Personal goals also influence career behaviours in important ways. Personal goals relate to one's determination to engage in certain activities to produce a particular outcome. Goals help to organize and guide behaviour over long periods of time.

The relationship among goals, self-efficacy, and outcome expectations is complex and occurs within the framework of:

Bandura's Triadic Reciprocal Model of Causality – these factors are all affecting each other simultaneously

- personal attributes,
- external environmental factors
- overt behaviour

In essence, a person inputs (e.g. gender, race) interact with contextual factors (e.g. culture, family geography) and learning experiences to influence self-efficacy beliefs and outcome expectations.

Self-efficacy beliefs and outcome expectations in turn shape people's interests, goals, actions, and eventually their attainments. However, these are also influenced by contextual factors (e.g. job opportunities, access to training opportunities, financial resources).

In this theory providing opportunities, experiences and significant adults to impact self-efficacy in all children becomes vital. Strategic career development interventions will positively impact young people in the context of this theory.

Super's Developmental Self-Concept Theory

Vocational development is the process of developing and implementing a self-concept. As the self-concept becomes more realistic and stable, so does vocational choice and behaviour. People choose occupations that permit them to express their self-concepts. Work satisfaction is related to the degree that they've been able to implement their self-concepts.

Career Maturity - Similarity between one's actual vocational behaviour and what is expected for that stage of development. Career maturity includes readiness to cope with developmental tasks at a given stage. It is both affective and cognitive.

Most career education programmes have been affected by Super's ideas. They provide gradual exposure to self-concepts and work concepts in curriculum that represents Super's ideas of career development/ vocational maturity. (National Career Development Guideline Standards)

Stages

Growth (Birth to mid teens) - Major developmental tasks are to develop a self-concept and to move from play to work orientation.

Sub stages:

- Fantasy (4-10 years old) - needs dominate career fantasies and little reality orientation.
- Interest (11-12 years old) - identifies likes/dislikes as basis for career choices
- Capacity (13-14 years old) - more reality incorporated; can relate own skills to specific requirements of jobs. (Vocationalizing the self concept)

Exploration (Mid teens through early 20's) - major tasks are to develop a realistic self-concept and implement a vocational preference though role tryouts and exploration; there is a gradual narrowing of choices leading to implementation of a preference. Preferences become CHOICES when acted upon.

Sub Stages:

- Tentative (15-17 years old) - tentative choices incorporating needs, interests, abilities are tried out in fantasy, coursework, part time work, volunteer, shadowing.
  - o May identify field and level of work at this sub stage.
- Crystallization of Preference (18-21 years old) - General preference is converted into specific choice. Reality dominates as one enters the job market or training after high school. Choosing a college major or field of training.
- Specifying a Vocational Preference (early 20's) - trial/little commitment; first job is tried out as life's work but the implemented choice is provisional and person may cycle back through crystallizing and specifying if not appropriate.

Establishment (mid 20's through mid 40's) - major tasks are to find secure niche in one's field and advance within it.

Sub Stages:

- Trial and Stabilization (25-30 years old) - process of settling down, if unsatisfactory may make 1-2 more changes before the right job is found.
- Advancement (30-40 years old) - efforts directed at securing one's position, acquiring seniority, developing skills, demonstrating superior performance, resume building actions.

Maintenance (40's through early 60's) - Major task is to preserve one's gains and develop non-occupational roles for things one always wanted to do; Little new ground is broken, one continues established work patterns. One faces competition from younger workers. Could be a plateau. Disengagement or Decline (Late 60's through retirement) - Tasks are deceleration of the career, gradual disengagement from world of work and retirement. One is challenged to find other sources of satisfaction. May shift to part time to suit declining capacities.

Development Tasks

Crystallization	*Forming a general vocational goal*
Specification	Move from tentative to specific preference
Implementation	Complete training, enter employment
Stabilization	Confirm choice through work experience
Consolidation	Advance in career

Rural Employment Strategies for India

The unprecedented commitment of the present Government of India to seriously address the need for employment generation is a propitious opportunity to implement strategies for generating full employment in the country. This report, which builds upon work done by the International Commission on Peace & Food in the early 1990s, confirms the potential to generate sufficient employment opportunities for all new entrants to the workforce as well as to absorb the current numbers of unemployed and underemployed. It includes strategies and policy recommendations designed to maximize the effectiveness of the Government's recently proposed initiatives for employment generation and rural prosperity. Implementation of these recommendations will be sufficient to generate 100 million additional employment and self-employment opportunities.

While many formal studies have been prepared to assess the growth and employment potential in India' formal private sector, less attention has been given to the conditions and strategies to promote rapid expansion and job creation in the rural and informal sectors. *This report focuses on strategies to increase employment opportunities in India's informal sector, with emphasis on agriculture, agro-industry, rural services and related vocations.* The report consists of three parts: an overview of employment in India, a business plan containing specific recommendations for implement¬ation, and a detailed discussion of employment opportunities and strategies in agriculture.

The major findings and recommendations can be summarized as follows:

1. The Indian economy is already generating approximately seven million employment and self-employment opportunities per annum, almost all of them in the informal sector, but in there is a serious lack of accurate information on the types and numbers of these jobs. The most effective strategy for employment generation will be to provide the missing links and policy measures needed to accelerate this natural process of employment generation.
2. There is enormous scope for raising the productivity of Indian agriculture, doubling crop yields and farm incomes, and generating significant growth in demand for farm labour. The report present evidence to demonstrate that improving plant nutrition through micronutrient analysis and improving irrigation through deep chiselling of soil can result in a tripling of crop yields.
3. Rising rural incomes consequent to higher productivity will unleash a multiplier effect, increasing demand for farm and non-farm products and services, thereby stimulating rapid growth of employment opportunities in other sectors.
4. Indian agriculture is constrained by weak linkages between agricultural training and extension, crop production, credit, processing, marketing, and insurance. The report presents an integrated strategy for bringing together all these elements in a synergistic manner by
   - Establishment of village-based Farm Schools to demonstrate and impart advanced technology to farmers on their own lands.
   - Establishment of a network of sophisticated soil test laboratories capable of high volume precision analysis of 13 essential plant nutrients coupled with development of expert computer systems to interpret soil test results and

recommend individualized packages of cultivation practices for each crop, location and soil profile.

- Establishment of Rural Information Centres to act as a medium for transmission of soil test data and recommended practices, access to current input and market prices, and other essential information for upgrading agriculture.
- Policy and legal measures to encourage contract farming arrangements between agri-business firms and self-help groups in order to increase small farmers' access to advanced technology, quality inputs, bank credit, processing, marketing and crop insurance.
- Measures to strengthen farm credit and insurance programmes, including creation of linkages between crop insurance, crop loans, and farm school training to encourage farmers who seek credit and crop insurance to adopt improved cultivation practices.

5. In order to ensure ready markets for the crops that are produced, the report focuses on the potential for linking crop production with huge untapped markets and specific agro-industries, including energy plantations to fuel biomass power plants, bio-diesel from jathropa, ethanol from sugarcane and sugar-beet, edible oil from Paradise Tree, horticulture crops and cotton.
6. The report argues that the India labour force suffers from a severe shortage of employable skills at all levels and that intensive development of vocational skills will act as a powerful stimulus for employment and self-employment generation. In addition to Farm Schools to impart advanced skills in production agriculture, the report recommends establishing a network of government-certified, rural vocational institutes providing training and certification in hundreds of vocational skills not covered by the ITIs. In order to offset the shortage of qualified trainers and the costs of replicating institutions throughout the country, the report advocates creation of a national network of 'Job Shops' linked to the Rural Information Centres and offering televised multimedia training programmes and computerized vocational training programmes.
7. The report recommends that the National Commission on Farmers arrange for employment surveys to provide accurate information on the growing demand for different occupational categories, the natural rate of employment generation by

category and skill level, and other issues required to promote full employment in the country.

Overview of Employment in India

Profile of the Indian Workforce

- *Workforce:* Although accurate measures of employment and unemployment are difficult in India's largely informal economy, the current labour force consists of approximately 400 million men and women.
- *Growth in Labour Force:* It is estimated that the work force is currently growing by 7 million persons per year.
- *Sector-wise:* Of these, about 56% are engaged in agriculture as their primary occupation which is down from 65% in the early 1990s. Another 13% are engaged in manufacturing and the balance are employed in the service sector, which has grown from 25% to 32% of total employment over the past two decades.
- *Organized vs. Unorganized:* The organized sector provides less than 8% of the total jobs, about 3% in private firms and 5% in the public sector. The informal/unorganized sector is provides the other 92%.
- *Skills:* Only 6-8% of India's workforce has received formal training in vocational skills, compared with 60% or more in developed and most rapidly developing countries.
- *Unemployment:* Depending on the survey measure applied, unemployment is estimated to range between 25 and 35 million. Youth unemployment is 13%, but reaches a high of 35% in Kerala. Unemployment as a percentage of the workforce fell in the 1980s and rose slightly in the 1990s. Authoritative published data was not available to indicate trends after 2001-2.
- *Migration:* According to sample survey estimates, approximately 27% of India's population are migrants, including those who move from one rural or urban area to another or between rural and urban areas. Approximately 57% of urban male migration is for seeking better employment opportunities. The net migration from rural to urban areas is approximately 2 million per annum, of which about 1 million may be job seekers.

Observations about Employment in India

Several significant conclusions can be drawn from this summary data:

1. *High rate of 'natural' employment generation:* In spite of a large influx of youth into the workforce, unemployment is not rising dramatically. This indicates that the Indian economy is generating a very large number of additional employment opportunities by natural processes that are not well documented or understood. An understanding of these processes is will assist the formulation of effective strategies to accelerate employment generation and eliminate the remainder of unemployment and underemployment in the economy. *If the unconscious process of employment generation can achieve this much, surely a conscious understanding and application can accomplish far higher rates of job growth.*
2. *Urban employment:* Since high rates of urban unemployment would almost invariably lead to rising discontent and violence, the relative stability of India's urban environment suggests that the urban economy is generating sufficient employment opportunities to absorb most new entrants and migrants from rural areas.
3. *Mismatch between Education & Employment:* While the number of employment opportunities is rising more or less as required to keep pace with the growth of the workforce, the type and quality of these opportunities does not match the expectations of many educated job seekers, which reflects inadequacies both in the type of employment generated and type of education being imparted to youth. Ironically, despite the surging number of graduates, many firms report difficulty in recruiting educated persons with the required work capabilities to meet the growth in demand for business process outsourcing, automotive component production and many other fields.
4. *Gap in Occupational Skills:* At the other end of the labour spectrum, it is increasingly difficult to obtain workers with basic skills in carpentry, masonry, electricals, mechanics, and many other trades. Although India operates a large vocational training system, it provides training to less than 2 million persons annually, which is grossly insufficient to impart skills to the 7 million new job entrants as well as the huge number of current unskilled workers. Absence of reliable information on the actual growth in employment by specific occupational categories makes it difficult to determine either the number of jobs being created in each field or the unsatisfied demand for various types of skills.

5. *Casualization of the workforce:* Evidence of an increase in casual and migratory employment reflects a deterioration in the quality of jobs in rural areas as well as rising expectations of the workforce that impels increasing numbers to abandon traditional occupations in search of better employment opportunities.
6. *Agricultural Employment:* While the percentage of the workforce employed in agriculture is declining, total employment in this sector continues to rise, though at significantly slower rates than in the past. A reduction in the proportion of the population employed in the primary sector is a natural and inevitable trend that is spurred by rising expectations and changing attitudes as much as by rising levels of farm productivity and mechanization. However, this does not mean that the potential for employment in this sector is being fully exploited. The findings of this report indicate that in the short term, strategic initiatives to modernize and diversify Indian agriculture can generate employment opportunities for very large numbers of people, thereby providing time for the more gradual expansion of employment potentials in other sectors.
7. *Surging Service Sector:* The traditional path of economic development was a progression from agriculture to manufacturing to services. India's recent success in IT and IT-enabled services is only one indication that this formula need not necessarily apply in the context of today's global economy where the demand for services internationally can rapidly expand employment opportunities domestically. In addition, changing social expectations within the country are stimulating rapid growth in demand for services that become prevalent in advanced industrial countries at a much later stage in their development, as indicated by the proliferation of courier companies, Xerox shops, Internet cafes, fast food restaurants and retail boutiques. The rampant clamour for education at all levels, surging demand for health care services, telecommunications, media, entertainment, and financial services are other expressions of this phenomenon. The publication of six English dailies and six Kannada dailies in the city of Bangalore is only one reflection of this wider trend. Research is required to more carefully document growth of the service sector, particularly its informal portion, to assess the

potential demand and most effective strategies for accelerating growth of employment. *These trends suggest that rural India has the opportunity to leapfrog over the traditional path to development, moving directly from agriculture into services.*

Theoretical Basis for Full Employment

The International Commission on Peace and Food, in its report entitled *Uncommon Opportunities: Agenda for Peace & Equitable Development,* examined the process of employment generation in society and concluded that full employment was a realistic and achievable goal for all countries in the foreseeable future. It observed that efforts to achieve full employment are constrained by a vague sense of helplessness or inevitability based on the erroneous perception that the number of employment opportunities generated in society is determined by forces that are either beyond the control of government and public initiative or too complex, costly and difficult to manage without severe adverse affects on the economy. Therefore, it may be useful to examine some of the major factors that presently limit the creation of new employment opportunities and the practical scope for action at these specific points.

Economically, employment generation is determined by how fully and productively society utilizes the material, technological, organizational and human resources at its disposal. The more productive the society is, the greater the quality and efficiency with which it produces goods and services, the greater the demand for those goods and services in the marketplace, the more employment opportunities and purchasing power created. This increased purchasing power then acts as an additional stimulus to the creation of new demand and employment opportunities.

Although early economists perceived that resources were limited, we now know that the potential for enhancing the productivity of resources is not. The Commission's report points out that the productivity of resources is the result of human resourcefulness. Since no society can or does fully exhaust its potentials for enhancing social productivity, the potential for employment generation is unlimited. Land, water and minerals may be limited, but the scope for increasing their productivity is not. Land is limited in India, but the scope for raising farm yields is not.

If this is the case for purely material resources, how much more true is it of technology, organization, knowledge, skill and other less tangible society resources? The enhancement in computer performance over the past 35 years according to Moore's Law is only one dramatic instance of a general truth about technological productivity in all fields. While the power of computers keeps increasing, the cost of producing them keeps falling because of technological developments that reduce their size, material consumption and labour inputs.

Technology alone does not result in human development. The application of technology through innovative social organizations has been the chief cause for the phenomenal gains of the past century. It was not the invention of the automobile but rather the innovation of a new organization of mass production by assembly line that enabled Henry Ford to transform the car from a luxury of the idle rich into a necessity for middle and working class families. It was not the invention of the computer, but the innovation of a new organization for electronic exchange of information in a standardized format that converted the Internet from the medium of academics and military planners into the most powerful communication tool in history and led to the emergence of the World Wide Web as a global library and global marketplace. India's dairy cooperatives, micro-finance self-help groups, STD booths, export processing zones, technology parks, and private computer training centres are all examples of organizational innovations that have stimulate development and create jobs.

What is true of technological and organizational resources is even more true for other social and human resources. Information is a resource that improves the quality of decision-making and makes possible the tapping of new opportunities. The quantity, quality and speed of all types of information exchange is multiplying exponentially. Through the enhancement of skills, knowledge and attitudes, the productivity of the human resource is growing by leaps and bounds. The USA, which awarded only a single PhD in 1880, now awards for than 35,000 annually. India produces more software engineers than the USA. Tamil Nadu, which had less than a dozen engineering colleges in 1980, has more than 200 today. Five lakh Indians are taking software training courses every year. Tens of thousands of four and five year old Indian children are surfing the internet or playing chess like future grandmasters. At the same time 45 per cent of the Indian population is still illitreate, only 60 per cent of 11-14 year olds are enrolled in school, two-thirds of children drop out before completing 10th Standard, and only five per cent of the workforce in the 20-24 age category have undergone formal vocational training, compared to 28 per cent in Mexico and 96 per cent in Korea. There is enormous scope for enhancing the knowledge and skills of India's workforce.

If the technological, organization and human potentials are unlimited, what is it that determines the actual extent to which a society develops these potentials? It is the awakening of the society. Socially, employment generation is determined by the aspirations of people, by rising expectations, by the urge to achieve and enjoy more. The higher the aspirations of society that actively yearn for fulfilment, the greater the energy and activity of the society and the greater the potential for employment generation. Government does not create jobs. No government can create and sustain full employment primarily by means of programmes. What government can and should do is to help awaken the people to the opportunities for higher accomplishment and to formulate policies and programmes that will help to release the initiative and support the efforts of the population for its own upliftment.

Guaranteed Employment

The generation of employment opportunities is as natural for a society as the spontaneous growth of plants on fertile soil. Every person born brings with him an assortment of material and other needs that natural create employment opportunities for himself and others to meet. The problem of shortage arises only when the structure of society prevents the spontaneous growth of employment opportunities. Employment is a problem of reconciling the potential with the actual. Like the shortage of water for agriculture in India, it is not a genuine question of economic scarcity but rather a problem of management.

Information about the actual process of employment generation in India is severely limited. We know that some seven to eight million persons are entering the labour force every year. We know that the rate of unemployment is relatively stable over time. Therefore, we must conclude that the society is spontaneously creating approximately seven million jobs a year, of which only a few percent are in the private organized sector. This fact shows that the Indian economy is vibrant and fully capable of creating the additional employment opportunities necessary to absorb the unemployed and underemployed. Minor adjustments in the structure of laws, policies and institutions can accomplish it.

It was with this understanding that the International Commission on Peace & Food first proposed to the United Nations in 1994 that employment be considered a basic human right to be constitutionally guaranteed. At the time, the proposal appeared visionary and unlikely to be given serious consideration. Now, a brief decade later, the proposal has been endorsed by the Government of India and is in the process of being converted into law. Naturally, it is neither possible nor desirable that Government tries to directly create all the necessary jobs. What it can do is to make the necessary adjustments in laws, policies and institutions and supplement them with some selected programme initiatives that will accelerate the creation of new employment opportunities by the society. The recommendations given in this report are conceived to accomplish this objective.

The growth of any sector of the economy depends on the growth of and support it receives from other sectors and the extent of integration between activities in different sectors. Until now the growth of Indian agriculture has been severely constrained by the weakness of its linkages with other key sectors, including industry, agricultural education, banking, insurance, marketing and infrastructure. A conscious effort to strengthen these linkages can stimulate rapid growth in this sector resulting in rapid growth in employment opportunities. The recommendations contained in this report are intended to provide or strengthen critical linkages for a quantum jump in the growth of employment and income opportunities in India's rural farm and non-farm sectors.

Skills Development for National Development

One need only walk through the streets and markets of any city or town in the developing world, from Asia to Africa to South America and beyond, in order to see the vast array of entrepreneurial skills on display. A core challenge facing those who rightfully view education as a powerful means of empowerment and development is how to effectively and successfully harness this work and life experience and channel it into formal education. It is a well established view that successful courses of formal education tend to be those that are relevant and meaningful to the lives of students. But how to encourage prospective students into such study when their formal schooling is not considered sufficient to gain direct entry into a course of post-secondary study? Likewise, business courses have an arguably well deserved reputation for being very expensive. This paper argues that partnerships are required between education providers and non-governmental organisations (NGOs) to provide affordable and flexible pre-tertiary business qualifications (diplomas and certificates) at a distance. This business focused education would seek to both formalise and expand the knowledge and experience of entrepreneurs. The resulting qualifications could then be used by such students, in combination with work and life experience, to gain entry into formal tertiary level studies. The drive, motivation and tenacity of entrepreneurs throughout the developing world represent a valuable human resource that would link well with formal distance business education. The current barriers to access must be lowered or removed if entrepreneurial success is to be matched by formal educational empowerment and longer term community development.

Defining Entrepreneurship

Defining what it means to be an entrepreneur is no easy task. Harding (2006, p. 5) contends that one must 'define the concept from the ground up'. Franco and Haase (2009, p. 637) maintain that a broader definition is required that views entrepreneurs as continual learners. A recent World Economic Forum report into entrepreneurship education defines an entrepreneur as someone who is creative, innovative and risk taking, and has an ability to translate 'ideas into action' (Volkmann et al 2009, p. 18). Dana (2001, p. 405) highlights the fact that 'there is no universally-accepted definition of entrepreneurs or of entrepreneurship' in the literature. This evident lack of a comprehensive and widely accepted definition does not detract from the reality that entrepreneurship possesses distinctive features including 'a capacity for innovation' (Bruni, Gherardi & Poggio 2004, p. 258). Nor does this apparent definition deficit alter the fundamental and important role that entrepreneurship plays in promoting economic development and vitality. Thus, linking entrepreneurship and education has for quite some time been considered crucial in limiting and reducing rates 'of long term unemployment' (Mueller et al 2006, p. 3). Entrepreneurship also widens and strengthens participation in economic activity, particularly for historically marginalised groups such as women (Hisrich & Ozturk 1999).

Research into entrepreneurship indicates that data and findings from the developed world 'need to be carefully examined and tested' prior to being utilised in the developing world (Hisrich & Ozturk 1999, p. 124). Education and training regimes need to be applicable and relevant to the local context and environment (Dana 2001, p. 405). Even so, Harding (2006, p. 6) points out that entrepreneurs are inherently flexible and adaptable and are not irreversibly linked to their ethnic, cultural or economic surroundings. In this context, knowledge is now seen as a central 'concept in social and economic advancement' (Franco & Haase 2009, p. 628). What do seem consistent and uniform are higher quality learning outcomes for those entrepreneurs who 'engage in action learning events' (Mueller et al 2006, p. 18). Action learning revolves around a pragmatic approach to education that seeks to provide students with opportunities outside the traditional classroom environment 'to meaningfully reflect on academic subjects' (Mueller et al 2006, pp. 4-5). Likewise, financial assistance alone is not sufficient to develop more effective and successful entrepreneurs, rather 'vocational education and training' are in many cases more beneficial (Dana 2001, p. 408).

Ascertaining what needs to be taught in terms of entrepreneurship education is no easy task as no formula exists for what constitutes entrepreneurship to begin with (Dana 2001, p. 414). Taatila (2010, pp. 56-57) highlights the need for learning to take place in the relevant business environment, while also detailing the need for real-life case studies based around student-centred and pragmatic pedagogical approaches. Plumy et al (2008, pp. 19-20) agree, stating that 'reality-based pedagogies' embedded in courses anchored to skill-building are better suited to entrepreneurship education than more traditional methodologies that focus on knowledge building, such as in accounting or management. Bringing together the workplace and learning, while 'integrating theory and practice', are key to implementing effective entrepreneurship education (Leppisaari, Tenhunen & Kleimola 2008, p. 6). Given that entrepreneurship represents an ongoing dynamic cycle of learning, it is surprising that there is somewhat of a gap in the organisational learning literature on this topic (Franco & Haase 2009, p. 629). Nevertheless, Plumly et al (2008, p. 19) detail a range of key skill building areas that they recommend covering, including communication, leadership, teamwork, negotiation, strategic planning, basic business law, innovation and technology, and product life-cycle and development.

NGOs and Entrepreneurship

Non-governmental organisations (NGOs) have a vital role to play in promoting economic development, and this is certainly the case when it comes to entrepreneurship education. In fact, both 'economic development and political empowerment' are now central themes amongst many development-focused NGOs, particularly when it comes to women and other marginalised groups in society (Rajasekaran 2009, p. 67). As Stefanovic (2007, p. 6) states, an increasing number of partnerships are taking place between NGOs, local and international businesses and government agencies. For example, NGOs are involved with 'small business management' education in India, while the

Entrepreneurship Development Institute of India (EDII) promotes through training and other activities 'development, employment generation and poverty alleviation' (Dana 2001, pp. 406-407). NGOs are also well placed to unite with other 'grass-roots agencies' and community groups to draw more people into formal training and education (Volkmann et al 2009, p. 92). In addition, NGOs are well situated to implement teaching and learning models and practices that are more organic and flexible than traditional education providers (Tesone 2004, p. 57). Rajasekaran (2009, p. 51) argues that NGOs over the past decade or so have contributed in more significant and lasting ways to the prosperity and development of poorer communities and countries through the provision of education, than the millions (if not billions) of dollars spent on more traditional aid programmes.

NGOs can help to make education more affordable and more accessible, helping to ensure 'that the poor are not priced out of the system' (Datt 2000, para. 31). Combined with this, the adoption of adult distance education (DE) is best placed to respond to ever increasing demands on the tertiary education sector (Kumi-Yeboah 2010, p. 20). Education and training can be provided across a broad spectrum from basic courses in literacy to 'training in livelihood enhancement' through to formal courses in entrepreneurship (Nuruddeen & Wada 2010, p. 11).

As Nuruddeen and Wada (2010, p. 11) point out, such a diverse range of courses when linked to microfinance programmes aimed at improving credit access, go a long way toward alleviating poverty. This being the case, it is not all about money, resources and access. Entrepreneurship distance students also require a supportive network of educators and fellow students to at least partially off-set the reality that most are 'first-generation learners' with a consequent lack of familial and social educational guidance and support, often taken for granted by middle class students (Datt 2000, para. 11).

Likewise, DE usually represents the only viable option available to most employed adults, such as entrepreneurs, with research indicating that many would not be able to undertake formal study without this option (Priebe, Ross & Low 2008, p. 11). NGOs and education providers need to work closely together and be acutely aware of the obstacles to DE and e-learning, namely, 'connectivity, equipment, software and training' (Daniel 2009). A holistic approach would likely see NGOs and education providers make powerful partners.

Partnerships: NGOs & Education Providers

The one important area that traditional education providers and NGOs can unite around to leverage their individual expertise is DE. Many education providers have a wealth of knowledge, experience and expertise in distance e-learning, with considerable growth expected well into the foreseeable future (Tesone 2004, p. 64 & Haley 2010, p. 58). Leppisaari, Tenhunen and Kleimola (2008, p. 77) maintain that entrepreneurship education requires collaboration between providers and the business world, as well as new pedagogical models that harness information and communications technology (ICT) 'in meaningful ways'. They go on to highlight the need for 'innovative online pedagogical learning solutions and authentic learning practices' (Leppisaari, Tenhunen & Kleimola 2008, p. 77). Volkmann et al (2009, p. 35) state that 'entrepreneurship education must continue to pioneer use of digital learning strategies and techniques'. In partnership with NGOs, entrepreneurship DE is likely to be promoted and implemented in ways that have a greater chance of reaching a much wider array of entrepreneurs who would otherwise not have access to such formal education. Partnerships with education providers and NGOs could also result in the design and implementation of a suite of short and medium term training regimes and packages with associated certificates and diplomas. These could then be entry points for participants into other levels of formal education and professional development.

The concept of open universities (OU) whereby access is open to everyone who applies is gaining traction in the developing world and highlights a range of valuable opportunities and pitfalls that are applicable to the ideas put forth in this paper. There is little doubt that opening access to higher education (and education more generally) would help to counter the barriers created by traditional entry systems that favour the elite in the developing world (Kember 2007, p. 73). The problem is that greater openness is only one part of the overall picture. A lack of infrastructure, particularly in terms of ICT, further widens the gap between those who have and those who do not, creating amongst other things digital, economic and educational divides (Gulati 2008 and Daniel 2009). Twigg (2002, p. 2) contends that it is possible 'to make online learning a tool to widen access without compromising cost or quality'. However, Kember (2007, p. 73) cautions that high rates of drop-out need to be acknowledged in order to develop a more holistic picture and more complete and effective strategies when it comes to reducing or abolishing entry barriers to higher education. Low adult literacy levels and dire economic circumstances mean that so many people in the developing world simply do not have the basic skills nor the resources to begin with (Gulati 2008). Even so, rapidly growing connectivity and the increasing importance of open educational resources (OERs) are likely to see at least some of these barriers greatly reduced in coming years (Daniel, Kanwar & Uvaliæ-Trumbiæ 2007, pp. 1 & 9).

Encouraging entrepreneurs into formal education is as challenging as trying to get them to transition from the informal sector to the mainstream economy (Dana 2001, p. 414). In this context, NGOs and education providers need to commit to long term approaches via ongoing collaboration, and by developing supportive networks for entrepreneurs (Leppisaari, Tenhunen & Kleimola 2008, p. 83). Entrepreneurs tend to know other entrepreneurs (Harding 2006, p. 6) and so the flow-on effects of introducing formal education and training to a particular entrepreneur or group are likely to grow with time. Stefanovic (2007, p. 8) points out that entrepreneurs from poor backgrounds (or the 'e-poor') might be living close to, or indeed just below, the poverty line; however, they often have the capacity to employ others. This job creation potential can be further enhanced through formal education and training. The ongoing growth in entrepreneurship education in the developed world, particularly the United States, is testament to the latent demand that exists for a greater focus on developing skills in entrepreneurial 'creativity and risk-taking', rather than solely on traditional-style business education (Plumly et al 2008, p. 18). NGOs are also better placed to provide 'access to credit' to marginalised entrepreneurs like women who often face enormous barriers when trying to access resources (Bruni, Gherardi & Poggio 2004, p. 263). Moreover, in India the EDII also demonstrates that although access to resources is very important, so too are programmes that improve personal confidence and motivate aspiring entrepreneurs, in the process, helping individuals to realise their hidden potential (Dana 2001, p. 407).

8

Vocational and Technical Education: International Context

Education and training have often been considered polar extremes, the first being the development of the mind and the latter the mastery of strictly practical endeavours. But the two worlds of practical and conceptual endeavours are less distant than they may seem, and these simplistic views of education and training are misguided.

Indeed, there are definitional problems concerning education and training, leading to misguided policies. There is a need for a clear understanding of the overlaps and contrasts between the two concepts. There is a long and old controversy in the literature opposing education and training. The Roman rhetorician Quintilian claimed that oratory was more useful than philosophy, thereby stating the superiority of training over education. But for many centuries education was closer to philosophy than to applied endeavours.

Some educators use the word *training* in a derogatory way, as if to suggest that the learning is intellectually shallow or that it goes with attempts to educate the poor. In contrast, some trainers refer to education as vacuous, fuzzy, and rambling learning that is good only for wasting the time of students.

What Vocational Training Offers

Both views, however, are too narrow and misleading. When dealing with less-schooled students, vocational subjects can be used to motivate and to create an environment that is familiar to them. Good training may function as a conduit for the best possible education for students less ready for abstraction. By using practical situations as start and end points, abstract concepts can be introduced and mastered by students who otherwise would be very low achievers in academic schools.

The environment created by good vocational schools can give students a sense of getting closer to a concrete job. This can in turn generate a degree of motivation and sense of self-efficacy that is conducive to the mastery of abstract concepts that would leave students cold and aloof when taught at academic schools that have difficulties in recreating environments that motivate low-achieving students.

Good vocational training makes use of the context of the practical subjects to teach mathematics, writing, reading, and science. Students are asked to read the instructions of what they are doing and write down the procedures they will execute. Concrete workshop situations are conceived, for instance, to have students convert inches to centimeters, Fahrenheit to Celsius, and so on. In other words, proportion is learned as a by-product of solving shop problems. Mathematics is smuggled into the practicalities of shop work. In fact, good training institutions have different versions of mathematics, one for machinists, another for electricians, and so on.

As research in the psychology of learning suggests, the mastery of subjects increases when the contexts in which phenomena are examined are fully familiar to the students. Experiments have shown that a physical principle is better understood when the students are given the broad context in which it applies. For instance, it has been shown that students acquired a better grasp of the concept of density when they were shown a clip from the film *Raiders of the Lost Ark* in which the hero, Indiana Jones, has to replace a golden skull sitting on a platform with his bag filled with rocks, both which weighed the same. Students were asked to estimate the weight of the golden skull by measuring the approximate volume of a human skull and multiplying it by the relative density of gold. What good training does is to present inside the workshop such concrete problems based on concrete needs arising in the practical tasks to be performed.

Nevertheless, what training offers is merely the possibility to tap into this potential. There is nothing automatic about it. Training can fail to use these opportunities. Training that is only training is bad training or merely too shallow to go beyond the transmission of some dexterity. How to put out a fire or how to unclog a pipe are useful pieces of knowledge in their own right and need to be taught. But they are essentially different from longer training programmes that contain more conceptual and theoretical structures.

The "basic skills" movement consists of improving the knowledge of the fundamental literacy and numeracy skills of workers who are learning a trade or have already mastered the more practical and manual aspects of their occupations. The essence of the successful strategies, however, is to use the same workplace operations as a scaffold on which to build the conceptual or cognitive skills that are missing. Workers learn how to read by reading the same manual that they need to read to perform their job correctly. Vocational contents can be an ideal context in which to plant cognitive development of a higher order. Thinking skills and good reading and writing habits can be developed while doing practical tasks that lead to marketable skills.

By the same token, academic education may also resort to practical endeavours in order to carry the more general message. Laboratory classes try to do this, and the *Indiana Jones* example illustrates more deliberate attempts to bring context to learning. Theory, after all, involves the generalization and conceptualization of real-world observations. Formulas written on the blackboard merely display packaged and sanitized versions of the intense intellectual effort that was required to arrive at them. The idea of having students "rediscover" physical principles goes in the same direction.

Developments in Technology and Work Organization

This reasoning implies that the differences between education and training have always been exaggerated and that most reputable training programmes are education as much as training. Recent developments in technology and work organization, however, seem to be blurring even further the distinction between education and training. In industrialized countries, a very significant share of manufacturing activities have changed considerably and incorporate new technologies, particularly those based on microprocessors and the variety of automation techniques that result from them. Some successful industrializing countries are definitely moving in the same direction.

New production technologies require more reading, more writing, more applied mathematics, and more science. In the past, these cognitive skills were, at best, a means to master a trade (e.g., one needs to know how to read to take the machinist course because some of the instruction is written in books or handouts). But these cognitive skills are becoming part and parcel of the occupational profile. For example, reading is directly useful for the performance of the core tasks of the occupation. Could it then be said that reading and mathematics are now vocational subjects? For that reason, most training programmes could benefit from a little more emphasis on language, mathematics, and science, as occurs in the best courses and apprenticeships. This is increasingly happening in Germany, in the American techprep programmes, and in the new generation of SENAI courses in Brazil.

While learning an occupation, the trainee may have an ideal opportunity to develop the same general skills that are taught in academic schools, that is, a general education. But this will not happen spontaneously. The integration of theory and practice, of shop activities with general principles of science, can be the result only of deliberate and well-informed efforts. Training programmes should not underestimate the potential offered by such integration or the difficulties of achieving it. But there are good examples of these ideas. For instance, the new versions of the traditional Latin American "methodical series," as well as new methods developed in countries such as the United States (tech prep, School to Work) and Germany (key qualifications), have good track records.

In short, vocational subjects can be used to motivate and to create an environment that is familiar to the students. Good training may function as a conduit for the best possible education for students less ready for abstraction. By the same token, academic education may also resort to practical endeavours in order to carry the more general message.

Differences and Similarities between Training and Education

There are conceptual differences between the roles of vocational training and education. Yet, as mentioned, the borderline between training and education is quite blurred. In its purest version, education is knowledge removed from practical applications (e.g., learning astronomy is pure education, except for those who plan to become professional astronomers). At the other extreme, pure training is a version of skill preparation that does not explore the theoretical implications of the tasks being learned (e.g., learning how to use a saw and a jack plane without learning drafting and the requisite mathematics). In most cases, however, the two are combined.

Good training and a good education are equally good–and actually very similar in nature–when they promote the broad conceptual and analytical development of the trainee. By the same token, a good education is often linked to applied endeavours that turn theoretical knowledge into a practical skill. The difference is mostly one of intention. Education uses the practical or occupational content to obtain a deeper mastery of theory, being somewhat unconcerned with the application of the knowledge in the marketplace. Training starts with the clear goal of preparing for an existing occupation, the theory being a necessary component to prepare a better worker for that position.

Yet, despite all the merits of training, it is not a cost-efficient substitute for good schools for all. By contrast, a solid basic education is the best preparation for a wide range of jobs. In addition, a good basic education shortens the length of training required. In other words, the need to develop a good training system does not replace the (perhaps) stronger imperative to develop a good general education system. Workers with a good mix of practical skills and conceptual understanding of technology can adjust more easily to new and different occupations, grow in their careers, and adjust to technological changes. The real issue is not general versus superspecialized training but the solidity and depth of the basic skills that go together with specialized training.

A first element to understanding the differences and similarities between training and education is to consider that the presence of training contents that may be applicable at the workplace does not vary inversely with the presence of fundamental concepts and abstraction. Both poetry and solid-state physics are rich in abstraction. The first has scarce direct applicability at the workplace. The second has ample utilization. Basket weaving has hardly any abstraction or conceptualization and finds little demand in modern societies. Cutting hair offers little in abstract thinking but there are ample economic applications for this skill. It is necessary to stress that theory and practice are not the extremes of a single continuum but independent concepts that admit all possible combinations of highs and lows, as exemplified above. Fortunately, to have the high theoretical and conceptual content that educates and sharpens the mind, one does not have to forego learning the practicalities of life and work. Both what is called vocational training and what is called education of all sorts have both the theory and the practice. The main point here is that occupational training that fetches a good market is as good or better than any other environment to educate the mind in the fundamental concepts that are usually found in good education.

Training should not be understood as something poor in theory and conceptualization. It can be rich or poor. Education should not be understood as something helplessly unpractical. In fact, it may be removed from immediate applications or it may be very close to them. There are no good reasons to be concerned with the differences between education and training instead of offering learning opportunities that have both.

Conclusion

Abstract subjects that are removed from the everyday life of students offer a more arid ground for learning. Such subjects as Latin declensions, French irregular verbs, underground geological layers, the successions of kings of France, and the capitals of African states are not topics that fascinate the average student. Hence, they are not the ideal place to graft the broad basic skills that constitute an education for a modern society. Vocational schools can avoid these motivational difficulties by bringing in the world of the factory, with its practicalities and the inherent motivation of learning some skills that have immediate market value. Nevertheless, not everything that happens in the factory is ideal for the process of learning. In particular, the factory routines teach mostly how to deal with repetitive activities. This is a worthy objective of short training courses and for the preparation of workers who lack the prerequisites for further development. This may be justified in many cases, but it is not what is considered the optimal environment for broad learning. But equally important to understand is that many interesting, motivating, or even fascinating practical applications of the concepts and theories taught in academic schools may fail to have immediate demand in the marketplace–even though, indirectly, all good education ends up being valuable in the world of work. Learning statistics by dealing with Formula 1 auto racing data is as good as any other method of motivating students and leading them to complex concepts. However, newspapers rarely include advertisements for jobs involving the analysis of Formula 1 data.

Technical Vocational Education & Training

Both vocational education and skills development have been known to increase productivity of individuals, profitability of employers and expansion of national development. A 'knowledgeable' workforce, one that is both highly skilled in a particular occupation and also exhibits flexibility, is seen as the most important human capital required for the development of a country.

India's workforce is characterized as having low skills and poorly prepared to compete in today's globalized world. Rapid technological changes now require individuals to *learn and relearn skills throughout their working lives by ensuring its relevance and effectiveness.* Hence it is inevitable to increase the knowledge, the skills and the institutional capacities within a time frame at the national and state levels. It's true that skilled workforce, impacts positively on economic growth, raises productivity levels and reduces unemployment.

Vocational and professional training system would have a major positive impact on national competitiveness. The Technical and Vocational Education is considered as an important measure for the development of trained labour force required for the socio-economic development of a country. It is argued that the elementary education must impart usable technical knowledge and vocational education can be used effectively to combat dropouts. More specifically, it is believed to be an effective answer to reduce unemployment and migration to urban centres. Technical education develops 'skill culture' in contrast to pure academic culture and preferences for white collar jobs and 'to serve simultaneously the 'hand' and the 'mind', the practical and the abstract, the vocational and academic'. The development of occupational skills leads to technological advancement that ensures optimum utilization of resources and leads to enhanced productivity and thereby increased level of growth, competitiveness and job satisfaction and reduction in gap between demand and supply.

Skills development is an increasingly important factor in adapting societies to changing economic and environmental conditions. It can bring innovation, enhance productivity, stimulate economic competitiveness and underpin inclusive approaches to development. Despite significant progress, too many developing countries still lack effective vocational education and training (VET) strategies, and are struggling with costly and outdated training systems, and have no culture of evaluation and knowledge-based policymaking and programme administration. In this age of liberalization, India is still way behind in training the people in different specializations. Vocational training is to impart specialized skills and knowledge, and instilling social and political attitudes and behavioural patterns essential for successful economic activities by people engaged in dependent employment, self-employment or subsistence work.

The Government of India in recent years has laid a lot of emphasis on streamlining vocational education so that it fulfils the emerging need of the market by focusing on employability skills.

The Prime Minister of India has suggested that India should set a goal to create 500 million certified and skilled technicians in the country by 2022. As we have the largest population of young people in the world, we need to invest adequately in their education and employability, to become the largest pool of technically trained manpower in the world.

Skill Development Targets

- To create 500 million certified and skilled technicians by 2020
- Invest adequately in their education and employability
- As envisaged in the 11th Plan:
  - Impart relevant skills to 10 million people annually
  - Create 70 million new jobs and gain industry support for the same
- Recognizing skills needs in the context of changing scenario
- Exploring possibilities & need for PPP and cooperation in the area of skills development
- Addressing employability issues imperative for inclusive growth
- Focus on quality and standardization and also quality of faculty / trainers / instructors

Briefly these are the Targets which have been set before us in the XIth plan. Even if these minimum targets are to be achieved in a substantial part, let alone as a whole, it will be important to critically review the existing Systems, Models and Best practices at the national and international level in the domain of Vocational Education and Skill Development to set as well as course correct the Road Map for the future.

Current Scenario

Access to VE & T – The Demand Supply Gap

Let us first look at the Availability *vis-à-vis* Demand of Skill Development and Vocational Education initiative.

- Between class 1st - 8th, about 50 % students drop out. Approx. 20-21 million drop out after Class VIII (target group)
- Formal training capacity is available only for - 2.3 million
- Gap - 18.7 million.
- 12.8 million persons enter the labour market every year.
- About 95% of the world youth (15 - 35 yrs) age learn any type of vocation / skill / trade, with a choice of 3000 vocational streams.
- In India we have identified only about 150 trades and only 2-3% of the youth (15-29 yrs) goes in for formal vocational training.

- Lack of new & innovative trades in VET to attract young children's and meet the Industry requirements

If we look at the current scenario we will find that, there is a Gap of 18.7 million. In India so far we have identified only about 150 trades with a choice of 3000 vocational streams and only 2-3% of the youth (15-29 yrs) goes in for formal vocational training. Obviously there is a big Gap between the Aspirations and the Availability.

There is another *Strange Phenomenon in terms of the Demand – Supply gap in India.*

- Skill development
  - India over the next five years will have surplus of un-trained and under-educated people - 1.3 million
  - India will fall short of real talent by about - 5.3 million
  - We will have a surplus that we will not need and a deficit that we cannot fulfill
  - Further crises to be caused by mismatch between jobs available and skill shortage
- *Thus there is a Gap between the Needs of the Industry and the Availability*

Although on one side as we can see from the *Bostan Study Group (2008)* that over next five years India will have a surplus of un-trained and under-educated people of 1.3 million and falling short of real talent of 5.3 million. That is there will be a surplus that we will not need and a deficit that we will not be able to fulfill.

From here it is equally important to see what will be the future of the Labour eco system in India in times to come.

Future of Labour Ecosystem in India

As per the Team Lease Services Labour Report 2006 *(The report mainly predicts the future of labour ecosystem in India, state wise.)*

- The potential working age population (20-59yrs)
  - Currently - 567 million
  - In 2020 - over 761 million *(estimated)*
- The govt. is talking about creating 10 million jobs every year
- However, the requirement is more than 15 million in a year.
- Even if we find 100 million new jobs, 170 million will be out of employment in 2020, this is nearly 30%.

- Only around 2.5-3% of persons aged 15 years or more had technical qualifications of even the most rudimentary kind
- 152 million persons who enter the in-formal sector for their livelihood have no access to vocational training
- The biggest challenge will be to provide formal education and employment to the huge work force in 2020

Even though enrolments in vocational education in India are small when judged by international comparisons, expanding the numbers or re-targeting the programme would not be justified unless a model is found that would substantially improve the outcomes.

India's Tremendous Potential- Demographic Surplus[1]

- Working age population to comprise over 63% of the aggregate by 2016.
- India only economy with declining age dependency ratios till 2030.
- A third of India's population below 15 years of age and 20 % of the population in the 15-24 age groups.
- In 2020, the average age in countries will be-

Indian	*Chinees & US*	*West Europe*	*Japan*
29 yrs	37yrs	45yrs	48yrs

- India with 69% of its population between 16-29 yrs – youngest country
- India's demographic surplus will be 47 million by 2020
- However Educated without professional skills constitute 69% of the unemployed.

Hence in order to make our Demographic Surplus become Demographic Dividend and not a nightmare it is important that our population is *adequately skilled to meet the growing industry demand and many more avenues of self employment are opened up keeping in view the national and global requirement.*

Skill Development - Challenges

- Acute shortage of Skill Development institutions/ Infrastructure
- Poor bankability of the skills due to poor training, resulting in low employability of trainees.
- Disconnect - Skills provided & Skills required by the industry.

- Outdated training modules & inadequate courses, machineries, tools & technology.
- Skill demands of the service as well as the organized sector remains largely unmet.
- Severe shortage of trained instructors; and
- Weak industry-institute interface

What is Preventing us from Meeting the Challenges?

- The challenges are immense and in order to achieve the goals there has to be:
- *Substantial expansion of quality - technical vocational education & training for raising employability & productivity*
- *Focus on Self-employment skills*
- *Models that would substantially improve outcomes.*
- The skills provided have to be attuned to:
- New business requirements: in India & abroad
- Improving quality of education and trainings at all levels;
- Make technical / vocational education system more flexible and inclusive for sustainable growth.

These and many more issues need to be addressed urgently. Keeping in view these challenges government has taken many initiatives. Are they enough?

Government Initiative (Including XIth Plan)

- 1600 new ITI's and Polytechnics
  - 1000 polytechnics – 300 by State Govt., 300 in PPP mode, 400 by Pvt. Sector
- 50,000 new Skill Development Centres (Rs. 2,000 cr)
  - It would enable 1 core students to get Vocational training.
- Strengthening of existing polytechnics
- Establishment of 125 new polytechnics (Rs. 1,125 cr)
- 580 new community polytechnics (Rs. 580 cr)
- Vocational education in 10,000 sec. schools (Rs. 1,000 cr)
- Organized training for 25 lakh BPL youths (Rs. 1,875 cr)
- Urban skill and employability programmes (Rs. 2,500 cr)
- Skill building and economic assistance (Rs. 3,000 cr)

- Incentivising State Govt. for expansion / up gradation of existing & new institutions.
- Greater public sector & private sector interface

Apart from these the Government of India has taken some bold and laudable initiatives of late, although much remains to be done:

Recent National Level Institutional Arrangement

- National Council on Skill Development to review and focus on policy direction by setting vision, and laying down core strategies
- National Skill Development Coordination Board to coordinate action for skill development in Public & Pvt. sectors and ensure that govt. agencies intensify actions for vocational education, technical training through Industrial Training Institutes (ITIs), and through promotion of public-private partnerships
- National Skill Development Corporation (NSDC) a non-profit company,
  - to promote skill development in the private sector
  - to promote technical training in the country in public-private partnership model
  - would set up world-class technical institutes across India.
  - private partners to hold 51 percent stake in the new entity
  - develop simple, easily understood "core" employability skills & competency standards
  - provide a common platform for collaboration amongst private sector employers, training providers and the labour force

Issue Still Remains

With Skill Development Mission initiative not much has taken off keeping in view employability & acceptability by the industry. Already entering in the third years of the XIth plan – but very little seen on the ground yet

- Skill Development is critical and immediate but the issue still remains that of Scalability in short time frame including emphasis on self employment with Quality & Relevance, and Systemic Transformation
- Hence Bold Measures need to be adopted Within the policy and New policies towards these Goals

For Scalability & Fulfilling Aspirations of the People & Needs of the Industry / Economy More Extra Efforts have to be Taken in the Skill Development Initiatives:

- Government Initiative- continue to be sustained and be hastened on the one hand and Strengthen Public-Private-Partnership and Encourage Private participation on the other.
  - In all these modes initiatives to encourage
- Programmes *other than pure academic university traditional education*, with *lateral linkages with higher education.*
- Popular employable programmes which attracts desirous students
- Testing, Certification through Industry / Chambers / Industry Associations
  - Institutions specialized in training and re-training (new providers)
- Independent Skill development Institutes i.e.(NIIT, APTECH)
- Specialist 'vendor-led' training, companies in partnership with other providers
  - Other New Modes

Keeping this in view it becomes evident to present few example of some of these currently taking place as Best Practices-nationally as well as Internationally under some of these Modes

Best Practices at the National Level

10.1 LG Electronics Ltd. with Mumbai it is:

- Model developed by L.G Electronics to meet their needs for skilled manpower of trade RAC / RTV/ Electronics/ ITESM etc for their Authorised Service Centres (ASC).
- This Model is initially applicable to 5 ITIs
- The key features of the model include:
  - L.G provides input to upgrade/ Modify/ Add-on to the curriculum
  - LG selects the trainees for appointment in Authorised service centre after completion of 1½ year of training (duration of training is 2 years)
  - Agreement between Authorised Service Centre & candidates for appointment
  - L.G gives scholarship Rs. 1000/- to selected trainees.

  - L.G provides training to ITIs instructors (Trainers) in the premises of L.G at their own cost (Including TA, Lodging & Boarding)

This is a collaborative model as opposed to adoption between LG Electronics and 5 ITIs in Mumbai developed by L.G to meet their needs for skilled manpower for their Authorised Service Centres

Model Adopted by the State & Bharat Forge Ltd (BFL)

- Bharat Forge (BFL) decided to adopt ITI Khed. The features are:
  - BFL *identified the requirement of Manpower for their Industry.*
  - Accordingly 6 Trades were selected.
  - Additional infrastructure facilities - building, equipment & power supply etc. in existing ITI by BFL.
  - BFL selects the Instructional Staff for the proposed trade & train them in their industry.
  - All non-recurring and recurring expenses borne by BFL for Initial 5 yrs.
  - BFL nominee is Chairperson of Institute Management Committee (IMC).
  - *Periodical audit of training by BFL.*
  - BFL engages pass out candidate for Apprenticeship Training and thereafter for Employment in their group of Industries.

This is a model of an ITI Adopted by Bharat Forg keeping in view their requirements of skilled Manpower and accordingly Six Trades were selected to engage the candidates for apprenticeship training & thereafter employ them in their industries.

Model adopted by Maruti Suzuki India Ltd. (MSIL)

To upgrade ITIs into Centres of Excellence to:

- Provide high degree of employability & creation of skilled technical hands.
- Encourage ITI Principals to good training institutes by way of personal visits.
- Frame comprehensive curriculum for holistic training as well as multi -skilling.
- Practical Training to students by visits to MSIL factory & driving schools

- Feedback from students to gauge the usefulness of training imparted.
- Modules for training the trainers with latest skills
- Attitudinal/Motivational training to staff ensuring empowerment & team efficiency.
- Skill test with admission test for admission in Centre of Excellence
- Thrust on selecting students with right aptitude.
- Suitable reward systems to recognize students, and meritorious service of faculty to retain/ train them.
- Adequate focus on infrastructural facilities of ITIs with respect to
- Tools, equipment, machinery, buildings, library, furniture,
- water storage facility, in-house power generation capacity,
- general repairs, including Civil & Electrical works,and
- identification and disposal of unusable assets, audio-visual teaching aids, computers etc.

This is a model adopted by Maruti Suzuki India limited to upgrade ITI into centres of Excellence to provide employability & creation of skilled manpower.

Learning from the Above Three Best Practices

The key to success here however are:

- Leadership provided by the head of the institutions/Industry
- Training & updation of Heads of the Institutes
- On going faculty development & training
- Absorption by Industry concerned with large part of the trainees
- Curriculum continuously updated & Practical Training on updated Industry Requirements
- Exposure to Best Practices for all bodies to collaborate /required state Govt. and other industries to adopt/initiate such partnerships

The key to success here however are the leadership and training by head of the institutions/Industry, the instructors in the Vocational System, and the ability for the industry to absorb trainees whether on the Shop Flore or in the office successful because of the availability of instructors who are up to date with and immune in Industry practical experienced background.

Scalability will be confined to only those larger industries with ITIs around it as SMEs may not have Surplus manpower and/or infrastructure and/or Skills to support this by themselves.

Collaboration can be more advisable than adoption because many may not be interested in running an ITI, but they can benefit by this kind of collaboration as a consumer of the trainees.

Best Practices : Infosys Campus Connect (PPP)

- Launched by Infosys in May 2004 with 60 colleges, as an industry-academia collaboration programme to align engineering student competencies with industry needs".
- Enhance the Quantity and Quality *(Technical Competency, Soft Skills, Process Orientation, Analytical Abilities, English Language fluency)* of its IT Talent Pool
- The Programme Approach has been to Provide
  - Students
- Access to Infosys Courseware, Projects and Case Studies
  - *Faculty*
- Industry Exposure & Experience
  - College Management
- Education Management Thought-Leadership
  - Educational Bodies
- Influence Higher Education Policies (*Access, Relevance, Scalability, Administration, Infrastructure, Versatility, Investments...)*
- Education Assets & Imperatives
  - Relationship Framework
- MOU with college/ University
- Campus Connect Annual Planning Process
- Stakeholder survey, Feedback and Information system
  - Infrastructure
- Campus Connect Portal
- Help desk, Email based request system, Survey Tool
- Webinar, Video Conferencing, Teleconferencing, Event Recording
  - Programme offerings and services
- Faculty Enablement Programme, Road shows

- Sabbaticals, Industry Visits
- Technology Seminars, Contests
  - Programme Management Practices
- Roll-out Planning and Execution Framework
- Deployment Tracking at National Level (248 Colleges)
- Regional and National level Review Methodology, Segmentation Model
  - Courseware and Methodology
- Foundation Programme Courseware, Soft skills Courseware
- Student Project Bank, Publications and KM System (Internal)
- Assessment methods, Lab Assignments Bank

Global Foundation Programme

- Customized to Meet Target Student Requirements
  - Generic courses; Open Systems Stream; Internet Stream; Mainframes Stream
- English Language Proficiency;
- Process orientation;
- Problem solving and orientation;
- Behaviroul Skills/Values

Foundation Programme Deployment for

- Scalability, Consistency and Repeatability

The Infosys Campus connect programme has grown rapidly to 500 colleges in Eleven India cities & Global presence in (North America, Asia Pacific & Europe) and has Trained over 25,000 students & enhanced skills of 2000 faculty.

The core of Campus Connect is the Foundation Programme, which is 130 classroom hour proprietary educational supplements for a batch size of 60-75 students integrated with the College's academic schedule and include Industrial Visits to Infosys Development Centres.

Course material provided by Infosys based on material used for its induction programmes, assignments, case studies and a Student Project Bank. Soft Skills Programme intended to develop students' skills in communication, team work, corporate work culture, etc.

12.1 Learning from the Infosys Campus Connect

- Colleges given incentives based on the performance of number of graduates joining Infosys and pass on the cash benefits received from Infosys to people, including faculty based on college-specific norms.

- Campus Connect reduces the learning time and training cost after employment by aligning the skill needs of IT services with the college curriculum,
- In determining its return on investment in Campus Connect, Infosys ensures that a sufficient number of Campus Connect graduates accept Infosys offers to make its investment in the programme worthwhile. It banks on its reputation as a superior employer and its large annual recruitment

Learning from German Model

The serious drawback with this model is that there is excessive specialization in a particular skill only. And it would limit the worker's employability due to lack of multi skills. However there are key advantages in customizing this model because, Trainees are being paid by the Industry and vocational education institutes and Training is being funded by the government. Secondly students are trained on updated industry infrastructure on the job and their Employability is guaranteed. Industry gets Low cost trainee with fixed timeframe and also gets Extra workers without incurring any long term liability

Community College – USA - (Govt.)

- Most technical & vocational courses are offered by Community Colleges as 60 % of the Higher Secondary School leavers prefer to enroll themselves in the Community Colleges
- Manpower needed at the lower & middle levels of various sectors of economic activity is easily prepared by the Community Colleges.
- These institutions are two year UG institutions (complete in it self) providing skill based and employment oriented education.
- Community colleges are unique in United States for the following reasons:
  - Enables students to learn varied trades/courses at a Lower Cost
  - Earn a two year degree which makes them employable immediately
  - Should they wish – provision to enroll into a degree college/ Univ. and continue & obtain their further degree any time
  - Excellent Transfer Opportunities

- Articulation or "2 + 2" transfer agreements allow students to transfer their community college credits toward a university degree.
- students first go to a community college for 2 years of study, obtain an associate degree, and then complete 2 years at a university to obtain a bachelor's degree.
- Many state universities give preference to qualified students who transfer from a community college in that state.
  - Unique features
- Flexible English Proficiency Requirements
- Focus on Teaching and Student Success
- Small Class Sizes (between 15 - 20)
- Additional Practical Training Opportunity
- Use of the Latest Technologies
- Hundreds of Programmes to Choose

The best part is that These institutions are two year UG institutions (complete in it self) providing skill based and employment oriented education which Enables students to learn varied trades/ courses at a Lower Cost and Earn a two year degree which makes them employable immediately. *Key is Lateral entry possibilities*

University of Phoenix - USA – (Pvt.)

- Provide education highly accessible for working students in almost every trades.
  - Flexible timing, flexible scheduling, continuous enrollment, a student-centred environment, practitioner faculty, online classes, online library, e-books, computer simulations
- providing instruction to bridges the gap between theory and practice through
  - advanced academic preparation
  - Courses/trades that more professional and are employable
  - skills that come from the practice of their professions.
  - relevance content helping students relate to the world of work and
  - make connections between theoretical and practical applications.
- Professional, VE & T that ensure - students receive a quality education that is applicable to the real world of work.

Education provided is highly accessible for working students in almost every trade generally not offered in University setup which is has flexible timing and scheduling. Education connects between theoretical and practical application and students receive quality education that is applicable to the real world of work. It can be called Vocational & Professional University

Learning from Community College & Phoenix University

The systems can be customized and attuned to our system

- It takes care of attitudinal perceptions - one has a degree.
  - This Degree is Part of the Academic Pyramid
- Enables students to learn varied trades/courses at a Lower Cost
- providing skill based and employment oriented education.
- instruction to bridges the gap between theory and practice
- Provide education highly accessible for working students in almost every trades generally not offered in Univ. setup
  - Flexible timing, flexible scheduling, continuous enrollment
- However for its success it must have involvement of Industry or the Private Sector in all aspects i.e. strong industry interface and effective trainers.

Kenya: Training for the Informal Sector- Jua Kali Experience

Distribution of vouchers to informal sector entrepreneurs to purchase training

- Aim of Jua Kali (Informal Sector)
  - Skills & technology upgradation for 25,000 informal sector manufacturing workers;
  - increase the access of informal sector entrepreneurs to services; and
  - improve the policy and institutional environment by removing restrictive laws and policies.
- Features
  - Voucher programme intended to introduce consumer choice, enabling informal sector operators to purchase the training they want.
  - Intermediaries—allocation agencies—selected by competitive tender to market, allocate, and redeem vouchers in a decentralized way throughout Kenya.

- Allocation agencies receive fee equal to 3 % of the value of vouchers issued.
- Vouchers to be used for any kind of training from any registered training provider.

As a result of the Jua Kali experience about 700 training providers became prequalified for providing training. By early 2001, some 18,000 training vouchers had been issued. The impact of the project, evaluated through two tracer studies, has been highly positive for the beneficiaries. Employment among the graduates had increased by 50 percent compared with employment before training, and the income of surviving enterprises had also increased by 50 percent.

The strong preference of Jua Kali workers for appropriate, accessible training by master crafts persons was revealed in the first phase of the project where 85 percent of all vouchers went to pay for the services of master crafts persons, and only 15 percent went to private and public training institutions.

Learning from the Best Practices - Kenya: Training for the Informal

Implementation experience underscores the importance of appropriate management arrangements that a project for the private sector is best managed by the private sector with government best playing a facilitating role.

- the use of a voucher mechanism enabled the project to
  - Stimulate demand for training, technology & management and marketing consultation among micro & small enterprises.
  - A supply response was generated & training market established to address the needs of micro enterprises;
- Unexpected Impact of the voucher training programme
  - Emergence of skilled craftsmen as the leading providers of training.
  - Entrepreneurs preferred the training services of master crafts persons in the informal sector to training in formal institutions.
  - The training by master crafts persons was usually well adapted to entrepreneurs' need for short, practical training.
  - These training providers were previously invisible to agencies that wished to pay for training directly;

Mexico: A Proactive Approach to Small & Medium size Enterprise Support

The Integral Quality & Modernization Programme (CIMO – now renamed PAC)

- Partnerships between public and private sector to provide Subsidized Training & Range of support services to
  - Enhance the productivity of the informal sector
  - Reaching and assisting small & medium-size enterprises to upgrade worker skills, improve quality, and raise productivity with specific sectoral needs.
  - Provide an integrated package of services, including (information on technology, new production processes, quality control techniques, and marketing)
- All States and Federal District have at least one CIMO unit, each staffed by 3 - 4 promoters.
- Most units housed in business associations that contribute office & support infrastructure.
- The promoters organize workshops on
  - training and technical assistance services, identify potential local and regional training suppliers and consulting agents, and
  - actively seek out enterprises to deliver assistance on a cost-sharing basis.
- Work with enterprises to conduct an initial evaluation of the firm, as the basis for training programmes and other consulting assistance.

The Integral Quality and Modernization Programme (CIMO – now renamed as PAC), was established in 1988, Set up as a pilot project to provide subsidized training, CIMO was evolved when it was apparent that lack of training is the only factor contributing to low productivity. By 2000, CIMO was providing a package of training and industrial extension services to over 80,000 enterprises each year and training 200,000 employees. Private sector interest has grown and More than 300 business associations now participate in CIMO, up from 72 in 1988.

Learning from Best Practices – Mexico

- CIMO has been effective in improving the performance of targeted companies.

- Its firms have increased investments in worker training,
- It had higher rates of capacity utilization, and adopts quality control practices.
  - These improved outcomes were associated with increased productivity.
- Is a cost-effective way of assisting small and medium-size enterprises.
  - increased profitability, sales and capacity utilization,
  - wage and employment growth,
  - reduced labour turnover, absenteeism, and rejection rates for products.
  - The most dramatic impacts were among micro and small firms.

Bangladesh: Underprivileged Children's Education Programme (UCEP)

The Bangladesh – Underprivileged Children's Education Programme (UCEP) Established in the early 1970s, with an objective to raise the living standards of poor urban children and their families.

- Focuses on the target group of working street children & providing skills to enhance their employability in the local labour market, often (informal sector)
- Conducted in 30 general schools for non-formal basic education working on three shifts per day in four major cities of Bangladesh.
  - Total enrolment about 20,000.
  - Skill training given in three training institutions working in two shifts each, training a total of 1,400 trainees
  - Extraordinarily high completion and employment rates for its graduates, both averaging about 95 percent.
- UCEP's programme (three stages)
  - Accelerated non-formal basic education starting at age 10 or 11.
- About half the graduates from the non-formal basic education programme are admitted into vocational training.
  - Fundamental skills training from six months to two years.
  - Placement in employment, and follow-up on the job.

Learning from Best Practices – Bangladesh

- *Locally based non-government training providers are often more effective in providing services that meet the needs of the informal economy.*
- Providing students with a solid base of general education;
- Focusing on the proper target group,
  - those with "blue collar working aspirations",
  - those who intend to enter the labour force after training as semi-skilled workers;
- Continuous linkages with industry, which ensure
  - trainees are trained in the knowledge, skills & attitudes sought by employers, and
  - employers are aware of the competencies of UCEP graduates
- Focus on acquisition of skills & competencies through
  - highly structured, supervised individual" hands-on" instruction (rather than being driven by credentials and certificates)
- Rigorous follow-up of each graduate in terms of
  - employment, earnings and performance on the job.

Best Practices - Chile: Vocational Education for Chilean Farming, CODESSER Model

- *Private sector participation in management.*
  - A directorate of 7 farmers or industrial entrepreneurs oversees each school.
  - This ensures greater job-skill matches,
- direct connection to the labour market for graduates and ;
- effective medium for bringing about organizational & productive innovations.
- *Teachers hired as private sector employees.*
  - Personnel policy *(including selection & promotion criteria & new contracts)* conforms to the Labour Code that regulates pvt. sector employees.
  - Teachers' salaries are about 50 % higher than in municipal schools
  - consistent effort to upgrade teacher training.
- *Educational programmes.*

- Basic general knowledge in humanities and sciences,
- prepare students to work in various occupations,
- teach students as problem solvers & encourage them to continue learning.
- Schools emphasize general growth and the development of responsibility, leadership and personnel management.
- Programmes updated after a thorough field study and approval by the Ministry of Education (to give the curriculum local relevance)

• *Curriculum revision.*
  - Periodic surveys of job requirements in the areas around each school.
  - Surveys used to adjust vocation-specific components in the curriculum and to prepare teachers in those areas.

• *Student selection. (Schools select their best applicants)*
  - selection examinations in Chile is graded from one to seven;
  - achieve at least grade five in each course to be considered for admission;
  - Prospective students must present a recommendation letter;
  - spend two days at the school to take written examinations in 4 basic areas;
  - go through a personal interview & psychological tests; and
  - undertake a farming activity.

• *Funding and budget allocations.*
  - The real value of public subsidies fell in the early 1980s;
  - declined again by about 15 percent between 1987 and 1991;
  - As a result, schools developed independent funding;
  - In 1982 the public subsidy represented the bulk of schools' budgets; and
  - it is now less than 50 percent.

Codesser: (Corporation for the Social Development of the Rural Sector) is a private, non-profit making corporation created in 1976 by the National Agricultural Society of Chile (Professional Association) in order to promote the global development of the rural sector. Its work involves two main areas of complementary action: training human resources and enhancing production. The former task aims to prepare people by offering formal education services and work training.

The latter aims to achieve greater economic efficiency and to boost the productivity and entrepreneurial competitiveness of the agro-forestry-livestock and agro-industrial sector.

Initially, it administered four schools whose reputations were poor and it was difficult to attract students but today, some schools receive more than 300 applications for 45 first-year openings and additional schools have been included because of the growing demand.

More than 75 percent of graduates from agricultural schools hold mid-level management positions in agriculture as against the far cry from the 15 percent match between vocational training and the job descriptions of the schools' graduates in the 1970s. In industry, where CODESSER's impact is more recent, this percentage is close to 62.

Learning from Best Practices – Chile CODESSER Model

- *CODESSER demonstrates that the key to success is a business arrangement that covers performance criteria and financing.*
- *Resulted healthy growth of labour demand in the Chilean economy*
- *Its management model has contributed and merits special attention.*
  - The high value placed on people and the tangible manifestation of this appreciation by providing scope for their participation are the basis of proactive management
  - educational institution, just as its students, needs to be able to understand, monitor & modify its own management processes, depending on its demands.
- applying knowledge to tasks, through continuous & collaborative learning.
- Establish effective & lasting bonds with bodies that have the knowledge, resources and also that have needs to satisfy.
- constant improvement and policy that fosters learning to live together with a clear institutional identification and shared expectations
- successful institution needs to learn self-governance

Several lessons can be drawn from CODESSER's experience. Educational organization requires a change of vision and the incorporation of models of modern proactive management. Its conceptual and operative approach and its service enterprise strengthen the possibilities of adaptation to the educational requirements of the society of knowledge. It's also important to learn that Network-management is an integral element of knowledge-management. It transforms methods of organizational and educational work; it opens exponentially the possibilities of knowledge; it accelerates the optimization of management; and it promotes the quality of education.

Ireland: Enterprise-led Approaches to Skill Development, Training and New Qualifications: the Irish Experience

It's important to explore the Irish context of public/private approaches to enterprise development with an example of stakeholder collaboration which is tackling skill development, training and qualification needs. It adopts the network delivery model functions as a collaborative investment initiative which adds value to existing provision and drive innovation and development. Skillnets was formed in 1999 as an Independent body – Industry Board (IBEC / ICTU / Chambers Ireland/CIF/SFA) as a response to the critical need for upskilling the workforce. It was eestablished to improve learning activity in enterprises leading to enhanced skills, employability and competitiveness and to facilitate training and development in Irish enterprises. From 1999 to 2005, a total of 114 networks have been operational with 6,122 companies participating and 35,315 workers receiving training. The network has been committed €24.24m grants out of which €12.76m has been invested by companies. Skillnets continue to adopt a broad based approach, and support training in a range of sectors from those with high growth potential, to workers in vulnerable sectors. Skillnets place a special emphasis on small and medium sized companies and provide higher levels of support to projects involving smaller companies.

The Training Networks Programme is funded through the National Training Fund and ensures that, insofar as possible, training is available to employees at all levels in participating organisations. In particular, Skillnets encourage firms to include the training needs of workers with low basic skills by piloting appropriate work based approaches.

In implementing its programme of activity, Skillnets focuses primarily on the strategic areas:

- Driving skills strategies through sectors and partnerships to encourage training participation at sector level.
- Growing the skills base by giving workers access to lifelong learning opportunities.

- Developing local learning responses to allow enterprises to develop training opportunities for employees at local level.
- Building best practice in learning and development in all aspects of the design, delivery, evaluation and dissemination of enterprise training.

Best-practice and Areas of Special Need

- Certification partnerships
- Measuring the impact of training
- Low basic skills and literacy
- New Possibilities for Small Business Training

Key Learning

- The enterprise-led approach is an effective means of addressing workplace learning
- When engaged, enterprises are in a strong position to determine and satisfy their own training needs
- Training networks require strong facilitation and support, both internally and externally

Six Basic Approaches in Training Systems around the World

- Japanese System
  - have the simplest design.
  - Students completing basic education go to general secondary education,
- thereafter either enter firms that provide entry-level training or go on to tertiary education.
- North American System
  - has no "streaming" until after secondary education and
  - it relies on post-secondary education to facilitate transition to work.
  - Students completing secondary education go to
- community colleges and polytechnic for short courses, and to
- universities, which provide both general and professional training.
- French System
  - Streams students into vocational courses at the secondary level.

  - Students in vocational courses are prepared for entry to the labour market,
  - Those in humanistic scientific streams are prepared for higher education.
- German System
  - Based on a long tradition of apprenticeships.
  - For secondary school students, instruction consists of ("dual" system).
- school-based general instruction and firm-based occupation-specific training
  - System, regulated by guilds, has set of qualifications that provides broad equivalency between
- graduates of the academic and the dual subsystems.
- Latin American System
  - training system is a hybrid of the French and German models.
  - For students completing basic education:
- it relies on autonomous vocational training institutes for those proceeding to the labour market,
- on general (humanistic-scientific) education at secondary level for those proceeding to tertiary education, and
- on school-based vocational education for others.
- Australian System
  - allows transitions between the vocational & tertiary education systems.
  - Employers play a key role in the management of the vocational system.

The question is whether India could adopt a particular framework, or develop a framework in its own way, or simply leave things unchanged. Leaving things unchanged seems unwise. Duplication and lack of coordination are already features of the system and if it is to grow substantially, some guiding framework is essential. Adopting frameworks used elsewhere is rarely possible, as too many precedents, and constitutional and institutional factors have to be taken into account. Customizing and developing a uniquely Indian framework keeping in view various available models would seem the only way to proceed, though this should be informed by international experience.

It is very clear from looking at the Best Practices and for these to succeed – involvement of Industry or the Private Sector is Critical – Their involvement is needed at every stage right from curriculum development, Source of trainers, the ultimate employer of the skills, optionally providing Infrastructure, etc.

Corporates / Private Sector in Skill Development

It is also true that Involvement of the Industry and the private sector is critical whether as Consumers, or as CSR initiative in partnering and as an Enterprise.

Corporates as Consumers

Corporates as consumers/users of trained/skilled manpower may partner with Skill development institutions not as a CSR initiative but to gain concrete benefits

- Training to students (generic & job specific skills) to employ them
- Academic supervised Internship
- Collaborative courses/Programmes keeping in view the demand of the market
- Training the trainers
- Funding collaborative Projects & Research
- Exchange Programmes
- Crossover of Faculty & Employees
- Infrastructural Support, Financial Support
- Promoting Industry – Academia Interface

Most of these of course only be possible by larger enterprises. We have already seen it in the PPP mode

As Corporates Social Responsibility

- Investing in Institution
  - Few corporates have the expertise, money or skill to invest in this mode
  - However very good institutions could come Independently or in PPP Mode
- Potential to become *Centres of Excellence,*
- Have Brand name to protect
- Done as a CSR initiative (not for Profit)

- Operational
  - *Helping, Administrative, Management –contribution in running of the institutions,*
  - *Volunteering, Academic contribution in form of Lectures, Research & Development and Training*- (may not be a long term model)
- Corporates put in funding only for
  - Autonomous independent institutions imparting quality education
- scholarships,
- naming buildings,
- invest in training only if they find it beneficial

As corporate Social Responsibility very few corporates would be doing so either as Setting up, or Volunteering or as funding.

Corporates/Pvt. Sector as Enterprise (FOR PROFIT APPROACH)

- This to be open to all provisions of Education
  - Either in form of setting up Training Centres, Skill Development centres, Vocational Education, part of Pvt. University System, Distance Education Institutes, New mode of Provision, companies/firms etc
- Nothing lost – Much gained: because Corporate/private sector is there to
  - Supplement govt.'s investment & effort and not to supplant it;
  - Supplement those who do it for Not-For-Profit as CSR
- As Market mechanism may be imperfect in education, hence
  - Transparent Autonomous Regulator like TRAI to ensure
- Consumers Interest (Students & Corporates)
- Promotion of autonomous Testing and Certification independent bodies

Bibliography

Allkins, M.T.: *Professional Development Programs, Leadership, and Institutional Culture: Lessons from a Study of Professional Development Programs for Community College Occupational- Technical Faculty,* University of California at Berkeley, Berkeley, CA, 1991.

Ambrose, S. A.: *Improving College Teaching,* Anker Publishing, Bolton, MA, 1995.

Brick, Jean: *Academic Culture: A Student's Guide to Studying at University,* National Centre for English Language Teaching and Research, Sydney, N.S.W, 2006.

Camp, W.G., & Heath-Camp, B.: *Professional Development of Beginning Vocational Teachers: An Introduction to the Professional Development Program for beginning Vocational Teachers*, University of California at Berkeley, Berkeley, CA, 1992.

Camp, W.G.: *Professional Development of Teachers of Vocational Education,* University of California at Berkeley, Berkeley, CA, 1988.

Chism, N. V. N.: *Faculty as Teachers: Taking stock of What We Know,* National Center on Postsecondary Teaching, Learning, and Assessment, State College, PA, 1994.

Finch, C.R., Gregson, J.A., & Reneau, C.E.: *Vocational Education Leadership Development Resources: Selection and Application,* University of California at Berkeley, Berkeley, CA, 1992.

Finch, C.R., Reneau, C.E., Faulkner, S.L. Gregson, J.A., Hernandez- Gantes, V.M., & Linkous, G.A.: *Case Studies in Vocational Education Administration: Leadership in Action,* National Center for Research in Vocational Education, Berkeley, CA, 1992.

Finch, C.R.: *Breakers: An Organization Simulation for Vocational Education Professionals*, National Center for Research in Vocational Education, Berkeley, CA, 1992.

Gillespie, K. J. & Robertson, D.: *A Guide to Faculty Development,* Jossey-Bass, San Francisco, 2010.

Grubb, W.N.: *School-to-work programs: True reforms of tired retreads?* University of California at Berkeley, Berkeley, CA, 1994.

Hanley-Maxwell, C., & Chadsey-Rusch, J.: *Enhancing Transition from School to the Workplace for Handicapped Youth: The Role of Vocational Rehabilitation.* ERIC Document, Washington, DC, 1985.

Heath-Camp, B., & Camp, W.G.: *Professional Development of Beginning Vocational Teachers: Implementation System,* University of California at Berkeley, Berkeley, CA, 1992.

Kolb, D.A.: *Experiential Learning: Experience as the Source of Learning and Development,* Prentice Hall, New Jersey, 1984.

Marcinkiewicz, H., & Doyle, Terrence, D.: *New Faculty Professional Development: Planning an Ideal Program,* New Forums Press, 2004.

McCann, I. & Radford, R.: *The Return of the Mentor: Strategies for Workplace Learning,* Falmer Press, Washington, DC, 1993.

Moeini, H., Alpsan, D. & Berberoglu, G.: *Proceedings of World Conference on E-Learning in Corporate, Government, Healthcare, and Higher Education 2005,* AACE, Chesapeake, VA, 2005.

Paris, K.A.: *A Leadership Model for Planning and Implementing Change for School-to-work Transition,* Center on Education and Work, University of Wisconsin-Madison, Madison, WI, 1994.

Paulsen, M. B., & Feldman, K.A.: *Taking Teaching Seriously,* The George Washington University Graduate School of Education and Human Development. Especially, Washington, D.C., 1995.

Phelps, L.A.: *NCREL Critical Issue Paper on School-to Work Transition: Business Partnerships,* Center on Education and Work-Madison, University of Wisconsin-Madison, Madison, WI, 1991.

Schmidt, B.J.: *Collaborative Efforts between Vocational and Academic Teachers; Strategies that Facilitate and Hinder Efforts,* National Center for Research in Vocational Educational Education, University of California at Berkeley, Berkeley, CA, 1992.

Schmidt, J.B., & Faulkner, S.: *Staff Development through Distance Education,* University of California at Berkeley, Berkeley, CA, 1989.

Sorcinelli, M. D., Austin, A., Eddy, P. & Beach, A.: *Creating the Future of Faculty Development: Learning from the Past, Understanding the Present,* Anker Publishing Company, Bolton MA, 2005.

Weimer, M.: *Improving College Teaching,* Jossey-Bass, San Francisco, CA, 1990.

Index

L

M

N

P

R

S

T

V

W

❑❑❑